Ferry

PALMYRA LAKE

HURRICANE IS.

DAVIS CUTOFF
1867

MISS.
LA.

Ark.

La.

Monroe

Davis Bend

Miles

THE PURSUIT
OF A DREAM

THE PURSUIT OF A DREAM

Janet Sharp Hermann

New York   Oxford
OXFORD UNIVERSITY PRESS
1981

Library of Congress Cataloging in Publication Data

Hermann, Janet Sharp.
The pursuit of a dream.

Bibliography: p. 275
Includes index.
1. Davis Bend, Miss.   2. Mound Bayou, Miss.
3. Afro-Americans—Mississippi—Economic conditions.
4. Afro-Americans—Mississippi—History.
5. Slavery in the United States—Mississippi—
Condition of slaves.   6. Plantation life—
Mississippi.   I. Title.
F349.D38H47   976.2'00496073   80-22539
ISBN 0-19-502887-2

For Kenneth M. Stampp

Printed in the United States of America

Preface

This is the story of an idea which survived for a century, reaching across national and regional boundaries, bridging political chasms, spanning differences of generation and race. The idea originated with a Scottish reformer whose newest utopian community in Indiana inspired a white slaveowner in the South. For thirty-five years this committed planter sought to develop an ideal "community of cooperation" at Davis Bend, his Mississippi plantation, never admitting that the most benign form of slavery could never be utopian. During the Civil War black veterans of the antebellum experiment prompted Yankee officers and northern missionaries to attempt their own version of the dream, but political and financial constraints as well as their own ineptitude foredoomed their efforts. Able black leaders then took command and, for a time, produced the fullest flowering of the utopian experiment, until natural disasters and external political and economic forces ended its prosperity. Still the idea persisted, and a new generation of Davis Bend blacks ventured into the wilderness to establish another model colony.

The community at Davis Bend and its successor at Mound Bayou differed significantly from other nineteenth-century black colonies. Unlike the antebellum ventures described by William and Jane Pease, such as Nashoba in the United States and Wilberforce or Elgin in Canada, the colony at Davis Bend was not designed primarily as a philanthropic project to benefit the poor Negro. The major purpose of the Mississippi community was always to provide increased economic productivity through harmonious cooperation; the fact that the colonists were black was merely coincidental. Except for a brief period during Union occupation, most colonists were neither refugees nor exiles but permanent residents, many of whom had been born at Davis Bend. And the fields they tilled were not marginal lands consigned to paupers, but rather some of the most fertile cotton acreage in the South. Only under the Yankees was the colony, like its counterpart at Port Royal, intended as a training school for a life of freedom. Before and after the war Davis Bend was first of all a hardheaded business venture run by experienced men of affairs seeking increased prosperity through cooperation. Furthermore, the members of the postwar association there were more sophisticated than the average freedmen. As slaves they had operated their own court system and managed incomes derived from individual business ventures. Experience during Union occupation helped prepare them to maintain their own interests in the face of predatory or bureaucratic forces. These enterprising colonists united in order to create a more prosperous place for themselves as free citizens of the South.

The Port Royal experiment in South Carolina, as described by Willie Lee Rose in *Rehearsal for Reconstruction,* was led by idealistic white Northerners whose encouragement of black initiative was limited by their low estimate of freedmen's capabilities. Federal officials and Gideon's Band of evangelical missionaries permitted little decision making by the blacks. Although the Northerners may have had a dream of an ideal community, they assumed that whites must lead it. At Davis Bend the antebellum slave community enjoyed enough autonomy to create expectations of complete self-government after freedom. The Union officers and missionaries who arrived to supervise them soon found their own assumptions about the unsuitability of black leadership contested by these capable freedmen. With great resourcefulness the blacks freed themselves from white management, salvaged the Davis Bend plantations and turned them into a model of prosperity.

The remarkably rich cache of source material for this drama of black success necessarily places the Montgomery family at center stage. Benjamin and his sons, Isaiah and Thornton, have left nearly two hundred delightfully articulate letters dealing with the affairs of the colonies at Davis Bend and Mound Bayou. Mary Virginia's diary provides a vivid picture of her life at the Bend, including much information about other members of their extended family. From these sources it is possible to draw unusually detailed characterizations of the leaders of the all black colony. It is much more difficult to ascertain the thoughts and feelings or to depict the daily lives of the ordinary colonists. From scattered references in letters, the files of the Freedmen's Bureau, census returns and tax rolls, contemporary newspapers, and the WPA slave narratives it is possible to learn a bit about more than one hundred members of the association at Davis Bend. More detailed information about these illiterate but not inarticulate black folk would be desirable. However, regrettable as it may be, the history of most societies, large and small, has been recorded in terms of the leaders and the recordkeepers. Even though it is incomplete, the story of the Davis Bend community is too fascinating to remain untold.

Each of the utopian experiments documented here was founded and led by a strong man who insisted that the inhabitants conform to his prescription for an ideal community. The slaveowner, Joseph Davis, practiced an unusually benevolent form of the paternalism cited by Eugene Genovese in *Roll, Jordan, Roll,* which allowed space for his slaves to develop a culture and world view of their own. However, essentially the same sort of entrepreneurial paternalism characterized the colonies established by Benjamin Montgomery for the freedmen and subsequently by Isaiah Montgomery for migrants from Davis Bend. Far from fitting the Genovesian model of pre-capitalist estates, each of these enterprises was equally as capitalistic as the factory towns of the paternalistic industrialists of the Northeast.

Benjamin Montgomery succeeded admirably in the world in which he found himself: he wrote better English with finer penmanship than his white correspondents, designed and built better devices of all sorts, and constantly outmaneuvered white businessmen and bureaucrats. He did not imitate whites, he excelled them! Nor did he accomplish these things at the expense of black interests; his success provided a measure of comfort and security not only for himself and his family, but also for the entire community. In many ways Isaiah Montgomery duplicated his father's accomplishments with equally beneficial results for members of his race. The remarkable Montgomerys had to surmount formidable obstacles of servitude and race prejudice to achieve notable success in nineteenth-century terms. They were not Uncle Toms but rather quintessential examples of the self-made men so widely admired by society at large. These leaders maneuvered the hostile white power structure to permit creation of an ideal black community whose citizens would be relatively free from racial harassment. The Montgomerys made it possible for the Davis Bend freedmen to share in the utopian dream.

Acknowledgements

This book would have been impossible without the assistance of a number of people who made the research both pleasant and productive. I am grateful to Elaine C. Everly, Assistant Chief of the Navy and Old Army Branch of the National Archives for skillfully leading me through a wealth of records from the Freedmen's Bureau. The staff of the Manuscripts Division of the Library of Congress provided valuable information, and I want to thank a fellow researcher there, Sadie Harlan, who shared her detailed knowledge of the vast Booker T. Washington Papers.

The staff of the Mississippi Department of Archives and History welcomed me with true southern hospitality. Michelle Hudson, in particular, made my several visits to Jackson pleasant. I also benefited from the warm and friendly cooperation of President and Mrs. George Owens and my former colleagues at Tougaloo College. The library there provided valuable information about Mound Bayou.

In Vicksburg I received generous assistance from Gordon Cotton and Blanche Terry at the Old Courthouse Museum. I also want to thank Judge and Mrs. Ben Guider for inviting me into their home to examine some of the original Benjamin Montgomery letters when photocopies at the Mississippi Department of Archives and History proved illegible. John E. Kerrigan and Mrs. Conrad Kuebel of New Orleans, direct descendants of Joseph E. Davis, kindly showed me family letters, jewelry made in Paris for Eliza Davis, and silver salvaged from antebellum Hurricane. I appreciate the encouragement I received from Percival Beacroft and Ernesto Caldeira at Rosemont, the family home of Jefferson Davis, which they are restoring so faithfully.

Others scattered about the country deserve my thanks: Conrad F. Weitzel at the Ohio Historical Society provided invaluable information about Samuel Thomas; he and W. E. Bigglestone of the Oberlin College Archives helped me understand many details of life at Oberlin in the 1870s. James E. Sperry, Superintendent of the State Historical Society of North Dakota, and Hiram M. Drache, my former colleague on the history faculty at Concordia College, Moorhead, Minnesota, each provided vital facts about Thornton Montgomery's years in North Dakota. J. Saunders Redding directed me to the Mound Bayou material in his works, and Marjorie A. Kierstead of Baker Library at Harvard uncovered the Montgomery entries in the R. G. Dun Credit Ledgers. Mrs. Betty White Wills of Tulsa, Oklahoma, promptly and generously granted permission to quote from her typescript, "Interludes," by Mary Mitchell White. Adele Hayes-Davis Sinton of Colorado Springs, Colorado, was equally gracious in allowing me to use the Jefferson Hayes-Davis collection of valuable letters.

I owe a debt of gratitude to several members of the faculty at the University of California, Berkeley. Leon Litwack generously shared his extensive knowledge of sources relating to the freedmen. Lawrence Levine asked penetrating questions about the folk, and Richard Sutch led me to the Dun Credit Ledgers and other sources of economic information.

The friendly helpfulness of the entire staff at the Jefferson Davis Association made my stay at Rice University both pleasant and productive. The continuing thoughtfulness of Editor Lynda Crist and Associate Editor Mary Dix in reporting relevant bits of information uncovered as they collect the papers of Jefferson Davis has contributed immeasurably to this study. I also appreciate their thorough reading and criticism of the manuscript.

I shall always be grateful to Frank E. Everett, Jr. for so generously sharing his detailed knowledge of the physical features of Davis Bend, Davis family affairs, and legal matters in nineteenth century Warren County. Frank and his charming wife, Clyde, befriended me with a warmth which enriched all of my visits to

Vicksburg, and, subsequently, Frank has provided painstaking and perceptive criticism of the entire manuscript.

I treasure the kind words with which Sheldon Meyer accepted this work for publication by the oldest press in the English-speaking world, and I have benefited from the astute editorial assistance of Susan Rabiner.

My greatest debt is to the two people who made this book possible. Kenneth M. Stampp, my major professor, provided the challenge with his uncompromising standards of scholarship and the incentive with his rare words of praise. W. D. Hermann, my husband, enthusiastically shared my ideas and gave me the benefit of an economist's point of view; his generous physical and emotional support and unfailing pride in my accomplishments sustained me throughout the project.

Berkeley, California   J. S. H.
July, 1980

Contents

1

Joseph Davis Has a Dream

1

An Antebellum Experiment

"Train any population rationally, and they will be rational. Furnish honest and useful employments to those so trained, and such employments they will greatly prefer to dishonest or injurious occupations."[1]

Thus did Robert Owen, the successful British industrialist and social reformer, explain to his fellow stagecoach travelers on a trip across the back country of Pennsylvania and New York in midsummer 1825 the basic philosophy that had led him to found the model factory town of New Lanark in Scotland. Now he was hurrying back to England, he reported, to wind up his business there and to enlist additional support for the brave new venture he had begun only a few weeks before at New Harmony, Indiana. He had left the leadership of this infant colony to his son William, and as he talked with his fellow passengers about his ideal "community of cooperation," he was full of enthusiasm for his experiment in this new American nation, a nation that seemed to him hospitable to innovations of every sort. After all, the young republic's most prominent men had welcomed Owen and had even encouraged him in his plans for creating a truly harmonious society free of poverty and crime. At well-publicized receptions the previous winter in New York, Philadelphia, and Washington, Owen had been entertained by many distinguished Americans, including President James Monroe and President-elect John Quincy Adams; at Speaker of the House Henry Clay's invitation he had given two addresses at the Capitol, each attended by members of

3

the Cabinet, the Supreme Court, and the Congress. With letters
of introduction from President Monroe, he had called on former
presidents Jefferson and Madison in the course of his triumphal
tour to New Harmony. Now this persuasive man expounded his
visionary theories of education and social organization with great
confidence, for he was sincerely convinced that New Harmony
was indeed the prototype of a new utopia.[2]

One of Owen's traveling companions, the noted British carica-
turist George Cruikshank, had heard his ideas often and was
more interested during the journey in noting the facial character-
istics of the people they met on the road. The other Owenite,
Captain Donald Macdonald, was preoccupied with the countryside through which they passed. However, a third passenger,
Joseph E. Davis, was fascinated by Owen's discourse. Davis, a
prominent lawyer from Natchez, Mississippi, enjoyed reading
treatises on political theory and social philosophy and subscribed
to the leading British and American journals. He had read
Owen's book, *A New View of Society*, as well as glowing accounts
of the author's appearances in American cities; he was much
impressed with this worldly figure. The opportunity to discuss
these bold theories with the author himself not only relieved the
tedium and discomfort of the stagecoach journey but planted in
Davis the seeds of an idea that would continue to grow for the
rest of his life.

Joseph Davis had every reason to be optimistic about man's
ability to reshape society; by age forty he had made his own fortune as a frontier lawyer in Mississippi. Earlier, his parents and
their large family had prospered as they followed the frontier
from Georgia to Kentucky and on to the Mississippi Territory.
Along the way, Joseph received a rudimentary formal education
that satisfied his lifelong thirst for knowledge by permitting him
to read widely on his own. He became a lawyer after a brief apprenticeship to a Kentucky merchant convinced him that law
was a more interesting and profitable field than business. In 1812
he joined the local militia to fight the British, just as his father
had done in Georgia during the American Revolution. Later Joseph helped shape the new state as a delegate to the Mississippi
constitutional convention of 1817.[3]

Davis's extensive reading kept him abreast of the reform sentiment then prevalent among intellectuals in England and New England, and he pondered their ideas about the nature of man and society. In the raw settlements of the Southwest he saw the chicanery and abuse that ruthless men were capable of in their pursuit of selfish gain. However, while maintaining a realistic understanding of man's imperfections, Davis was optimistic about the human potential for improvement; experience had led him to believe that any progress was possible in this expanding New World. Therefore, he probed Owen's thoughts eagerly for a blueprint which might prove applicable to his own situation.

Owen asserted that "man is the creature of surrounding circumstances" and will respond to humane acts of generosity and cooperation. He believed that character was formed early in life; therefore, the way to build a harmonious society was to treat children from infancy with perfect kindness. Even the youngest pupils should be taught that their main purpose in life is to try to make others happy. A teacher must never indicate by word or facial expression annoyance with a child because, Owen asserted, children misbehaved only because of failure to understand the reasons for good behavior. A rational explanation delivered in a patient manner would soon transform the wayward child into a model pupil. Applying this same philosophy to adult factory workers at New Lanark brought gratifying results, though not the utopia Owen had hoped to achieve. He treated his workers as reasonable human beings while maintaining, as one biographer noted, "the attitude of a master and not of one feeling any remote sense of equality with his employees." He treated them with the same imaginative paternalism that he used with school children, and they frequently responded with cooperation and even affection. Many prominent people journeyed to Scotland to visit Owen's model village. His theories were especially popular with the post-Napoleonic enlightened despots of Europe.[4]

Although Owen's only experience had been in textile manufacturing, he was convinced that his methods could be used to increase agricultural production as well. Joseph Davis must have been especially interested in the reformer's plans to combine agriculture and light industry at New Harmony. The idea of employing humanitarian means in the pursuit of profits appealed to the ambitious lawyer from Mississippi. As the oldest of ten children and the mainstay of the family, Davis learned early that it was preferable to gain one's ends through persuasion rather than compulsion. A rather slight, small-boned man, he had relied on nonviolent tactics in his climb to the top of a highly competitive profession in a rough and violent society. Owen's methods of harmonious cooperation sounded eminently sensible to him.[5]

During the next few months Joseph Davis meditated on Owen's utopian ideas as he made up his mind to give up his law practice and leave Natchez. In 1818 he had bought from the federal government a large tract of rich bottomland on the Mississippi some thirty miles by river below a settlement called the Walnut Hills, which later became the town of Vicksburg. By acquiring several existing small farms, he soon owned the entire 11,000 acres of the peninsula, which came to be called Davis Bend. He sold sections to a few friends he thought would make good neighbors, but reserved for himself 5,000 acres of the most fertile land on the southwestern side of the peninsula. Soon he commissioned his brother Isaac to begin development of a plantation there. However, shortly after construction of the first dwelling, a devastating storm struck the Bend, crippling Isaac for life and killing his infant son. Isaac moved his family to another county, but Joseph continued to develop the place, which he now called Hurricane. There, with a nucleus of slaves inherited from his father in 1824, he began to build a labor force as rapidly as his finances permitted. Finally, in 1827, at the age of forty-two, Davis married a sixteen-year-old girl from New Orleans and, with his three young daughters, retired to Davis Bend. Here he proposed to establish a model plantation where he could combine idyllic living with profit and prestige.[6]

One might wonder why Joseph Davis, in the prime of life, would leave a highly successful professional career for the isolation of a rural plantation. It is not surprising, however, that he decided to become a cotton planter, because in the new Southwest of that era the ownership of a flourishing plantation was considered the true mark of success. It was not unusual for men to abandon thriving business or professional careers and turn to planting. J. H. Ingraham, a contemporary observer, asserted:

> A plantation well stocked with hands, is the *ne plus ultra* of every man's ambition who resides at the south. Young men who come to

this country, 'to make money,' soon catch the mania, and nothing less than a broad plantation, waving with the snow white cotton bolls, can fill their mental vision. . . . Hence the great number of planters and the few professional men. . . . As soon as the young lawyer acquires sufficient to purchase a few hundred acres of the rich alluvial lands, and a few slaves, he quits his profession at once, though perhaps just rising into eminence, and turns cotton planter.[7]

According to this description, Joseph Davis had moved quite slowly; he waited until his career was well established and he had acquired more than "a few hundred acres . . . and a few slaves."

However, in view of his eminence, he might have chosen to leave the management of his plantation to an overseer while remaining in Natchez to pursue a career in politics. Had he followed this course, he might soon have been elected governor or senator, with good prospects for a national career. In fact, Joseph Davis only stood for elective office three times: once in 1817 when he was chosen as a delegate to the first Mississippi constitutional convention, again in 1820 when elected to the legislature, and finally in 1832 when the state constitution was revised. He lost the last election, apparently because he opposed the popular election of judges. Although Davis remained active in the Democratic Party as a delegate to state and national conventions and as a member of numerous committees, he never again faced the electorate.[8] Nevertheless, prominent men frequently consulted him concerning political affairs, for he had the reputation of being "one of the best informed politicians of his time." In later years, his knowledge, skill, and lifelong fascination with politics proved an invaluable asset to his youngest brother, Jefferson, in the latter's career as a U.S. congressman, senator, cabinet officer, and, ultimately, president of the Confederacy.

Joseph Davis evidently preferred the challenge of life as the patriarch of an elaborate plantation to that of an active politician. By the mid-1820s he had tired of his position as a respected lawyer, former legislator, founder of the Mississippi Bar Association and of Trinity Episcopal Church in Natchez; he was now ready to establish a suitably fine home for his family. All available evidence indicates that he did not marry until 1827, although he had three young daughters, ranging in age from four to fifteen, when he and his bride moved to Hurricane. These girls may have been the product of a common-law relationship, but there is no mention of a previous marriage in the large Davis family correspondence, nor is there any known legal record of one. It is also possible that the children were adopted, though that, too, is absent from family tradition.[9] In any case, with characteristic independence, Joseph acknowledged them as his daughters in 1827 and seemed determined to make a home for them and his new wife in the model community he proposed to create.

Although Davis had accepted many of Robert Owen's ideas for social reorganization, by late 1827, when the lawyer moved to Davis Bend, the British reformer's community at New Harmony was already in trouble, and by 1829 it had failed.[10] Davis undoubtedly read the bitter attacks on Owen which filled the national press. The reformer was criticized not so much for his practical failures as for his open rejection of orthodox religion and the institution of marriage. Although Davis did not agree with these radical ideas, he continued to admire the Scottish utopian for his innovative theories. However, the new planter proposed to adopt only the elements of Owen's philosophy that would promote his goal of an efficient, prosperous plantation community.

The idea of applying these cooperative principles to a slave colony was not unheard of at that time. Many concerned Southerners such as Davis were still seeking a practical alternative to slavery. Some seized upon Owen's communitarian plan as an adjunct to their scheme for the colonization of freed slaves in Liberia, which had been founded in 1822. Others proposed to set up black colonies in the United States, where slaves might earn their freedom while learning the skills and attitudes deemed necessary for success as free men. The only practical attempt to implement such a plan was the short-lived Nashoba community established near Memphis by Frances Wright, a young Englishwoman, who unwisely sought to combine religious and sexual freedom with emancipation. Her uncompromising radicalism swept the colony to an early death on a wave of public indignation.[11] Although Joseph Davis never aimed to duplicate the experiments at Nashoba or New Harmony, they provided the climate in which he established his community at Davis Bend. He based it on a conviction that all men, white and black, are capable of living harmonious, productive lives through rational cooperation.

By 1850 Joseph Davis had created at Davis Bend the sort of cotton plantation that was the goal of most ambitious young men of the Deep South. A visitor arriving by steamboat saw first the substantial warehouse complex at the Hurricane landing, where busy workers unloaded supplies used in plantation operations and shipped out the large cotton crop and other produce. From the landing, a walk crossed a wide green lawn and led into a grove of live oak and pecan trees where, a quarter mile back from the river on a low rise, stood a massive brick mansion with galleries around both the first and second floors. In the main section of the house the thick walls, low ceilings, and small windows gave the rooms a dark, cavelike feeling that was welcome after the humid heat of the riverbank. The front door opened onto a wide hall with a drawing room and tearoom for the ladies on the right. On the left was the master bedroom and behind it the book-lined office to which Davis often retired with male guests for wide-ranging discussions of political and plantation affairs. Here, on many evenings, Joseph and his younger brother Jefferson reportedly "talked of books, of elementary law, of agricultural experiments, commented upon the day's doings, and made and perfected theories about everything in heaven and on earth." The second and third floors of the mansion each contained four large bedrooms, with a sweeping view of the river presented from the third-floor dormer windows.[12]

To the west of the main building stood a large, two-story wing containing only two rooms, each forty-three feet long and twenty-five feet wide. The lower one was the red-brick-paved dining room where large groups were seated comfortably for lavish dinners, often lasting most of the afternoon. Above was a high-ceilinged music room lined with family portraits and housing a piano, guitars, and music books. Here nieces, nephews, and young guests sometimes gave impromptu concerts, played charades, and improvised games. The west wing was connected to the main house by a second-floor gallery that provided a covered walkway to the dining room below. Although the spacious mansion lacked the architectural grace of many in Natchez, it contained some surprising innovations. For example, Davis had brought plumbers from Cincinnati to install bathrooms on each floor that were supplied with water from a huge tank in the attic. The tank was kept filled by a slave-powered force pump connected to a well in the yard.[13]

Behind the dining- and music-room wing stood a brick building containing the kitchen and laundry on the ground floor and six bedrooms for the house servants above. Beyond this, another structure accommodated the overseer's office, a storeroom, and two upstairs bedrooms. A short distance from the house, toward the river, Davis had constructed a large garden cottage designed to resemble a Greek temple with square Doric columns on all four sides. Each of its two spacious rooms had a huge fireplace at one end opposite a bay window, and French doors along two sides. This building served as a more commodious library and as "bachelor quarters" when the big house was overcrowded.

A broad walk shaded by crape myrtles led from the back gallery of the house to a twenty-five-acre flower garden filled with rare roses and shrubs, surrounded by a thick hedge of intertwined roses, honeysuckle, and jasmine. This was a favorite strolling place in the early morning coolness or at dusk because, as one relative recalled, "the whole family was addicted to gardening." Many of the plants were imported from Europe, and Davis brought over an English gardener to plan the landscaping and supervise its maintenance. The garden was so beautiful that sometimes riverboats would stop to allow their passengers a better view.[14]

Beyond the flower garden were eight acres of well-tended peach, fig, and apple trees flanked by an extensive vegetable garden. Behind the house, intersecting the crape myrtle walk, was another broad path leading to the gates of the large coach house and stables containing some thirty stalls filled with blooded horses. Guests were often taken there to admire the latest acquisition from famous American and foreign racing stables. The ladies sometimes fed sweets to a favorite as he arched his neck over the fence appealingly. The men were more likely to go for a fast canter along the smooth, flat road to test the mettle of Black Oliver, the Canadian racehorse, or Highland Henry, the beautiful red bay. However, they were rash indeed if they chose the strong, muscular, but vicious-tempered Medley; he had already killed a groom who handled him carelessly. These fine horses were a source of great pleasure to Joseph Davis, who had inherited his father's appreciation of the animals. However, while the elder Davis had raised horses and tobacco to make a living in Kentucky, horse breeding was only a hobby for Joseph, who often gave them to friends but never sold one.[15]

Near the stables stood a group of utility buildings, including a blacksmith shop, corncrib, large cotton gin, gristmills, and sawmills. Davis was proud of the fact that he was among the first to acquire a steam gin when they were introduced into Mississippi in the 1830s. Later he used the same steam engine to power the mills. He was always alert to technological innovations, just as he was to improvements in agricultural methods.[16]

Beyond the gin stretched a long row of neatly whitewashed cabins for the black community. The Davis slave force had grown rapidly since 1827, when Joseph moved to Hurricane. According to the Warren County tax rolls, which counted only those slaves over age five and under sixty, Joseph Davis paid taxes on 82 slaves in 1828. After some fluctuation, he was charged for 115 in 1834 and for 163 five years later. The extent to which the tax rolls undercounted the total seems apparent in the 1840 federal census, which lists the Joseph Davis slave force at 226, while the 1841 tax rolls show only 168. By 1850, according to the census, he owned 242 slaves, and ten years later the total had reached 345. That put Davis in the top 12 percent of Mississippi slaveowners—those who held over 200 slaves. In fact, he was one of only nine men in the state who owned more than 300 slaves.[17]

It was in his treatment of the slaves that Davis showed the greatest originality, for his methods were unusual even among wealthy, enlightened planters. This fact was evident in the physical appearance of the slave quarters. The cottages were well built, with plaster walls and large fireplaces, and they contained two large rooms and two shed rooms behind them. Even the ideal slave houses recommended in agricultural journals contained only one large room. The Davis cottages had front and back galleries, often shaded by fruit trees, and were near a large cistern house from which pure water was readily available. Since each house accommodated no more than the average number of slaves quartered in a single dwelling in that area, the unusual size of the buildings meant that the Davis slaves were housed more comfortably.[18]

Davis exceeded the recommended limits on food for his slaves, too. Instead of the usual peck of cornmeal per week, each slave was allowed to take as much as he wished from the gristmill for his own use and to feed his chickens, kept in the henhouse behind each cabin. In addition to eggs and chickens slaves were plentifully supplied with pork, and occasionally with beef and mutton raised on the place. Sweet potatoes were always in ample supply, as were vegetables from the garden and fruit from the orchard in season. In addition, the Davis slaves were well clothed and supplied with comfortable bedding.[19]

However, Davis went beyond providing generously for the physical comfort of his work force. In the organization and management of the slave community he reflected the influence of Robert Owen and his enlightened paternalism. As an individualistic Jeffersonian, Davis abhorred authoritarian methods of command. He was fond of saying, "The less people are governed, the more submissive they will be to control." He heartily disagreed with the prevalent philosophy among slaveowners, which maintained that "the most important part of management of slaves is always to keep them under proper subjection. . . . Unconditional submission is the only footing upon which slavery should be placed."[20] Instead Davis sought to maintain order and productivity by gaining the cooperation of the slave community through a form of self-government. He established a court, eventually held every Sunday in a small building called the Hall of Justice, where a slave jury heard complaints of slave misconduct and the testimony of the accused in his own defense. No slave was punished except upon conviction by this jury of his peers; Davis sat as the judge and seldom intervened except to ameliorate the severity of some of the sentences. One contemporary observed, "[Davis] gave it as his experience that the tendency of his plantation juries, like those of other courts, was to find a verdict not from the evidence adduced, but from their opinion of the character of the accused, a disposition which it became necessary for him to check by the most careful charges and an un-judgelike defence of the criminal."[21]

Not only did the court adjudicate disputes among slaves, it also reviewed complaints from the overseers, who could not punish anyone without court permission. This meant, as one former slave noted many years later, "the overseers had only a partial power."[22] As a result, overseers at Hurricane were often dissatisfied, claiming that they could not maintain discipline without authority. However, Davis was able to insure that his system was followed, because he resided on the plantation most of the time, keeping the reins of control tightly in his own hands. His brother had serious problems with overseers when his political career kept him in Washington for long periods.

Jefferson, who was twenty-four years younger than Joseph, decided to resign his army commission in 1835 when Joseph offered him a tract of land adjacent to Hurricane. There the younger Davis and his trusted body servant, James Pemberton, cooperated in the difficult tasks of clearing land and constructing buildings, with the help of a small, newly acquired slave force. Pemberton had served Jefferson during his army career on the frontier, and they had developed a warm relationship. According to Jefferson's wife:

> They were devoted friends, and always observed the utmost ceremony and politeness in their intercourse, and at parting a cigar was always presented by Mr. Davis to him. James never sat down without being asked, and his master always invited him to be seated, and sometimes fetched him a chair. James was a dignified quiet man, of fine manly appearance, very silent, but what he said was always to the point. His death, which occurred from pneumonia in 1850, during our absence, was a sore grief to us, and his place was never filled.

From 1850 until the Civil War, Brierfield, the Jefferson Davis plantation, struggled along under the supervision of a new overseer almost every year; sometimes they left in disgust even before the end of the season. The elder Davis was always vigilant to protect the slaves on both places and often saw to it that Jefferson dismissed overseers whom he considered too harsh.[23]

Jefferson adopted his older brother's methods of slave management, including the establishment of a court with slave jurors. An historian of Mississippi slavery found only one other slave-owner, A. S. Morehead, a lawyer from Copiah County, who gave his slaves trials before punishing them.[24] If the concessions annoyed the overseers, no doubt the neighbors, too, found them unwise, considering their fear of slave unrest in a region where the blacks far outnumbered the whites.

The court system was not Joseph Davis's only innovation. He firmly believed that each person should be allowed to develop his full potential, and therefore he encouraged his slaves to acquire skills in areas that interested them. Moreover, skilled workers were allowed to enjoy the benefits of their more valuable labor; Davis ruled that each slave might keep anything he earned beyond the value of his labor as a field hand. While only a handful of slaves took advantage of this generous offer, all were able to profit from the various incentives provided at Hurricane. The Davis slaves were permitted to sell their chickens and eggs to the family or to anyone else they chose; most probably traded them at the Hurricane store. Sometimes they sold poultry as well as garden produce and wood from the vast swamps to steamboats plying the adjacent river.[25]

Davis also provided special rewards for superior performance in work assignments such as picking cotton. At harvesttime he kept a daily record of the number of pounds each field hand picked and let the work force know that they were competing not only among themselves but with others in Mississippi. In 1845, a visitor, noting the proficiency of one who picked 468 pounds in only part of a day, remarked, "Mr. Davis thinks that the boy will make the highest picker in the State, as he is only 19 years old." However, Davis discovered that too much competition could be counterproductive. One year he permitted a race between hands at Hurricane and those at Brierfield for the largest gleaning in a single day. Unfortunately, he found that in the heat of the contest they had picked "bolls, stalk and tap root," requiring another day's work to sort the trash from the cotton.[26]

The master of Hurricane was fond of giving little presents to particular slaves not only as a reward for achievement but also as a birth or wedding gift, or consolation for a death. He usually made a dramatic ritual of the presentation, adding to the excitement. One family member recalled:

> There was a little store-room adjoining Mr. Davis's bedroom below stairs, out of which came, in the most astonishing and unexpected variety, candy, negro shoes, field implements, new saddles and bridles, fancy plaid linsey or calico dresses for the negro women who needed consolation for a death in their families, guns and ammunition for hunting, pocket-knives, nails, and screws. This little closet was an ark, of which Mr. J. E. Davis kept the key, and made provision for the accidental needs of "each one after his kind."

Special feasts were always provided for holidays and family celebrations. For a slave wake at Brierfield, the mourners were given "a large quantity of flour, several pounds of sugar, the same quantity of coffee, a ham, a 'shote,' and half a dozen or a dozen bottles of claret." They expected less for a baby's wake, but more for a wedding, in addition to a fine wedding dress, of course.[27]

Davis was more than normally vigilant about the health of his colonists. The Bend was a swampy river bottom area where disease flourished, especially among those not acclimated to the place. At least one of Joseph Davis's friends declined to buy land there because he feared the location was too unhealthy. Most of the white residents tried to leave the Bend during the summer "sickly season," when it was almost impossible to avoid malaria. Jefferson Davis himself became seriously ill and his first wife died, probably of malaria, just three months after their early-summer wedding. Joseph was reluctant to leave the plantation, but after repeated summer illnesses finally acquired the habit of taking his family to a cooler climate, usually some spa in the mountains.[28] The slave community, of course, did not have this option.

Still, Davis agreed with the planter who wrote, "The great object is to prevent disease." His slaves had all the advantages of a good diet, adequate clothing, and snug houses, as well as reasonable working conditions. Nonetheless, sickness was a problem, and Davis provided a hospital and practical nurses for those requiring medical care. The more seriously ill were treated by the same doctor who cared for the white families on the plantation. Both Joseph and Jefferson Davis sought new ways to improve health care. When a Brierfield slave failed to respond to conventional treatment, Jefferson sent her to New Orleans for several months of treatment by a popular specialist in slave maladies. While touring Europe, Joseph discovered the apparent benefits of hydrotherapy; he promptly persuaded his Swiss physician to return to the Bend to supervise construction of a large "Water-Cure Hospital," complete with steam-powered machinery and accommodations for ailing slaves. The Davises were also among the few planters who provided regular dental care for their work force.[29]

One testimonial to the effectiveness of health care on the Davis plantations is the unusual number of aged slaves who lived there. The 1860 census lists at Hurricane one male aged 80, another 90, and "Betsy, aged 100." At Brierfield there were females aged 85 and 90, and "Robert, aged 104."[30] These elders were treated with a great deal of respect by everyone on the plantations, white as well as black. "Old Uncle Bob," the oldest resident, was especially revered. He had been a slave driver "in George Washington's time" and was brought to the Bend with the earliest group of slaves that Jefferson acquired. By the 1850s he and his old wife lived in semiretirement in a cottage that the Davises carefully furnished with extra blankets and a special rocking chair for the rheumatic old man's comfort. Although he did no manual labor, he served a useful function for his master: Varina Davis, the wife of Jefferson Davis, reported, "He had a quiet horse, and used to ride over Brierfield every day, and at the end of a nine months' session of Congress he could, with the utmost accuracy, tell the course of events on the place during our absence."[31]

Old Uncle Bob also served effectively as the resident black preacher; his mistress pronounced him "eloquent in prayer, faithful in all things, and fit to be, as he was, a shepherd of his people." White-led religious services were available for the Hurricane and Brierfield community only sporadically and for short periods. Neither Joseph nor Jefferson Davis seemed to be as committed to the provision of spiritual care as they were of physical care for their blacks. For a time they paid the salary of a white missionary sent out by the Southern Baptist Church to work among slaves. Later, Joseph, who was an original communicant of Christ Episcopal Church in Vicksburg, brought an Episcopal clergyman to live at Hurricane. The latter conducted Sunday services in the morning for the whites and in the afternoon for the slaves, though Jefferson sometimes preferred to attend the afternoon meeting. Regardless of the temporary ministers, however, Old Uncle Bob continued to inspire respect among whites as well as blacks. Jefferson considered him "as free from guile and truthful a man as I ever knew." The remarkable old man survived to enjoy five years of freedom, dying at Hurricane in 1870 at the age of 114.[32]

By 1850 the most influential slave at Hurricane—and after the death of James Pemberton, at Brierfield as well—was Benjamin Thornton Montgomery. He was the beneficiary of Joseph's encouragement of individual talent, the finest flower of Davis's utopian experiment. Born in 1819 in Loudoun County, Virginia, Montgomery spent his boyhood as the companion of his young master, who was about his own age. The white boy had lessons every morning with a tutor; in the afternoon, when the two boys were playing beside the river, he would yield to Ben's urging and trace in the sand the letters he had learned that day. Thus the eager slave boy mastered basic reading and writing.[33]

This routine life ended abruptly in 1836 when, without warning, Ben was sold to a trader who took him south to Natchez. Traveling overland for seven or eight weeks with a gang of strangers and arriving at the teeming slave market on the Mississippi to face an uncertain future must have been a traumatic experience for the seventeen-year-old lad. Although he was well fed and clothed in order to make a good, salable appearance, he must have been filled with trepidation as he listened to older slaves tell of hardships on the large plantations of the Southwest. It was a boom period for slave trading in the area; in the three years from 1834 to 1837 the slave population of Mississippi more than doubled, from 70,000 to 160,000, at an average price of more than $1,000 each.[34] Both Joseph and Jefferson Davis added substantially to their slave forces during these years. Ben Montgomery was only one of many whom Joseph took from the Natchez market to the rapidly growing community at Hurricane.

Ben did not like the change from town life in Virginia to the isolated plantation on the Mississippi, so he promptly ran away. Davis soon recovered him and, applying the rational approach that Owen advocated, "inquired closely into the cause of [Ben's] dissatisfaction." As a result of this unusual conference, Ben's son later reported, the master and the young slave "reached a mutual understanding and established a mutual confidence which time only served to strengthen throughout their long and eventful connection."[35]

With access to the Davis library, Montgomery improved his literary skills and even accumulated a small library of his own. He also became proficient in other areas. He learned how to survey land so that he could plan the construction and maintenance of the levees that were essential for flood protection. He learned to draw architectural plans and participated in the construction of several large buildings on the plantation, including the elaborate garden cottage. In addition, he became an adept mechanic and was soon managing the steam-powered gin for his master, who asserted that Ben had "few Superiors as a Machinist." In the late 1850s he invented a boat propeller that promised to be an improvement on the paddle wheels used on river steamboats. Acting on "the canoe paddling principle," the blades cut into the water at an angle, causing less resistance and therefore less loss of power and jarring of the boat. With this propeller, which weighed a fraction of the conventional paddle wheel, there was no need for a wheelhouse. Ben made a prototype which he operated by hand on the Mississippi for a couple of years before the Civil War, but he dreamed of powering it with a steam engine so that its advantages could be truly tested. Jefferson Davis apparently tried to patent the propeller in Montgomery's name and was told by the U.S. Patent Office that a slave could not receive a patent. He reapplied in his brother's name and was refused because admittedly Joseph was not the inventor. One of the early laws enacted by the Confederate Congress provided for the registration of slave patents by their masters, but there is no record that either of the Davis brothers secured a Confederate patent on the Montgomery propeller. Nor did Ben succeed in getting a U.S. patent on it during or after the war, although he had applied in 1863, when he displayed a model of the invention at the Western Sanitary Fair in Cincinnati.[36]

However, Montgomery enjoyed his greatest success as a retail merchant. In 1842 he established a store on the plantation, selling dry goods and staple items to the slaves in exchange for the wood, chickens, eggs, and vegetables they produced on their own time. Davis guaranteed Ben's first consignment of goods, but from then on he maintained his own line of credit with New Orleans wholesalers. His store provided a convenient place for the entire community to buy goods; it saved a costly trip off the peninsula for the slaves and allowed the whites to buy a few luxuries without waiting for a visit to Vicksburg or Natchez. "The ladies of the family used to 'shop' at his store," a visitor recalled, and one year the account of a family member amounted to $2,000. Soon Ben was marketing the fruit crop from the Davis orchards and acting as Davis's agent in purchasing supplies and shipping the huge cotton crop. He sold food and fuel to the steamboat captains who carried freight for the Bend. In time he became the actual business manager for Hurricane and, in the absence of the Jefferson Davises, for Brierfield as well. Ben's power and influence exceeded that which had been exercised by James Pemberton when Ben first arrived at the Bend.[37]

With some of his accumulating profits, Montgomery built a combined store building and living quarters near the steamboat landing. Here he established his wife, Mary Lewis Montgomery, whom he had married on December 24, 1840. She was the daughter of Virginia slaves who had been among the earliest arrivals at Davis Bend, where she had grown up surrounded by a large family. The Lewises continued to play an important part in the Hurricane community as long as it existed. Perhaps membership in his wife's family helped Ben accept his new way of life. Soon he was able to pay his master the equivalent of Mary's labor, and she remained at home, occasionally sewing for the white ladies but usually just caring for the five children that were born to them by 1851. Their second son, Benjamin Osmond, died before he was three, but the others, two boys and two girls, lived to adulthood.[38]

These literate slave parents were very much concerned about the education of their children. Their youngest son, Isaiah, left an account of his early training. He remembered that his mother read to him from the time he was a tot; while he was still quite small his parents arranged for him and his brother to have lessons on Sundays from "the old fashioned Websters blue back spelling book" taught by George Stewart, an educated slave belonging to Jefferson Davis. At night Ben drilled the children in the alphabet by "making letters on cardboard and covering [them] with tissue paper." He was a strict taskmaster, giving them assignments one night that they had to recite perfectly the next; thus they learned to write. When Isaiah was about seven years old, his father discovered a well-educated white man, George Metcalf, who had recently moved to a small farm some three miles from Hurricane, where he was making a poor living cutting wood. Ben had no difficulty hiring him to tutor Isaiah and his sister, Mary Virginia, who was then about five. When Joseph Davis learned of this arrangement he moved Metcalf and his wife nearby, where he taught four or five white children along with the Montgomery youngsters; two of the pupils were Davis relatives, including one of Joseph's nephews. However, in antebellum Mississippi even the master of Hurricane could not protect indefinitely this daring venture in integrated education. Isaiah recalled, "The school was finally discontinued because of its existence being too publicly known of."[39]

When the promising young Isaiah was ten years old, Eliza Davis decided that he should come to live in the mansion to be trained as Joseph's valet and private secretary. Ben wanted to keep him at home under parental supervision to continue his studies, but even financial independence did not remove the Montgomery family from Davis control. Joseph promised to see that the lad continued his education, and promptly put him to work filing letters and papers and caring for the office. At night he slept on a pallet in Davis's bedroom so that he was available when needed. Soon Isaiah began the tedious task of copying letters and documents for the files. He said later, "There were no typewriters in those days, and frequently four or five copies of a long speech or plea or account would have to be made by hand." This exercise and his wide reading in the large Hurricane library gave Isaiah unusual literary competence. However, his abrupt removal from his family home must have reminded Ben of the galling fact of his inability to control his own life or the lives of his children. Although Isaiah asserted, "We just barely had an idea of what slave life was," Ben must have been acutely aware of his lack of freedom.[40]

Great as were the privileges granted to this remarkable man, and despite the responsibility he was given, there were many jarring reminders of his true status. Some people resented Montgomery's success and the need to do business with him as though he were a white merchant. In 1856 the captain of one of the large steamboats who had contracted to carry the mail to Davis Bend wrote to the postmaster general objecting to the fact that the post office was kept "at the store of Ben F. Montgomery who is a slave." The captain considered it improper to deliver the bag of mail to a black man and requested that "a Free White man" be required to handle it in the future.[41] Joseph Davis's efforts to broaden Ben's knowledge and experience sometimes led to his encountering obstacles imposed by his race and status. In the 1850s Davis took Montgomery to Vicksburg to inspect and study the machine shops there. While staying in the home of the shop manager, Ben acted as his master's valet and even asked permission from the lady of the house to wait on the table. She recalled that he did the job "most dexterously," but it must have been an unwelcome interruption of his engineering lesson. Ben won the respect and approval of the whites he contacted by being sensitive to their needs while meticulously observing the rules of caste behavior. His generous gifts of delicacies for yellow-fever victims in Vicksburg in 1853 accompanied by "such beautiful letters" won him the admiration of the recipients, especially since they knew that in his master's absence he was acting on his own initiative. He was an expert at playing the game.[42]

The first Union officer who got to know Ben Montgomery in early 1863 was captivated by his intelligence and ability; he later remarked, "I don't see how so inteligent [sic] a man could have consented to remain so long a Slave."[43] This is indeed a valid question. By the 1850s Ben made enough money annually to buy his freedom and that of his family, and it seems probable that Davis would have accepted this natural culmination of his permissive policies. If his master refused to emancipate him, Ben had enough money, contacts, and mobility to make good a flight to freedom for himself and his family. It seems unlikely that so sophisticated a man could have been held in bondage against his will.

However, Montgomery's wide knowledge of existing conditions made him realize the dismal alternatives to his situation. The

handful of free Negroes in antebellum Mississippi lived a precarious life on the fringes of society, maintaining their freedom and a
meager livelihood with great difficulty. Ben knew George
Fitzgerald, a free black carpenter on the neighboring plantation,
who was constantly under suspicion by the whites. He had to
persuade his employer, Colonel Wood, to file his free papers each
year, and he was restricted in all his contacts with the slaves,
including his own wife. If Ben had moved North, he would have
encountered intense race prejudice in a strange community without the backing or protection of Joseph Davis. There was probably nowhere else and no other status whereby he could have enjoyed the prosperity and security he had as the only merchant,
business agent, and engineer at Hurricane, and Montgomery,
who read the Vicksburg and New Orleans newspapers and magazines, knew this full well.[44] Although the reminders of the limitations to his freedom must have rankled, Ben enjoyed the complete confidence and even companionship of his master. Davis
was delighted with his most brilliant pupil and discussed all of
his hopes and plans with the slave. After many years of partnership, Ben came to share Joseph's dream of creating an ideal
community from which all could profit. This common goal must
have done much to compensate Montgomery for his bondage.

How successful was Joseph Davis in creating an ideal community with slave labor at Hurricane? How close did he come to
realizing the dream that had first captivated him during the
stagecoach journey with Robert Owen so many years earlier? In
terms of material profit, a prime goal of all of Owen's early
schemes, the Davis Bend experiment was a great success. There
in the fertile Mississippi bottom lands Davis developed a plantation that was among the most prosperous in the state. Although
cotton was the major cash crop, Davis never equaled the quantity
per acre produced by his immediate neighbors on the Bend. For
example, in 1850 John A. Quitman raised almost the same
number of bales on less than two-thirds the cleared land, and
Quitman's brother-in-law, Henry Turner, produced half again as
much as Davis with slightly less improved land (see Table 1).
Again, in 1856, both of the Davis plantations, with a total of
slightly more than 2,000 acres of improved land, produced only

1,265 bales of cotton, while the combined Turner-Quitman estate realized 2,200 bales on 2,500 acres (see Table 2). One contemporary later observed that, although Davis "was not famous for the number of his cotton bales, they were always of the best quality."[45] However, the figures cited do not necessarily indicate a low productivity per acre for the Davises, because they experimented with a wide variety of crops and therefore planted fewer acres of cotton. For example, in 1850 Joseph raised 15,000 bushels of Indian corn, while the Turner plantation of comparable size produced only 10,000 bushels. Davis also raised 1,000 bushels of sweet potatoes and 100 hogs to make his plantation more nearly self-sufficient. The unusual quantity of orchard produce not only supplemented the slave diet but provided another small cash crop.

Joseph Davis was also noted for breeding fine-quality cattle, sheep, and horses; the census data for both 1850 and 1860 confirm his large investment in livestock (see Tables 1 and 3). He bred both beef and dairy cattle, adding meat and butter to his annual products. He was the only planter on the Bend to raise a substantial number of sheep; by 1860 his flock produced 2,000 pounds of wool. Davis also experimented with unusual crops such as buckwheat. He was always eager to apply the latest theories of scientific agriculture, even if it meant sacrificing some assured short-run cotton profits.[46]

The Warren County Personal Tax Rolls reveal Davis's success in providing luxuries for himself and his family (see Table 2). In the decade of the 1850s he owned more clocks, watches, gold and silver plate, carriages, and pianos than any of his neighbors. His investment in fine horses far exceeded that of the others and probably explains the large production of oats and hay in 1850. There is further evidence of the affluence of the master of Hurricane in a detailed statement of goods he purchased from a New Orleans merchant in the first six months of 1861. It included such exotic materials as silk, linen, organdy, and lawn, as well as quantities of ribbon, braid, tassels, pearl and "porceline" buttons, net, silk thread and hose, Valencienne lace, and handkerchiefs of silk and Irish linen. For April, apparently an average month, the bill totaled $328.75, a sizable sum for luxury items Ben Montgomery evidently did not stock in his store.[47]

Table 1   PRODUCE FOR 1850 AT DAVIS BEND

	PLANTATIONS				
	Jos. E. Davis	Henry Turner	John A. Quitman	F. A. Freeland	Jeff. Davis
Acres improved	1,600	1,500	1,000	600	450
Cotton bales (400 lbs.)	152	219	150	152	99
Indian corn (bu.)	15,000	10,000	6,000	4,000	5,000
Oats (bu.)	1,000	—	—	150	—
Hay (tons)	100	100	—	—	—
Irish potatoes (bu.)	100	30	25	—	—
Sweet potatoes (bu.)	1,000	30	25	—	—
Peas and beans (bu.)	—	200	—	—	—
Market garden ($)	—	100	100	30	—
Orchard produce ($)	1,000	—	30	—	100
Horses	150	25	8	20	10
Mules	50	60	45	28	12
Milch cows	50	25	20	15	5
Working oxen	50	24	16	12	8
Other cattle	50	—	40	20	34
Sheep	200	75	—	—	—
Swine	100	60	6	—	100
Wool (lbs.)	300	100	—	160	—
Butter (lbs.)	500	300	2,000	500	100
Implements and machinery ($)	3,000	20,000	500	2,000	1,000
Animals slaughtered ($)	1,000	—	—	300	200
Value of stock ($)	20,000	15,000	8,000	5,000	1,500
Value of farm ($)	100,000	50,000	40,000	20,000	25,000
No. of slaves	242	290	133	66	72

SOURCE: 1850 U.S. Census, Agriculture Schedule, Mississippi, Warren County; Population Schedule, Mississippi; Mississippi Department of Archives and History.

Table 2   WARREN COUNTY PERSONAL TAX ROLL

	1848	1854	1856	1857	1858	1859	1860
Joseph E. Davis							
Pleasure carriages	1	2	2	2	2	2	—
Value ($)	250	250	250	300	300	300	—
Watches	2	1	1	2	2	2	—
Value ($)	150	100	100	150	150	200	—

	1848	1854	1856	1857	1858	1859	1860
Clocks	—	—	—	2	2	1	—
Value ($)	—	—	—	60	60	100	—
Cattle (over 20 head)	300	25	75	100	100	100	—
Race, saddle, carriage							
horses	3	1	1	2	2	2	—
Value ($)	200	150	150	600	500	500	—
Value of gold & silver							
plate (over $50)	400	—	—	100	100	200	—
Pianos	—	—	—	1	1	1	—
Value ($)	—	—	—	100	100	100	—
Slaves (under 60 yrs.)	210	217	238	290	308	300	316
Amount of State Tax ($)	143	85	93	125	131	129	244.20
Jefferson Davis							
Pleasure carriages	—	1	1	1	1	1	—
Value ($)	—	150	150	75	75	100	—
Watches	1	2	2	2	2	—	—
Value ($)	100	100	200	100	100	—	—
Cattle (over 20 head)	50	20	40	100	100	69	—
Race, saddle, carriage							
horses	2	—	—	1	1	1	—
Value ($)	200	—	—	125	125	300	—
Slaves	79	83	98	94	102	102	113
Amount of State Tax ($)	51	33	39	42	45	44	88.45
Turner & Quitman							
Pleasure carriages	1	—	—	—	—	—	
Value ($)	50	—	—	—	—	—	
Clocks	2	—	—	—	—	1	
Value ($)	75	—	—	—	—	5	
Cattle (over 20 head)	110	50	50	60	134	108	
Race, saddle, carriage							
horses	—	—	—	—	—	1	($100)
Slaves	311	291	310	338	348	359	
Amount of State Tax ($)	189	110	117	136	140	145	
R. Y. Wood							
Cattle	15	20	50	43	63	—	
Slaves	12	131	310	120	120	121	
Amount of State Tax ($)	7.55	49	117	49	49	48	

Number of Bales of Cotton (for 1856)			
Joseph E. Davis	815	Turner & Quitman	2,200
Jefferson Davis	450	R. Y. Wood	650

SOURCE: Personal Tax Roll, Warren County, Mississippi Department of Archives and History.

Table 3 PRODUCE FOR 1860 AT DAVIS BEND

	PLANTATIONS				
	Joseph Davis	Jeff. Davis	Turner and Quitman	Mrs. Freeland	R. Y. Wood
Acres improved	1,700	800	2,000	600	996
Unimproved	1,000	1,000	4,000	700	230
Value ($)	100,000	75,000	200,000	35,000	25,000
Implements and machinery Value ($)	500	400	1,000	500	350
Livestock:					
Horses	50	7	9	16	4
Mules	90	30	120	25	39
Milch cows	24	25	30	12	10
Oxen	65	18	30	8	14
Other cattle	65	60	100	20	15
Sheep	275	5	—	80	—
Value ($)	15,000	5,000	10,000	6,000	6,000
Cotton bales (400 lbs.)	12*	220	325	168	213
Indian corn (bu.)	—	1,000	1,000	—	4,000
Peas and beans (bu.)	100	—	100	50	—
Irish potatoes (bu.)	50	—	50	50	—
Sweet potatoes (bu.)	150	—	1,000	100	—
Buckwheat (bu.)	100	—	—	—	—
Wool (lbs.)	2,000	—	800	—	—
Butter (lbs.)	500	—	2,000	150	—
Animals slaughtered ($)	—	—	50	100	—
Home manufactures ($)	—	—	100	1,500	—
Number of slaves	355	111	308	80	171
Slave houses	76	28	80	35	25

*[sic]
SOURCE: 1860 U.S. Census, Warren County, Mississippi; Agriculture Schedule and Slave Population Schedule, Mississippi Department of Archives and History.

Although Davis may not have maximized profits in any one year, it is obvious that he operated a thriving plantation that made possible an affluent style of life for his large family. Contemporaries commented upon his wealth; Zachary Taylor said that Davis had "made himself a little paradis [sic]," and others referred to him as "a man of great wealth surrounded with all the comforts and luxuries that money could command."[48] In a material sense, there is little doubt that the plantation experiment at Hurricane was an unqualified success.

But Joseph Davis expected to reap more than physical benefits from his model plantation. He seemed to find much psychic satisfaction in his position as one of the leading planters in Mississippi. Although there is no evidence that Davis claimed a more illustrious ancestry than the Welsh and Scotch-Irish working-class folk from whom he descended, he adopted the life-style of the planter aristocracy. His lifelong hero was Thomas Jefferson, and the gracious hospitality of Hurricane rivaled that of Monticello half a century earlier. He welcomed a constant stream of visitors for stays that often lasted several months, and the dining room and the music room above it rang with the sounds of merriment at parties honoring these guests. One member of the family later recalled that the big house at Hurricane was always full: "There were enough visiting relations alone to keep it crowded." The master of the plantation, though he avoided overindulgence, was known to delight in fine food and drink, especially in the company of charming ladies. Davis undoubtedly enjoyed the role of gracious host.[49]

As a wealthy cotton baron, Joseph Davis became a person of some importance in local and state affairs. His word carried a great deal of weight in matters ranging from cotton taxes and state-constructed levees to the regulation of dueling. Although his mild manner was often spiced with sharp satire, he acquired a reputation as an able arbiter of disputes. He was rather rigid in his political views and, after he had explained his reasons, suspected that anyone who still differed with him was insincere. Davis displayed this same confidence in his own judgment in the treatment of his large family. As the eldest of ten children and one of the wealthiest, he was very generous with his siblings and their families; when he deemed it appropriate, he showered them with gifts ranging from clothes and vacation trips to large plantations. He took in a widowed sister and raised her seven children along with his three motherless grandchildren. He educated a number of nieces, nephews, and wards, and quietly gave financial assistance to many who were in need. Davis relished his role as *pater familias* and treated his dependent relatives in some ways as he did his slaves, with benevolent firmness.[50]

Thus, the model plantation appeared to provide both financial and psychic benefits for its master. But what did it do for the other participants in this utopian experiment? Was there true harmony in this "community of cooperation"? There is consider-able evidence that Davis's methods at times created dissatis-faction among some members of the family. Those who had ben-efited from Joseph's generosity were grateful, but there was also some resentment of the conditions he attached to his gifts. For example, Davis usually kept title to the lands he gave away, thus maintaining control over their use. Although he probably hoped to protect the beneficiaries from their own business ineptitude, it led to veiled bitterness and frequent quarrels among his depen-dents. However, even with the friction and resentment of Davis's authoritarian management, most members of the family probably considered the plantation experiment a success.

The parade of white overseers who spent a year or two there undoubtedly would have dissented from this judgment. By the 1850s Joseph Davis had divided his slaves into two groups, each with its own overseer; Jefferson employed only one to manage his smaller work force. As we have seen, these men lacked the au-thority to punish any slave until he had been given a hearing before the slave court. Most of the overseers felt that this restric-tion undermined their power to an unacceptable degree. Varina Davis recalled the open contempt in which some of their slaves held these white men and their families. One young slave girl refused to serve the overseer's family because their table man-ners were too crude, she said, and they had called her by a nick-name. A Davis field hand so frightened another overseer that he sought protection from Varina, claiming the slave had pulled a knife on him; Varina discovered the accused with a bladeless knife handle thrust into his belt, chortling over the cowardice of the white man.[51] It is not surprising that these poor men were eager to move to plantations where they could exercise more con-ventional control. They and the white artisans who occasionally sojourned on the Davis places must have felt threatened by the relative independence of the slaves. However, all the white peo-ple taken together formed an insignificant part of the experi-mental community.

By far the most important segment of the plantation population in terms of numbers was the slave community. How successful did the experiment seem to them? With all the innovations and concessions, did they form a true "community of cooperation"? It is very difficult to determine the prevailing attitude among the

Davis slaves. As previously noted, Isaiah Montgomery reported many years later that he and his family "just barely had an idea of what slave life was." But the Montgomerys clearly were not typical Davis slaves. In 1931 another member of Joseph Davis's work force gave an equally glowing assessment of antebellum conditions. Aunt Florida Hewitt supposedly said, "Did dey treat we well? Sho dey did. Beter dan I has bin treated since." However, she claimed to be 107 years old at the time of the interview, and the interviewer was a prominent white man, a former governor of Mississippi, with whom she was unlikely to be candid. Even the way he transcribed her dialect seems to indicate that he held a stereotyped view of blacks; such testimony is suspect at best. The other former Davis slaves interviewed in the Federal Writers Project failed to give a general appraisal of conditions on the Bend. George Johnson, who was only a young child when freedom came, labeled his master "as good as they get." James Lucas belonged to Jefferson Davis for only a short time and merely noted the contrast between the talkativeness of Varina and the calm, quiet manner of her husband in dealing with their slaves.[52]

With only limited testimony from the slaves themselves, their attitude toward Davis's experiment must be inferred from their actions. One positive indication is the fact that apparently there were no runaways from Hurricane or Brierfield after Benjamin Montgomery fled soon after his arrival in the mid-1830s. Many years later, when *Century Magazine* reported that Jefferson Davis kept a pack of bloodhounds on his place, which the Yankee troops had to destroy, Isaiah Montgomery wrote indignantly that Davis "had no hounds of any kind on his plantation, and absolutely no use for negro dogs, as none of his slaves were runaways."[53]

Nor is there any evidence of open discontent among the slaves at Hurricane or Brierfield. Varina Davis described the slaves' usual displays of affection for the master and his family. They were greeted effusively when they returned to Brierfield, whether from a brief trip or from long absences in Washington. When their first baby was born, the mistress of Brierfield reported:

> Every negro on the plantation, great and small, came up with little gifts of eggs, and chickens and a speech of thanks for the birth of a

"little massa to take care of we, and be good to we," from the year-old, open-mouthed, glossy little tot, with an egg in his fist, to the old women with a squawking hen, or a dozen large yam potatoes in their aprons.

Before Jefferson left to assume his duties as president of the Confederacy, he made "an affectionate farewell speech" to his assembled slaves, and they responded warmly "with expressions of devotion." However, common sense tells us these demonstrations undoubtedly stemmed as much from the slaves' concern for their own welfare as from genuine affection. Varina frequently suspected feigned illness among the workers and dosed them with bitter medicine to discourage it. If, as one historian asserts, such malingering was a sign of the slave's passive resistance to his lot, then the black community may not have found Davis's experiment completely satisfying.[54]

Even the jury system did not ensure perfect justice, for, on at least one occasion, an overseer managed to circumvent it. At Hurricane the two slave squads and their overseers were in constant competition. One day one of the overseers bet the other a box of cigars that he could secure Joseph Davis's permission to have one of his best and most cooperative slaves punished. The next Sunday at court the overseer accused the slave of insubordination and of using insulting language to him. Davis called the hand to the witness seat and questioned him. The man denied the charges, telling Davis, "You know me and know what kind of man I have been." The master then closely questioned the overseer, but the latter made an issue of the case, insisting that he could not be responsible for keeping order if such acts went unpunished. Finally, without forcing the jury to choose between the slave and the overseer, Davis reluctantly agreed to the punishment. Although such injustice was probably uncommon, there were frequent instances when the jury prescribed and the master approved punishment for a slave. The usual sentence required the culprit to wear a heavy iron band for a prescribed time; although he still worked in the fields during the day, at night and when he was not working he was chained to the wall of the jail. For these convicts, Hurricane was certainly less than utopian.[55]

However, the slaves undoubtedly knew that their situation

compared favorably with that of most of their fellow bondsmen. They knew that their food, clothing, housing, work load, and privileges were better than their neighbors'. They also had other advantages. Many years later, Isaiah Montgomery told a fellow freedman that Robert Wood, master of an adjacent plantation, had raised two families—a white one in the mansion and a mulatto one in the quarters. Isaiah was very critical of the practice and clearly implied that, on the Davis plantations, sexual exploitation of the slaves was not permitted.[56] Such details of slave life on other plantations must have been well known to the Davis work force.

They probably also knew of Joseph Davis's reputation as an unusually indulgent master. When they left the Bend or encountered whites, they frequently heard themselves referred to as "Mr. Davis's free negroes." When hoop skirts became fashionable, they may have heard local whites joke that "Mr. Joe Davis would have to widen his cotton rows to allow the [slave] women to get through."[57]

His slaves also recognized that, unlike most masters, Joseph Davis respected them as people. Undoubtedly it was generally true, as one historian of slavery asserts, that "to enjoy the bounty of a paternalistic master a slave had to give up all claims to respect as a responsible adult." However, Davis adopted Robert Owen's method of rational treatment, which allowed his workers to maintain their dignity. As his brother said, Joseph had higher hopes for the Negroes' "moral and mental elevation" than did "most men of his experience." He expected his slaves to work hard for their own benefit as well as his, and he was quick to commend and encourage those who performed well. He and his brother were careful in little things; for example, they respected a slave's wish to be called by his full name rather than a shorter nickname, and they always referred to them as servants, never as slaves. The courtly politeness with which Jefferson treated James Pemberton probably also characterized Joseph's dealings with Ben Montgomery. There is no evidence that the Davises demanded or even permitted the demeaning subservience commonly required by masters.[58]

The black community was well aware not only of what the Davises thought of their capacity but also of what they thought of the institution of slavery itself. Isaiah claimed that slaves knew of the "various shades of opinion prevailing among their masters," and they recognized the difference between the brothers. They knew that Joseph "considered slavery an evil that was a vexing problem to get rid of." After the war, the elder Davis asserted that he had wanted to free his slaves for more than twenty years but could think of no adequate way of guaranteeing their welfare. He had reached adulthood and formed his opinions in the early years of the nineteenth century when there was strong sentiment for reform, and slavery was condemned as inhuman. Joseph shared Thomas Jefferson's dilemma regarding the peculiar institution and never accepted the later doctrine of Southern apologists that slavery was a positive good.[59]

On the other hand, Jefferson Davis, a generation younger and repeatedly forced to win the approval of a Deep South electorate, "considered [slavery] as ordered of Divine Providence for the benefit of both races involved." He shared the prevalent assumption that Negroes were inherently inferior to whites and were protected by slavery from unequal competition with their superiors. As one biographer concluded, "Jefferson Davis regarded Southern planters like his brother and himself as providing a beneficial tutelage for a childlike race unprepared as yet to take care of itself in a white man's world." In fact, he did not believe that blacks could ever become the equals of the whites, and so he regarded slavery as an essential means of regulating the races in society. Despite his differing views, Jefferson accepted the management methods established by his brother. After 1845 his political duties took him away from Brierfield most of the time, and his attitude had little impact upon the treatment of the Brierfield work force.[60]

Although Joseph believed that some of his blacks were capable of independent living and may have thought that he was training all of them for eventual freedom, there is no evidence that he took steps toward manumitting a single one. Ironically, it was Jefferson who gave his most trusted slave the option of freedom in case of his owner's death. James Pemberton chose to take care of Jefferson's wife with the provision that he would be freed at her death.[61] Since James predeceased both of them, there was no manumission of a Davis slave.

In spite of all the special treatment enjoyed by blacks at Hurricane and Brierfield, they were still aware that they were not free. In fact, the more independent and self-sufficient they became, the more galling it may have been to realize the limits to their freedom. Frederick Douglass expressed this reaction from his own experience:

> Beat and cuff the slave, keep him hungry and spiritless, and he will follow the chain of the master like a dog, but feed and clothe him well, work him moderately and surround him with physical comfort, and dreams of freedom will intrude. Give him a bad master and he aspires to a good master; give him a good master, and he wishes to become his own master.[62]

There is no reason to believe that the members of the slave community at Davis Bend were satisfied with their condition.

Although most of them probably maintained a general longing for freedom, there was one immediate cause for anxiety among the slaves. In addition to the normal nineteenth-century fear of the death of loved ones, there was a very real dread of their master's death. Joseph Davis was considered an old man even before the decade of the 1850s. There must have been general apprehension among the slaves about the consequences of his impending demise. His financial success meant that, during his lifetime, no slaves were likely to be sold away from the expanding plantation; however, all knew that there was no assurance of a continuation of his benevolent policies after his death. No one was more aware of dissension within the slaveholding family than the observant servants; in the case of the Davis blacks, self-interest must certainly have added to their curiosity about conflicts among the whites. They were haunted by the specter of a major family quarrel around Joseph's bier, resulting in the division of his slaves among his heirs. Added to the horror of possible separation from loved ones was a dread of leaving Hurricane, to which many had a deep attachment. Above all, there was the fear of being sent to any one of the plantations in the South where there were virtually no checks on the cruelty that might be meted out by owner or overseer.

Joseph Davis succeeded in establishing a financially successful cotton plantation from which he derived considerable psychic satisfaction. The other white inhabitants of the plantation enjoyed many of these same benefits but were plagued by a bickering and jealousy quite naturally engendered by their dependent status. The slaves, while appreciating their benevolent master, recognized quite clearly the limits to their autonomy and the dangers inherent in their condition. Perhaps only the father is the ultimate beneficiary of paternalism. Joseph Davis realized that there was discontent within the family and anxiety among the slaves. He had hoped to create an ideal community using some of Robert Owen's visionary ideas, but he insisted upon combining them with his own demand for profits substantial enough to bring him social status and material comfort. Since, in Mississippi, this meant the use of slave labor, there was never any possibility that the plantation might become truly utopian. The continuance of slavery was inherently incompatible with the creation of a voluntary "community of cooperation." Although Davis modified the peculiar institution as much as possible to accommodate some degree of individual initiative and freedom of choice, perfect harmony could never be achieved where any member of the community remained, in reality, a chattel. The master of Hurricane must have known that his model plantation was only comparatively benign and its members only relatively happy. However, as a pragmatic utopian he continued to strive for improvement, and his unfailing enthusiasm for his dream inspired emulation by those upon whom he had the greatest influence.

II

Federal Officers
Usurp the Dream

2

The Chaos of War

The Civil War destroyed Joseph Davis's model plantation experiment and replaced it first with chaos and then with several innovative communities established by federal officers for the benefit of the freedmen. In each case, the ideal of modified self-government through community cooperation, implanted and nurtured by Davis, survived as one element in the Yankees' experimental colonies. Although these abortive attempts failed to create the utopias they sought for the freedmen, they managed to preserve and perpetuate the dream through times of great upheaval.

The first year of war brought no appreciable change in the even tenor of life at Hurricane and Brierfield. When Mississippi seceded from the Union in January 1861, Jefferson resigned his seat in the Senate and returned to Brierfield, only to be summoned to Montgomery, Alabama, to head the Confederacy. His emotional farewell to his slaves and the departure of the family seemed to portend momentous events, but the plantation routine continued as it had for more than a decade during the Davises' absence. The Joseph Davis family spent the summer months in Richmond as part of the gay society centered around the executive mansion. However, the excitement and the underlying anxiety of the First Family of the Confederacy scarcely impinged upon the Davis Bend community, where cotton still ripened luxuriantly in the fertile fields.[1]

Suddenly, in April 1862 the effects of the war reached Hurricane and Brierfield, bringing changes that gradually destroyed the old way of life. The Confederate defeat at Shiloh opened northern Mississippi to the Union army, while the losses of New Madrid and Island No. 10 exposed the mid-Mississippi Valley to Union gunboats. Jefferson Davis became concerned for the safety of his family and possessions at Davis Bend, but Joseph was more worried about the threat posed by rising floodwaters. The seventy-seven-year-old planter personally supervised the reinforcement of a neighbor's levee where seepage seemed to threaten the entire Bend. He shepherded cattle and slaves to high ground while fulminating against the stupidity of Confederate generals whose unexpected losses might further threaten his domain.[2]

Word of the fall of New Orleans on April 25 reached Hurricane just as the river topped the record flood stage of two years earlier, and Davis decided the time had come to flee. Leaving white overseers at both plantations with Ben in charge of the Hurricane house and grounds, he commandeered a place for himself and family and a few slaves aboard the last Confederate boat upriver from New Orleans. He found temporary shelter for his retinue with O. B. Cox, friend and former overseer, whose plantation lay between Vicksburg and Jackson. Realizing that the twin threats from flood and war jeopardized all their possessions, Davis immediately arranged to send two flatboats towed by a small steamer under Cox's direction to bring their books, papers, and other valuables to Vicksburg. Cox was instructed to evacuate as many slaves as the boats would carry, but by the time the family possessions were loaded, most of the Negroes had disappeared; he brought only seven from Brierfield and ten from Hurricane. This unprecedented act of insubordination demonstrated the rapid breakdown of the old authority structure. Obviously the slaves preferred the hazards of flood and war to the uncertainties of refugee life with their master. Surely they had been reminded of their continuing slave status by the arrival the day before of a Confederate boat to conscript slaves for work on the fortifications at Vicksburg. Montgomery wrote Davis that the overseers had been forced to send ten from Hurricane and five from Brierfield, although none wanted to go.[3]

As an expression of their new sense of independence, as soon as Cox left with the boats the slaves broke into the mansions and seized items of clothing and furniture for their own use. Davis blamed the white overseers for failing to stop this lawlessness, even hinting that Nicholas Barnes at Brierfield had encouraged the looters. Evidently Davis did not expect Ben Montgomery to control his fellow blacks, assuming perhaps, that he had his hands full protecting his store from the mob.

Although it should have been apparent to both men that the antebellum dream was shattered, Davis clung to the hope that he could rebuild it in the interior. After another futile attempt by an agent to recover some of the slaves, Joseph went down to the Bend himself in an open boat. His personal authority was still strong enough for him to remove more than a hundred blacks to his place of refuge, including both of the Montgomery boys. But the expedition was so taxing to the old man that it may have contributed to a brief illness that followed; Davis never again visited his beloved Hurricane.[4]

Davis's spirits were further lowered by the loss of his entire 1861 cotton crop, which he had held in storage at the Bend. When Confederate authorities ordered the destruction of all cotton along the river that might fall into enemy hands, Davis instructed Ben to send some 200 bales thirty miles up the Big Black River (much of the remainder of the cotton was under floodwater, and therefore Davis figured it was unlikely that it would be confiscated). However, the local newspapers learned of the arrangement and suggested that the Davis brothers were trying to save property that less prominent Confederate planters were required to destroy. Incited by this publicity, a mob located and burned the cache on the Big Black. A short time later, a squad of Confederate soldiers visited the Bend and, despite the protests of Montgomery and Barnes, burned the rest of the Davis cotton, 841 bales in all. Stung by this financial loss, Davis complained bitterly to his brother and the newspapers about what he termed wanton destruction.[5]

However, the Confederate depredations soon seemed minor in comparison with Yankee destruction. On June 24, as Admiral Farragut's fleet steamed up the Mississippi from New Orleans, a raiding party landed at Davis Bend. Perhaps seeking retribution against the First Family of the Confederacy, the Yankees stripped Hurricane mansion of its costly furnishings, keeping what they liked for souvenirs and destroying the rest. They carried out the sets of china and glassware, dumped them on the grass and shattered them with their bayonets. All of the family portraits were slashed and the books from the adjacent library building were thrown into a bonfire on the lawn. Finally, they put the torch to the great house and departed, leaving behind the flames, which were visible through the darkness all the way to Vicksburg. The frightened slaves who wandered aimlessly among the debris noted that only the empty library at Hurricane and the looted mansion at Brierfield remained of the Davis family dwellings.[6]

During the next few months there was great uncertainty and confusion within the diminished black community on the Davis plantation. Joseph finally located an alternative home for them near Bolton in Hinds County, between Vicksburg and Jackson. However, when seventy blacks from Hurricane were taken there in November, they discovered that the twenty slave houses were little better than shacks, and the barren farm had produced only a fraction of the corn and hogs for which Davis had contracted. Although the master set men to work planting corn and improving the housing, many of the slaves slipped away and returned to the more familiar surroundings of the Bend. An even larger group of Brierfield slaves defected from the neighboring place that Joseph had bought for his brother's use. Food was scarce and difficult to procure; tools and farm animals were frequently stolen by the roving marauders that menaced the countryside. In all the confusion, the health of the people and of the livestock suffered. A measles epidemic started by a fugitive from the work crew on the Vicksburg fortifications swept through the quarters, claiming at least a dozen lives. Inadequate housing and irregular meals probably contributed to the high incidence of pneumonia, which also took several lives. During a three-month period that year, the doctor treated from two to ten seriously ill slaves on each of his eleven visits to the Joseph Davis place in Hinds County. Eliza Davis was bedridden much of the time, and Joseph himself was incapacitated for three weeks late in the year. It was a dismal time for the entire community.[7]

Back at the Bend, the white overseers fled after repeated Yankee raids took several blacks and terrorized the inhabitants. Ben Montgomery assumed command of the remaining people and set about providing subsistence. By January 1863 he could report to Jefferson Davis that they had produced 300 bushels of corn. However, he calculated that that would not see them through till the next harvest; he was negotiating with a woman across the river in Louisiana to buy some rain-damaged corn, which he proposed to boil with cottonseed to provide cattle feed. In order to earn some money for necessities, Montgomery started a small shoemaking business on the place, tanning his own leather and selling shoes to the neighbors. He was assisted by fifteen-year-old Isaiah, whom he had kept at Hurricane on one of the boy's liaison trips from Fleetwood, Joseph Davis's Hinds County refuge. Montgomery was doing his best to provide for the blacks in a rapidly disintegrating society.[8]

The events of war soon provided another source of authority at the Bend. In February 1863 Admiral David D. Porter, commander of the Union fleet on the Mississippi, sent an ironclad, the *Indianola,* downriver past the Vicksburg batteries at night to try to recapture a ram* that the Confederate Navy had recently taken. However, on February 24, two Rebel gunboats apprehended the unescorted *Indianola* just opposite Davis Bend, rammed and sank her.[9] Porter was especially anxious to recover two large cannons that had been thrown overboard before the ironclad was sunk. When he heard that Isaiah Montgomery had watched the entire operation, the admiral had the black lad brought aboard his flagship, *Black Hawk,* for interrogation. Although efforts to find the cannons were unsuccessful, Porter was captivated by the intelligence and charm of young Montgomery and his family. He virtually adopted them and assumed responsibility for the entire black community on the Bend. On April 22 he enlisted Isaiah as his cabin boy and personal attendant, taking the lad with him on various ships during the next six months as the Union navy assisted General Grant in capturing Vicksburg and freeing the Mississippi from Confederate control. For a time the admiral made use of Ben Montgomery's mechanical skill to repair gunboats, but soon persuaded him that he and his wife and daughters should seek refuge in the North. Ben had closed

---

* A ram was a warship with an armored protuberance at the prow that was used to pierce the hulls of enemy ships.

his store several months earlier rather than accept inflated Confederate currency; now he boxed up the remaining merchandise and entrusted it to his father-in-law, William Lewis. By June the Montgomerys had settled in Cincinnati under sponsorship of Mrs. Richardson, wife of the captain of the transport that took them up the river. There Ben found a job as carpenter in a canal-boat yard, and Mary Virginia, his eldest daughter, worked for Mrs. Richardson. In October, when Isaiah's health was threatened by a persistent attack of dysentery resulting from drinking impure water in the Red River campaign, Ben's written request prompted Admiral Porter to discharge the boy and send him to join his family in Cincinnati. With both Admiral Porter and Captain Richardson, Ben demonstrated his skill at winning patrons that had been so useful in his dealings with white Southerners. Porter called the elder Montgomery "an ingenious mechanic" who was "as well educated as most white people and as sensible a man as I ever met with."[10] There is no evidence that Montgomery regretted leaving Hurricane or abandoning the Confederate cause. He probably felt fortunate to be able to take his accumulated store profits and at least part of his family to safety. However, he must have felt some trepidation at leaving young Isaiah in combat and Thornton in the interior with Joseph Davis. It was a time of wrenching decisions for all.

Porter was favorably impressed with the intelligence of the entire black community at Davis Bend and took steps to provide for their welfare after Ben's departure. In July, after the fall of Vicksburg, the Union army moved east and the Joseph Davis family fled from their Hinds County plantation with the retreating Confederate forces. Although some of the slaves chose to go with their old master, many made their way back to the Bend. Porter enlisted some of the able-bodied men in the gunboat service as mechanics, firemen, coal heavers, or servants; on July 15 Thornton Montgomery signed up as an officer's steward on the USS *Carondelet*. However, most of the former Davis slaves elected to remain and cultivate the plantations for their own benefit. Perhaps as a result of long conversations with Ben Montgomery, Porter decided to foster an independent colony of contrabands, as the government called the freed slaves, under the supervision of the commander of the gunboats that patrolled the adjacent river.

The latter drew up rules and regulations for the colonists and left "an old Patriarch," probably Uncle Bob, in charge. They were employed cutting wood to meet the insatiable demand of the steamers, and the navy officers saw that they received fair compensation. The blacks also guarded a large herd of confiscated cattle, which they slaughtered for the gunboat crews on command, retaining an adequate share for themselves. Some fifteen of them leased plots of land from the government, but the season was too far advanced to plant more than garden vegetables. However, the admiral was optimistic about future prospects of the colony. He told the adjutant general that next spring "they will all go to work planting cotton on their own account, and . . . will raise more than they ever did before."[11]

The successful recovery of the *Indianola* from the river bottom led to the departure of a permanent Union contingent, and the occasional presence of a cruising gunboat proved insufficient to protect the colony from Rebel raiders. For months Joseph Davis had been pressing Confederate commanders to rescue "his people," and, finally, in early September, a small raiding party under Lieutenant Harvey made its way overland to the Bend. They were surprised to be met by armed Negroes, not knowing that the Union officers had provided them with guns to protect their cattle. The blacks may have feared that the raiders were there to reenslave them. At any rate, the Confederates began firing and killed some ten blacks, capturing a few more. In reprisal for black resistance and as an example to others, they hanged poor, retarded Alleck Flynn and then fled. Davis was furious at what he considered a slaughter of innocents and continued for the rest of the year to try to persuade some armed Confederates to recover the slaves from the two plantations on the river. After this raid he admitted that he could properly take only those willing to join him, but he still believed it was his duty to offer all of them protection from the Yankees.[12]

Ben Montgomery had been in Ohio for more than two months before his former master learned of his absence. The remaining blacks told Jim Green, Davis's emissary, that the Yankees stole Ben's money and "carried him off" when he failed to produce large sums which they believed the Davises had left in his care. Reporting this story to his brother, Joseph added, "I have little confidence in any of them."[13] It stunned him to see many of his most trusted slaves abandon the family after Union troops looted and burned the Hinds County plantations. He was touched to find that a house servant had saved some of his granddaughter's beloved books, but it disturbed him to note that O. B. Cox's favorite family cook had led the enemy to the Davis silver and to Jefferson's papers and books. In those disturbed times the old man continued to worry not only about the handful of blacks who had joined him on his hard journey into exile in Alabama, but also about those who had gone to the Yankee contraband camp at Blake's Plantation on the Yazoo River or back to Hurricane and Brierfield.[14]

However, the problem of caring for the former slaves had now been assumed by the Yankees. As Grant's army moved south into the Confederacy, hordes of contrabands swarmed into the lines seeking freedom, protection, and subsistence. By November 1862 their numbers so impeded military operations that Grant appointed Chaplain John Eaton, Jr., as superintendent of freedmen to deal with the problem. Eaton set up refugee camps that soon became sinkholes of misery and degradation, providing inadequate food and shelter with uncertain protection from enemy raids. Samuel R. Shipley, a Quaker philanthropist who toured these camps in the Mississippi Valley in late 1863, described the appalling conditions at Blake's Plantation, eight miles from Vicksburg. There, "from 600 to 700 poor creatures," including some of Davis's former slaves, were gathered in wretched huts that differed from hog pens only in the leaky roofs that partially covered them. The smoke from poorly built chimneys was dispersed somewhat by the cold north wind, which swept in through open sides, chilling the two or more families huddled on the bare dirt floor of each hut. These ill-clothed, hungry, idle people were subject to disease and despair.[15]

As the number of Union victories mounted, the flow of black refugees became a flood, and pressure grew to find an alternative to the refugee camps. The War Department's American Freedmen's Inquiry Commission, in its preliminary report, recommended that all contraband camps "be regarded as places for reception and distribution only." The blacks should be put to work either on military projects or as plantation laborers under government or private supervision.[16] Eaton had already recognized the advisability of moving the refugees to healthier surroundings where they could be more productive. He set out to employ as many as possible picking and ginning cotton on abandoned plantations. The profit made from the sale of this valuable commodity went into a fund to provide relief for other destitute blacks. This new enterprise, using private lessees to manage the plantations, created many additional problems for the superintendent of freedmen. He had to prevent fraud by unscrupulous speculators and had to protect the ex-slaves from exploitation, while following shifting government policies and providing low-cost, humane relief. His efforts were further complicated by the difficulty in securing capable officers to assist him. As he noted later:

> The feeling against serving the Negro in any capacity still prevailed among the officers of our troops. . . . It was exceedingly difficult to find men adapted to the task. . . . To get a man who could be kind to the Negro and just to the Negro's master was all but impossible.

Men who accepted assignments in the Freedmen's Department were hampered and ridiculed by fellow officers who called them "nigger men."[17]

However, Eaton found one man "of character whose services would be willingly offered and capably administered" in Samuel Thomas, a young captain of Eaton's own 27th Regiment of Ohio Volunteers. Thomas had been born of Virginia parents who became prosperous landowners on the southern border of Ohio. He was an ambitious youth who, after attending public schools in Marietta, went to work at age seventeen as a junior clerk for an Ohio iron company. Four years later, when he joined the army, he had advanced to the second highest position in the firm. Meanwhile, he had privately studied geology and metallurgy as well as law. Thomas quickly caught the eye of his superiors in the army; Eaton and the commander of the 27th Ohio agreed that he was "the most promising young man" among the lower-ranking officers. When Eaton needed an assistant in the Freedmen's Department he asked for Samuel Thomas because, he said, "I believed he would devote himself with willingness to the Negro cause."[18]

Eaton's confidence was well placed, for Thomas worked diligently to bring order out of the chaos that faced the Freedmen's Department during the last years of the war. He was placed in charge of the freedmen in the Vicksburg area in August 1863 when, according to Eaton:

> The scenes were appalling: the refugees were crowded together, sickly, disheartened, dying on the streets, not a family of them all either well sheltered, clad, or fed; no physicians, no medicine, no hospitals; many of the persons who had been charged with feeding them either sick or dead.

Thomas used all the resources of private charities and the meager aid allowed by the government to alleviate the worst suffering while trying to relocate the freedmen on plantations along the river. Newly formed black regiments were used as a home guard to protect these planting ventures from Confederate and guerrrilla attacks. Thomas was promoted to colonel and given command of the 64th U.S. Colored Infantry while continuing to serve as superintendent of freedmen and provost marshal at Vicksburg.[19]

Even before the fall of that key city, General Grant had decided that the fertile land at Davis Bend should become a haven for freedmen because it included the plantations of the president of the Confederacy and his brother, as well as those of the late General Quitman and several other wealthy Southerners. Grant told Eaton that he would like to see it become "a negro paradise."[20] Eaton accepted this suggestion with enthusiasm and sought ways to implement it. In November he proposed to Samuel R. Shipley that the Friends' Association of Philadelphia sponsor a model freedmen's colony at the Bend, dividing about a thousand acres among some one hundred blacks for their own cultivation. The Quakers would provide the necessary mules, equipment, housing materials, and subsistence for the season, keeping an account with each freedman to be settled when the cotton crop was marketed. Shipley estimated that the scheme would require a capital outlay of about $10,000, which would be repaid at the end of the year and thus become available for another group of freedmen the next year. Noting that only by such means could the black race rise above its present state of destitution and dependence, he recommended that the Quakers seize the opportunity to lend a helping hand. Like a true utopian, Shipley predicted that this experiment would have far-reaching consequences. He asserted:

> We may hope that if successful, the good results of our beneficence would incite others to the same good work, and, that the ability and good conduct of our lessees would silence and put to shame the calumnies against this unfortunate race.[21]

However, by the time Shipley formally presented this proposal to the Philadelphia Quakers, Colonel Thomas had persuaded the Freedmen's Department of the Union army to sponsor a similar experiment. On December 18, 1863, General McPherson ordered Thomas to take two companies of colored troops and occupy Davis Bend. Thomas landed at Hurricane and later testified that he found the condition of the Davis blacks "about as usual where negroes are alone." They were well housed but lacked food and clothing. He claimed that he issued rations to 900 people the first day of his occupation.[22]

The colonel noted that a minority of the destitute were former Davis slaves. Even before the army occupation, refugee blacks had begun to gather at Hurricane and Brierfield. Some were friends of Davis people or had heard of the comparatively pleasant conditions there before the war. Others probably were attracted by the independence and relative security provided by the navy-sponsored colony. Soon the army had built fortifications across the narrow neck of the peninsula and, for the next year, kept two to eight companies of black soldiers there to guarantee security from guerrilla raids. By the end of 1863 a New York newspaper headline could proclaim "Jeff's Plantation Turned into a Contraband Camp." The reporter found an ironic justice in the conversion of the Davis estates to a colony of freedmen who, he felt sure, would demonstrate their ability to maintain themselves as free people and thus prove the absurdity of slavery.[23]

Early the next year Thomas began dividing the land at the Bend among lessees; the government would provide supplies and equipment on credit in a scheme similar to the one rejected by the Philadelphia Quakers. However, the black lessees had scarcely begun to work their plots when a shift in government policy halted the experiment. As Union troops had moved into the South, there had been a great deal of fraud and profiteering by officers who confiscated Confederate property. The lure of bales of valuable cotton proved irresistible to many who neglected their military duties to enrich themselves. Describing the situation in the lower Mississippi Valley, Admiral Porter contended:

> It was not an army and navy entering a rebellious State to put down insurrection and bring people back to their duty; it was an army of cotton speculators, commanded by General Greed, General Avarice, General Speculation, and General Breech of Trust, with all their attendant staff of harpies, who were using the army and navy for the vilest purposes.[24]

The speculators were not limited to military personnel but included "ex-governors of States, ex-senators, relatives of people in Washington, rich merchants from New Orleans" who swarmed into the river valley "like so many hungry wolves seeking food in midwinter." Porter concluded with some exaggeration, "Ah! no man can imagine what a fascination there was in a bale of cotton, especially at a time when each was worth one thousand dollars."[25] Those who were not so fortunate as to find baled cotton scrambled to secure land on which to grow the magic crop the next season. Colonel Thomas noted: "Men from the North, by hundreds, flocked here eager to get a chance at the golden prospect, thoroughly convinced that to get a lease and a permit for hands was all that was to be done in order to secure a fortune."[26]

In March 1863, in an attempt to curb these abuses, Congress gave the Treasury Department responsibility for collecting all abandoned property. By September an order of that department expanded its agents' control to include all abandoned lands within Union lines, and authorized them to lease plantations to applicants who were loyal to the federal government. Since the only labor available to work these lands was that of former slaves, the army was directed to assign refugees from the camps to the white lessees. Although the plan devised by William P. Mellen, supervising agent of the Treasury Department, in collaboration with James E. Yeatman, president of the Western Sanitary Commission, sought to protect the freedmen-laborers from exploitation, the results fell far short of their goal. As Eaton later noted, many of the northern lessees "came on the ground to make money, whether the Union cause—not to mention the Negro—suffered by their operations or not."[27] These budding capitalists resented the Treasury order, which, through a complicated system of classification by age, sex, and ability, prescribed a much higher wage for the freedmen than required by the army. The lessees contended that $10 to $25 per month to each laborer was excessive in view of the risks incurred by the planters. Furthermore, these newcomers generally ignored the provisions that required them to supply adequate shelter, food, and clothing, the latter to be deducted from the laborers' wages at nominal increases above cost.

The Freedmen's Department officials, seeing their authority undermined by Treasury interference, echoed the lessees' contentions that wages were too high. In March 1864 General Lorenzo Thomas persuaded Mellen to reduce the wage scale to between $3.50 and $10 per month plus rations and clothing. A short time later Treasury officials agreed to remove the provision for clothing. Thus freedmen who had contracted at the first of the year to work for $25 per month were instead forced to accept $10 or less. It is not surprising that many of them became discouraged. In addition, the Treasury agents took most of the able-bodied freedmen as plantation hands but did nothing for their helpless dependents. The army, which had lost the productive capacity of both lands and workers, claimed it had no means of providing for the destitute, and benevolent societies withdrew their aid in the confusion. Eaton took the Freedmen's Department case to Washington and, finally, in the fall of 1864 persuaded President Lincoln to restore their authority over both the blacks and the plantations. However, this year-long dispute took a heavy toll of projects to assist the freedmen.

At Davis Bend all work was halted by black lessees early in the year when Treasury agents claimed jurisdiction over the area. By February 2,000 acres had been taken from the freedmen and restored to Mrs. Rosa Duncan and other heirs of the Turner-Quitman estate. They had sworn to the requisite loyalty oath, although Eaton claimed that they "confirmed it only by disloyal acts." Following a common practice, Mrs. Duncan took a Northerner, Alexander Warwick, as her partner and liaison with Union authorities. In addition, two northern men, David Lombard and J. H. Carter, leased 1,200 acres on the Hurricane plantation.[28] This meant that almost half of the cleared land on the Bend was taken from the jurisdiction of the Freedmen's Department, and blacks who had expected to work it for themselves were required to work it for others.

In March General Thomas ordered all land on the Bend except for the Turner-Quitman holdings to be "reserved for military purposes," and cultivated by freedmen on their own or as part of the Home Farm for the destitute.[29] However, since it was late in the spring and the white lessees had incurred considerable expense, Colonel Eaton directed Samuel Thomas to leave them undisturbed and proceed with the experimental colony on the 2,000 acres unclaimed by either the white planters or the Home Farm. Thomas immediately divided this land among seventy of "the best negroes," and they set to work. At the time of this allotment Thomas carried out another provision of the general's order and confiscated all "the horses, mules, oxen, wagons and carts and farming implements" held by the freedmen.[30] The government regularly seized all animals and tools from contrabands who entered their lines on the assumption that they were stolen goods, since slaves could not legally own property; the army hoped thereby to secure more supplies for their own use and keep them from falling into enemy hands. This peremptory confiscation of their property infuriated the Davis ex-slaves and left them unable to continue farming on their own. Colonel Thomas explained that the purpose of the measure was "to furnish every thing necessary through the Government, charge to the recipients, and receive payment from them at the end of the year." The Freedmen's Department was determined to maintain tight control of every aspect of its model plantation at the Bend. A few wily freedmen salvaged something by selling their animals to resident whites at bargain prices, but most lost their only valuable possessions. This act permanently embittered many Davis blacks who subsequently regarded Yankee officers as less trustworthy than their old master.[31] Thus the Union-sponsored utopian experiment began with a serious impediment to wholehearted cooperation.

After the army occupation in December 1863, the number of refugees at Davis Bend increased rapidly. On January 4, 1864,

950 were reported, under the direction of a single white private. A month later 3,000 freedmen were registered there, and in March Captain Gaylord Norton assumed direction of the colony under the personal supervision of Colonel Thomas at Vicksburg. The number of refugees continued to grow as Sherman moved through Mississippi and into Alabama, releasing from bondage an estimated 8,000 former slaves. The Union expedition up the Red River brought another 2,500 fleeing to Vicksburg. Since Davis Bend was considered the safest haven, most of the new arrivals were crowded into the inadequate accommodations there. In November the commanding general stated somewhat optimistically that the Bend could easily support "not less than twenty-five thousand" refugees.[32]

In April 1864 Henry Rountree, an agent for the Cincinnati Contraband Relief Commission, in his requests for supplies, vividly described conditions at the Bend. On the edge of Brierfield he found a cattle shed without siding that housed six adults and twenty-nine small children, all in miserable circumstances. The only male adult was blind and could do nothing for the group. One of the women had an advanced case of smallpox, another was too ill to stand up, and a third woman was caring for a dying young son while neglecting several smaller ones. The refugees had no furniture and were forced to sleep huddled together on the dirt floor with only two old quilts and a worn army blanket to cover them. The nearest water was more than a half mile away, and the children, all under twelve, could scarcely carry the heavy two-gallon stone water jug when empty. Total cooking equipment for these thirty-five people consisted of one pan and an iron kettle. They often ate raw bacon with their hard biscuits because of lack of fuel and utensils. This forlorn group had followed Sherman back to Vicksburg, where their men had been enrolled as soldiers. Rountree concluded, "I never saw such degradation."[33]

Passing on, the missionary found neat but crowded cabins on the Lovell place, one of the Turner-Quitman plantations. Here the primary need was for cooking vessels. In contrast, about a mile into the woods near the riverbank he saw about 150 "poor, miserable, hovels or sheds, each filled to overflowing." They were simply built of a framework of sticks covered with brush and strips of sod for a roof. One hut not more than twelve feet square housed 17 refugees; many contained a dozen or more. Rountree estimated that about 2,000 freedmen lived there in great need. He requested bolts of cloth, thread, needles, and pins so that the women could make clothes for themselves and their families. They also needed burlap to make bed ticks and a bale of blankets, as well as all sorts of tinware. Rountree suggested that a supply of six- and twelve-quart pails would ease the burden of the children, who were compelled to carry water "on their youthful necks and heads."

Next Rountree visited the "Joe Davis quarters," which he said "speak plainly of their former owner being a man of system, good order and large wealth." The missionary was impressed with the beauty of Hurricane and spoke regretfully of the destruction of the mansion and use of fences for firewood, which allowed the lovely, rare garden to be trampled. The inhabitants of the pleasant slave houses were comparatively comfortable though crowded, but they directed him to the henhouse, which was occupied by a family of sixteen destitute blacks, "also newcomers with Genl Sherman."

Later Rountree visited the 1,300-acre Wood plantation, where he found the same division observed on the other places. The former slaves of the plantation, living in neat, comfortable cabins, "were generally well supplied unless it was with shoes, which are universally needed." However, scattered around the place were some one hundred brush and sod shanties, which Rountree deemed "not fit to shelter cattle in during a storm." These were occupied by recent refugees, mostly women and children with a few old, crippled men, all in great need.[34] This split between old residents and newcomers helped fix the social levels of the new black community on the Bend. As in most societies, the older residents knew the system and were determined to preserve their comforts. The recent immigrants had to struggle with their own poverty as well as the resentment and sometimes open hostility of the old settlers. The Davis blacks complained about the dislocation caused by the hordes of refugees, but they managed to maintain their superior position. Although some were evicted by black soldiers' families or by inmates of the Home Farm, most of them were able to build other housing quickly, aided by their own comparative wealth and the help of friends in the established community. However, the old resident-newcomer antagonisms provided still another barrier to the creation of a true "community of co-operation."[35]

The Home Farm was reserved for those freedmen who were incapable of caring for themselves. From the first, Union officials had thought it fitting that these unfortunates should find a haven on the plantation of the president of the Confederacy, so some 500 acres of Brierfield were reserved for their use. Here the old, crippled, orphaned, or indigent were expected to contribute what labor they could toward their own support either in the cotton fields or the vegetable garden. Although it never provided care for all of the indigent refugees, in 1864 the Home Farm accommodated some 955 people, according to a detailed record book. The vast majority of them were females of all ages. There were many male children and quite a few men over sixty; some were in their eighties, and one was age ninety-two. But there were only a handful of males in the eighteen-to-fifty age group, and most of those were labeled "unfit for work."[36] The typical family consisted of an adult female and her children, although there were some families with two adult females, either sisters or mother-daughter groups. The overwhelming majority were described as black; there were three listed as yellow, one brown, and three white. The last, a mother and her two children, were identified as "refugees from Cap West." Most of the adults listed their occupation as field hand, although there were a few house servants. The only skilled laborer was a shoemaker. A few older children were called schoolboys or girls. These ex-slaves had had a great variety of former owners, most from other counties in southwestern Mississippi or across the river in Louisiana. The only former residents of Warren County were a woman and her two daughters, and they were not from Davis Bend. So Brierfield contained an enclave of destitute outsiders, most of whom probably had never heard of the Bend and had no idea of the tradition of independence and enterprise that the Davis blacks cherished.

There continued to be a great deal of sickness among the refugees on the Bend. The case of smallpox that Henry Rountree had found at the cattle shed was not unusual. Even Joseph Davis, in exile in Alabama, heard that smallpox and other diseases were so severe at Hurricane and Brierfield that a Yankee lessee gave up his plan to settle there.[37] On March 5, 1864, Freedmen's General Hospital No. 2 was established to augment the one at Vicksburg "for the benefit of the Sick Freedmen at Goodrich's Landing La. and Davis Bend Miss. and all intermediate camps and plantations on the Mississippi River." A few days later Dr. Charles A. Foster, an army doctor from Chicago, set up the Davis Bend branch in the old hospital building at Hurricane; Colonel Thomas had dismantled and removed the water-cure facility shortly after Union occupation in December. Within two weeks Foster had treated 89 patients: 12 were able to return to their jobs, 6 died, and the other 61 remained in the hospital.[38] In its first year of operation the hospital accommodated an average of 200 to 250 freedmen each month. Rountree found it well managed and remarkably neat and clean, thanks to the diligence of the white couple who served as matron and steward there. The greatest need, according to the missionary, was for a larger supply of medicine. He noted that Dr. Foster "was greatly pleased" when Rountree reported that he had ordered castor oil and other remedies from his agency in Cincinnati.[39] Foster's hospital helped relieve the suffering and incidentally provided employment for some freedmen as cooks and nurses. Also it proved convenient for the lessees, who were obliged to furnish medical care for their hands.[40]

The freedmen seemed universally eager to read and write, and were especially interested in the schools set up by agents of the benevolent societies on the Bend. In April Henry Rountree reported three schools in operation. At the one on Wood's place 260 children were taught by three young ladies from the North. Rountree observed a spelling class, another which read "very nicely," and a third whose students "acquitted themselves creditably in Arithmetic." He found they needed a larger schoolroom with proper benches for the pupils. He also requested some primers, slates, pencils, and a supply of "McGuffie's Electic [sic] Speller and Reader." Rountree noted that the other two schools were equally large, and the three were so distributed that every child on the Bend could reach one. Throughout the next year ten or twelve missionary teachers operated three or four schools on the Bend with combined enrollments of 700 to 1,000 pupils.[41]

It is difficult to assess the work of these teachers. Judging by the books ordered by Rountree and others, the curriculum was limited to basic instruction in reading, writing, and arithmetic, although one teacher added *Montieth's First Lessons in Geography* to his order. Since the vast majority of the freedmen were totally illiterate, a more advanced curriculum would have been inappropriate. However, there were several obstacles to effective education in this situation. One was the mobility of the black population. Many of those brought to the Bend fresh from slavery chose to leave or were sent as hands to other plantations or drifted to the cities. Often a promising pupil disappeared after a few weeks, perhaps to return several months later to begin again. Another impediment faced by the teachers was the bureaucratic interference of government personnel who demanded endless reports and forms before even the simplest arrangement was made or supplies sent. Joseph Warren, superintendent of education for the Vicksburg district and a Union army chaplain, was forever returning monthly reports to the teachers with niggling criticism. Eventually, some of the young women seem to have deliberately made mistakes to needle this exasperating official. Warren returned one form to Miss Maggie Littell with the stern warning that the government "does not intend the Monthly Reports of Schools to be jokes." She was ordered to "correct the item Race and return the Report today."[42]

A third obstacle to the educational effort was the friction between teachers from different religious denominations or benevolent societies. Samuel D. Barnes, a young lieutenant stationed at the Bend, commented on this problem when describing the funeral of one of the teachers. Neither the body nor the ceremony had been well prepared; Barnes was shocked to note that they even had to call in a freedman to help carry the coffin. In explanation, the lieutenant said, "She had no particular friend here, and a good many did not belong to her society, hence seemed to care little whether she lived or died."[43] This detriment was removed the next year when the superintendent of education assigned to the Bend only teachers from the United Presbyterian Board of Missions. However, the example reveals still another hazard to good education: the unhealthy environment of that swampy river bottom land. Less than a month before the funeral noted above, Barnes had attended one for Miss Trimbly, a teacher from Pennyslvania. The next year Warren reported that Davis

Bend was so unhealthy for Northerners that he thought schools should close at the end of May and not reopen until October. "Two or three estimable persons have lost their lives by endeavoring to prolong their work on the Bend, and others have suffered severely."[44] However, even these measures did not prevent serious illness among the teachers, which kept the schools closed a number of days each year.

What sort of people were these emissaries from the North who formed the new white elite at Davis Bend? The majority of them were young women from middle-class families who came South with a sincere desire to help the poor victims of slavery. The conditions under which they had to live and work must have tested their enthusiastic commitment. The only housing available was in the deserted mansions, which had been stripped of furniture and were in sad disrepair. On the Davis plantations the teachers were housed in the Brierfield mansion, where souvenir hunters had removed even the door locks and the marble mantels. Although the missionaries brought essential items of furniture, there were few comforts. Besides fostering disease, the hot, humid summers must have made work difficult for these unacclimated newcomers. In May Lieutenant Barnes reported "the gnats are biting most terribly and it is almost impossible to write at all."[45] Horses, mules, and any other forms of conveyance were scarce, so the teachers often walked several miles to their schoolrooms on dusty roads under a scorching sun in summer, or through ankle-deep mud in freezing rain in winter.

Despite physical discomforts, many of the missionaries maintained an enthusiasm fueled by their piety and patriotism. Here was an opportunity to bring Christ's teachings to the poor, exploited blacks, about whose welfare the abolitionists had taught them to feel deeply. Furthermore, this assignment allowed the women to work in the war zone under conditions little better than those of the soldiers in combat, while contributing to the common cause of victory for the North. They must have felt a sense of kinship with male relatives and friends who were sacrificing so much in this bloody war.

Drawn together by the shared experience of life in a strange and hostile land, these expatriates made the most of every opportunity for a party or celebration. On July 4, 1864, the whites at

Davis Bend gave a gala party to commemorate both the independence of the nation and the first anniversary of the fall of Vicksburg. Colonel Thomas and his staff provided a steamboat, which left Vicksburg early in the morning loaded with missionaries and army officers. After a pleasant three-hour cruise downriver, the guests reached the Bend, where local teachers had decorated the entrance to Brierfield mansion with the inscription THE HOUSE THAT JEFF BUILT. Outside, tables were spread under the trees, and both before and after a sumptuous dinner the visitors were entertained by lengthy speeches and patriotic songs. The steamboat did not return the weary party to Vicksburg until almost midnight.[46]

In the long newspaper account written by an army officer who was present, the freedmen were scarcely mentioned. The reporter described the Bend as a "Freedmen's paradise" where missionaries superintended black cultivation of small plots on which the crops looked promising. He expressed the collective joy of the whites that "the sable sons, by a guard of whom we were surrounded. . . had been brought out of the House of Bondage." But no blacks participated in the ceremonies or even attended the party except, perhaps, as servants.

How did the white missionaries and teachers regard the blacks? Usually this was their first close encounter with another race, and they often had the abolitionists' idealized view of the noble, primitive black man. The teachers seemed eager to report the rapid progress of their pupils, comparing it favorably with that of whites in the public schools of the North.[47] However, few fully appreciated the difficulties in attempting to transform illiterate, agricultural laborers into educated, sophisticated city folk like themselves. Henry Rountree wrote to his agency that he considered the missionary teacher to be "the keeper of the minds and interests of many truly helpless [freedmen]." This attitude of benevolent paternalism led the Northerners to attempt to dictate every phase of the freedmen's lives, and, predictably, they were disappointed when results did not match expectations. Some were able to maintain their enthusiasm through disappointment, but most came to feel that their efforts were in vain; they frequently blamed their failure on the inherent incapacity of blacks to learn quickly.[48]

Not all of those who came South to aid the freedmen were impelled by idealistic motives. Among the preachers, teachers, and agents of northern charity were some who succumbed to the cotton fever rampant among military officers and government lessees. Henry Rountree told his sponsors that he intended to protect the blacks on Wood's plantation from exploitation by marketing for them the raw cotton that filled their storehouses. At the same time, he wrote to financiers in the North, offering to act as their agent in buying cotton at low prices. While stationed at Vicksburg, Rountree was reprimanded by his agency for selling relief supplies that he was supposed to have distributed to freedmen. He claimed that he had only been trying to avoid pauperizing the refugees and intended to use the profits for charitable purposes. But, at the same time, he had ordered expensive furniture, carpets, and glassware from St. Louis for his own use. A Quaker friend wrote Rountree that a mutual acquaintance who had visited Vicksburg was spreading the story at home "that thou had been in the practice of sleeping with thy housekeeper, a colored woman, and had been selling the goods intrusted to thee and appropriating the proceeds to thy own use."[49] Although Rountree hotly denied the charges, there is reason to question the sincerity of his commitment to the freedmen. No doubt most of the missionaries, like most humans, had within them elements both of idealism and venality. The freedmen gained some temporary but vital relief and some basic education from these people, but must have found their racial attitudes very similar to those of the southern master class before the war.

In November 1864 Colonel Eaton set out to determine how well the former slaves were performing as free laborers. He addressed questions to planters, military superintendents, teachers, and freedmen, seeking their appraisals. J. H. Carter's answers give some insight into his relationship with his hands. Cultivating the northern half of Hurricane plantation, he claimed to follow army regulations carefully but seemed to provide the minimum of food while charging the maximum markup on goods sold to workers. He complained that he had kept all who were in the quarters when he arrived; hence he had more children and incapacitated blacks on his place than normal. Nonetheless, he claimed to have provided for all sick hands, while dependents were rationed by the government. All had received medical care from the government hospital. He admitted some difficulty in getting his hands to work diligently. Middle-aged laborers were generally reliable, he said, but the teenage girls wasted a great deal of time. He tried "by exhorting and precept. . . to inspire all with the desire to labor," but found that the greatest "quickener to their zeal [was] to find the amount to their credit insufficient to procure a coveted calico dress, or straw hat." Carter concluded that free laborers worked one-third less time per day than had the slaves; hence cotton could never be produced as cheaply again.[50]

Carter maintained that a planter was more likely to win the respect of his laborers if he kept his temper and avoided profanity. He deplored the "almost utter want of chastity or modesty" among them and their preference for concubinage over marriage. He shared the missionaries' conviction that "it will take stringent laws rigidly enforced to break up the licentious habits of this generation, and a patient teaching of the young. . . to eradicate such practices in the next generation." Carter also complained about the freedmen's habits of lying and stealing, which he considered "other fruits of the accursed institution" of slavery. He believed that, in fairness to them, blacks should be subject to the same punishment, as white offenders. Although Carter was engaged in planting for profit, his report gives no indication that he was unfair to his workers. As a subsequent complaint by one of his hands shows, there was little opportunity for black workers to accumulate any money under that low wage system, even when the planters were honest.[51]

How did the black lessees fare? How effective was the experimental system in which the government supplied mules and equipment on credit and the lessees worked their assigned land with the assistance of their families and as many other hands as they could afford? In July 1864 Colonel Thomas had reported that " the enterprise promises success." The black lessees' crops were as far advanced and as healthy as those on any white-managed place on the Bend.

In mid-August disaster struck in the form of the army worm. According to the Vicksburg *Herald,* "They devoured as the locusts of Egypt. Five-sixths of the crop was thus destroyed."[52] The Davis Bend cotton was especially vulnerable because it was planted late as a result of the army-Treasury dispute. The loss was discouraging both to the white planters and to the black lessees. Still, the blacks did end the season with a profit. The seventy freedmen produced 150 bales, which paid their debts and left each lessee with $500 to $2,500 for his year's work. In addition, they had grown enough corn and vegetables to see them and their stock through the winter. Many had built comfortable homes and were well settled as small farmers.[53]

The experiment had been so successful that Thomas and Eaton persuaded General N.J.T. Dana to issue an order on November 5 reserving the entire Davis Bend peninsula to the military to be "exclusively devoted to the colonization, residence, and support of the Freedmen."[54] He ordered all white persons not connected with the military service to leave before January 1, 1865, after which no unauthorized whites would be admitted. Colonel Thomas was given responsibility for carrying out this order. Now Thomas had a free hand to create the ideal colony that he and John Eaton had talked about ever since Grant's suggestion a year and a half earlier. Some members of the black community at the Bend and in Vicksburg, noting the prosperity of the black lessees, were fired with enthusiasm for the project. Thomas reported:

> The more intelligent part of the Negro population are beginning to see the immense advantages of such a scheme, and are engaged in organizing a colony, which proposes to take at least one thousand acres, divide it on the plan adopted this year, build their houses, secure the land for one year certainly, and, if possible, a sure vested title to it.[55]

Thus the stage was set for a larger utopian experiment in 1865, to be conducted by the blacks themselves under the supervision of the Union officers.

3

The Problem
of Reconstruction

The nest in which the rebellion was hatched is to be the Mecca of "The Freedmen." The home of Jeff. Davis, who represents the rebellion for slavery, is consecrated . . . as the home of the emancipated. . . . [This experiment] will strike an answering chord in all the loyal North, as it points out the fitness of the place for the humane and economic work of elevating thousands of an oppressed race, and of saving a vast and needless expense to the Government.

—*New York Times,* December 4, 1864

With this characteristic blend of economic and philanthropic motives, Freedmen's Department officials began implementing their optimistic plans. Following the navy's precedent of a written constitution, Captain Gaylord Norton, provost marshall of freedmen at Davis Bend, with Colonel Thomas's approval, drew up a set of "Rules and Regulations" by which some 5,000 acres, all of the cleared land except the Home Farm, would be leased to freedmen to work on their own account. They were to form themselves into companies of from three to twenty-five hands and select one of their number to be the head; all business was to be transacted with this head person as soon as a company with all its dependents was registered with the department. The quantity of land allotted to each company depended upon the number of its workers, but additional hands could be hired only with official approval. Each company could draw rations, teams, and equipment from the government or from private capitalists, to be re-

61

paid from the crop. Every able-bodied member of a company had to do his share of the work; those with disabilities were required to have a certificate to that effect from the chief surgeon of the hospital. Under this plan, 181 partnerships and companies were formed including some 1,750 men, women, and children.[1]

Although Colonel Thomas was later to claim that the colonists "were left free to manage their own affairs," they were closely watched by white superintendents on each of the three plantations. One of these men, A. W. Hunt, had been a Louisiana planter with Union sympathies who fled North during the war. His previous experience with cotton culture and Negro labor caused federal officials to employ him at seventy-five dollars per month "to exercise complete supervision over all the people" on the 3,000-acre Palmyra plantations, formerly held by the Quitman heirs. Similarly, John Lackey supervised the freedmen of the 1,100-acre Wood colony, and John Werts was put in charge of the 1,200-acre Hurricane place.[2] They were instructed to see to it that each company planted all of its land, at least two-thirds of it in cotton. They were to supervise the arrangements by which freedmen borrowed teams and equipment, seeing that they lived up to their contracts and were not cheated. These supervisors were to require the blacks to keep their houses and grounds "swept every morning and the filth removed." Rations were to be issued with the utmost economy, excluding all the able-bodied, and a detailed census was to be taken of the entire colony each month. While carefully regulating most aspects of the freedmen's lives, Norton admonished the superintendents to listen to their complaints and try to get along peaceably with them.[3] There seemed to be little confidence in the notion that the freedmen could or should manage their own affairs without white intervention.

Norton was especially concerned about "the present disgraceful and bad conduct" of many residents of the Bend who were "stealing, plundering, killing stock, and living in idleness and vagrancy." In an attempt to restore law and order, Norton ruled that each planatation was to elect a sheriff who would receive complaints and make arrests in disputes among citizens. The sheriffs would then bring the cases before a court of three judges, each elected from one of the plantations for a three-month term. The court was authorized to swear and examine witnesses and decide cases "according to their Ideas of justice and the evidence produced."[4] The judges could prescribe a variety of punishments: fines up to $1,000, forfeiture of crop, expulsion from the Bend, confinement in the guardhouse or hard labor on the Home Farm. Although Norton reported that the court system was successful, his record keeping was haphazard. Only nine court sessions, which heard some nineteen cases, are recorded. Most of them involved petty thefts or assaults in domestic quarrels, although several were related to stray animals that had damaged neighbors' crops. The penalties imposed were usually small fines, a few days' imprisonment in the blockhouse, or labor on the Home Farm. Each sentence was reviewed and approved by the post commander.[5]

These elected judges decided cases between freedmen but seldom handled disputes between whites and blacks. In only one instance did a white man, John Lackey, superintendent of Wood colony, take a freedman to court. He accused one Frank McCall of breaking into his house and stealing goods worth about fifty dollars. Among the items taken was a bag of meal, which ruptured and left a trail from the scene of the crime to the defendant's house. A subsequent search revealed the rest of the stolen goods inside, and McCall was convicted and sentenced to thirty days in the guardhouse. However, freedmen did not have such a convenient means of redressing their grievances against whites. Henry and Isaac Green were forced to write a complaint to the post commander when two superintendents, John Werts of Hurricane and Finley McDonald of the Home Farm, broke down the gate to Green's field one midnight when it obstructed their passage. The freedmen maintained that they kept the gate open until eleven each night and would have opened it later for the men if they had asked. Instead, the superintendents pried the gate from its hinges and left it on the ground for the rest of the night, allowing cattle to damage Green's corn. There is no record that the post commander took any action in this case.[6] It seems clear that equal justice was available only among freedmen, not between the races, even in this Union-sponsored utopia.

Visitors from the North often cited this court system as evidence of a unique experiment in self-government; few realized that it was simply a continuation of a tradition established by Joseph Davis more than a generation earlier. The ease with which the older residents, who may well have suggested and helped plan the court system, adopted this form of community control stemmed largely from their previous experience under Davis's tutelage.

According to Samuel Thomas, the black planters at Davis Bend took a great deal of interest in their elections and chose the best men for office. By the end of the summer of 1865 they had expanded their self-rule to include education. They elected a board of directors to serve for six months "for the purpose of arranging about school houses, the residences of teachers, the collection of money as necessary," and other related problems. Although State Superintendent of Education Joseph Warren doubted their ability to raise as much money as they proposed, he felt sure that they would provide material assistance to the teachers' agency, and he welcomed their independent initiative.[7]

The major national events of April 1865 had repercussions even in this quiet and isolated community. Lee's surrender and the impending end of the war were cause for celebration among the officers, superintendents, and teachers on the Bend. However, the news of Lincoln's assassination quickly shattered this happy mood and brought grief to the entire colony. Lieutenant Barnes reported that "all the colored people, men, women and children have crape [sic], black string or mourning of some kind for as Uncle Sam, Massa Lincoln is dead."[8] But the tragedy brought no immediate change in the government experiment at Davis Bend.

Soon after the war ended, John Eaton persuaded the commissioner of the newly created Freedmen's Bureau in Washington to appoint Samuel Thomas to the post of assistant commissioner for Mississippi, thus providing some continuity from the earlier Freedmen's Department of the army. On June 20, 1865, Thomas took over the formidable task of providing for the physical, legal, educational, and economic needs of the 400,000 freedmen in the state. By late September, relying heavily on the core of men retained from the Freedmen's Department, Thomas had some 50 officers and 160 civilians working for the bureau in Mississippi.[9]

Under Commissioner O. O. Howard's direction, Thomas urged the freedmen to be industrious and patient and strive for self-sufficiency, while commanding the whites to accept emancipation as a fact and treat their free laborers fairly. He attempted to regulate in an evenhanded manner relations between the major elements in a fractured society. As might have been expected, he encountered monumental problems. This twenty-four-year-old official had to cope with the demands of a hostile white population, a vacillating and perpetually suspicious administration in Washington, a reluctantly helpful local military force, and a corps of assistants of uncertain ability and tenure while trying to serve the vital needs of the mass of former slaves. In the summer of 1865 neither the government nor the bureau had established policies, and everyone seemed to have a slightly different answer to the vexed question of what to do with the freedmen. Thomas's response, like that of his superiors in bureau headquarters, tended to be paternalistically protective. Perhaps his extensive wartime experience with helpless refugees made this inevitable. At any rate, he appeared confident of his ability to decide what was best for the poor, ignorant blacks, and he demanded conformity to his decisions. At times he jeopardized his rapport with his superiors by eloquently opposing those bureau policies he feared would abandon the blacks to persecution by their former masters. In one instance Thomas took drastic action to make sure that a white planter did not escape punishment for murdering a freedman.[10] He was a resourceful and courageous bureau chief.

The one place in the entire chaotic state where the assistant commissioner felt altogether successful was at Davis Bend. On frequent visits there he must have enjoyed the deference of the black leaseholders as well as the respect of the sizable white community. Perhaps their quiet accomplishments restored his confidence in the wisdom of his policies. When General Strong, the inspector general for the Freedmen's Bureau, toured Mississippi that summer, Thomas took him to the Bend and later told Eaton, "He never saw anything like it in his life. He says I have the best start of any one; professes to be incapable of seeing how we have accomplished so much."[11] A few weeks later two newspapers of the state echoed this rosy assessment: "The success of the plan of colonization, as adopted and practically carried out on the Bend, realizes all that could be expected. . . . It has been a task of no small magnitude."[12]

When this pet project seemed threatened by the wholesale restoration of property that followed President Johnson's amnesty proclamation, Thomas sent a fervent plea to General Howard to set aside Davis Bend for the blacks for another three years. He noted that the self-governing colony, operating entirely apart from the white community, won commendation from every intelligent visitor. He continued: "The Freedmen have built houses, and expended money on the land, with the expectation that the Government would sustain their claim to it in preference to that of the rebel owners." If the plantations were restored, this promising project would have to be abandoned.[13] Because of uncertainty about the president's policy, Howard postponed a decision, but Thomas continued to badger the bureaucracy to protect the interests of the Davis Bend colony.

By midsummer Thomas's authority over his model community was challenged from another quarter. An organization of black lessees proposed to increase their profits by ginning and baling their own cotton. The leader of this movement was the redoubtable Benjamin Montgomery, who, with his sons, had recently returned to the Bend from two years as a refugee in Ohio. After Thornton's discharge from the navy in July 1864, all three Montgomery men worked in a canalboat yard near Cincinnati. But the family never felt at home there, though they were kindly received and Ben was invited to exhibit his boat propeller, labeled AN IMPORTANT INVENTION, at the Western Sanitary Fair in December.[14] According to Isaiah, the entire family waited eagerly "until times settled so that we could return to the old Hurricane Plantation." Even before the war ended, Ben sent Thornton back "to see what outlook there was for the resumption of business." By February 20, 1865, twenty-two-year-old Thornton was registered as head of a company at Hurricane, receiving 200 pounds of bacon, 196 pounds of flour and 50 pounds of sugar from the government for his group. On March 7 he received another allotment, but subsequent rations evidently were purchased through the Montgomery store, which Thornton had reopened with government permission. There was great demand for all sorts of goods that had been scarce or unavailable during the war. Now that the Bend was crowded with freedmen eager to borrow against their new crop, there was a ready market for the items in the Montgomery store. Isaiah said that "father invested all our little capital in merchandise to be shipped South by river—while I came via Cairo." Soon Ben himself followed, and by summer he was established there, using all of his administrative skills to manage both the store and their planting operations under difficult postwar conditions.[15]

There were many changes on the Bend that must have been disturbing to the man who had managed the smooth functioning of the Davis Plantations before the war. As previously noted, the rapid influx of refugees had displaced many former Davis slaves, resulting in overcrowding and friction between old residents and the newcomers. It was among the nucleus of Davis people, bound together by memories of more settled times under a benevolent master, that Montgomery found an undercurrent of discontent that he could mobilize in an attempt to restore some of the old order under his leadership. Already some of the literate new men were coming to the fore; men such as Thomas Bland and Thomas M. Broadwater, who signed the register themselves when they received rations as heads of companies. The court also provided potential leaders in the three elected judges, especially J. A. Gla, who signed his own name to the court record at each session and assisted bureau officials in maintaining school buildings.[16] Ben was careful to include these new leaders in his projects to increase the freedmen's autonomy. The Montgomerys formed a partnership with them to operate the Hurricane sawmill during the spring of 1865.

By July Ben was ready to undertake a larger project; he proposed to form an association of reliable black planters to lease and operate the cotton gin at Hurricane. In 1864 this concession had been held by a white man, E. S. Bedford, who charged twenty dollars per bale to gin and press the freedmen's cotton, an increase of some 300 percent over prewar charges. Costs of supplies, such as rope and bagging, had increased as a result of wartime shortages, which made all business ventures in the South difficult and expensive; however, the freedmen felt that Bedford's charge was exorbitant. They also complained about his inefficient manner of ginning, which resulted in damage to the machinery and an unusual waste of cotton, further reducing profits. They were receptive to any scheme which promised improvement.[17] Montgomery could make a persuasive case for the advantage of cutting out the middleman, especially when he was a carpetbagger obviously bent on quick gains at their expense. The Davis Negroes were confident of Ben's ability to manage the gin successfully, since he had supervised its operation during the prewar years.

The gin concession was evidently a lucrative prize. As early as May Colonel Thomas had written the army commander at the Bend that he had had many applications for the lease but proposed to wait until he found exactly the right person. He wanted someone who could invest as much as $5,000, because the gins "must be well repaired if they do the work on the Bend as it should be done." He hoped to have somebody at work on them by the first of August and promised "to get a reliable party, who will conduct the business right."[18] Benjamin Montgomery and his group hoped to meet this requirement.

On the evening of July 15, "The Colored Planters of Hurricane Plantation" presented a petition to Colonel Thomas requesting the use of the plantation gin for their new cotton crop. They wrote, "From many years experience of a portion of the undersigned in arranging, repairing, & operating said machinery . . . we feel competent to take charge of & do promise to keep the same in workmanlike order so long as entrusted to our care & use." They further agreed to "most cheerfully submit to all legal charges for both land and machinery."[19]

The petitioners complained about the confiscation of all their animals and farm equipment by the army the previous year. As evidence of their business ability, they cited the fact that they had been resourceful enough to resupply themselves and make a new crop. Furthermore, they asserted that the requested grant would encourage projects like the Davis Bend colony by allowing black planters the greatest possible reward for their labors. They humbly requested the gin concession "to prevent the imposition of superfluous and unnecessary charges." The document was signed by fifty-six planters.

Here was a well-organized, articulate letter outlining very persuasive reasons for assigning this coveted concession to the people for whom the colony was designed. It reflected both their pride in past accomplishments and their confidence in future successes. There was a hint of blame for the confiscation of their animals and tools, with the implication that the gin concession would give bureau officials an opportunity to make amends. All of it was couched in meticulously polite terms. This document would have done credit to any business group in the country petitioning the government.

To underline the urgency of their petition and perhaps to add the weight of personal persuasion, four of the planters visited Colonel Thomas in Vicksburg on the eighteenth. At this interview Thomas told them that he had asked Major Meatyard, the post commander at Davis Bend, to determine whether the majority of the lessees really favored these plans for the gin.[20] The committee returned to the Bend the next day and asked Meatyard how he planned to discover the sentiment of the planters. They were surprised to learn that he had received no official instructions to conduct an investigation.

Hoping to expedite matters and perhaps fearing that their petition would be ignored, the four leaders sent a letter to Thomas on July 20 reporting what they had learned. They concluded, "In order to remove your suspicions respecting the correctness of our position, & in justice to us as the Representatives of the people's wishes, we hope you will re-advise Major Meeyard [sic] at your earliest convenience." The letter was signed by J. A. Gla, Thomas Bland, B. T. Montgomery, and Thos. M. Broadwater.[21]

The planters waited impatiently for eleven days and then drew up a second petition. Their stated purpose was "to enter our protest against the efforts presistently [sic] & as we think, unfairly being made to misrepresent to you our views & wishes with regard to the ginning of the cotton raised by us on the Plantation."[22] They then listed and refuted the arguments made against their competence and again asserted, "We have among our members those who while slaves successfully conducted not only the ginning of the cotton but also all the business transactions connected with the same." If they could do this as slaves, there seemed no reason to doubt that, as free men, they could do as well.

They described the cooperative they planned to form with "each member paying his share in proportion to the amount of cotton he may have ginned." Such an organization would show the world that they were capable of preparing their crop for market as well as raising it. They were fearful that otherwise "mere speculators" might rob them of their hard-earned profits. This petition contained some seventy names, seventeen of whom signed for themselves. The names of the committee were scattered among those of the other planters, as though by their obscurity to establish the true grass-roots nature of the project.

Finally, their efforts brought a response; three days later Colonel Thomas wrote a long, formal reply stating his decision: "After careful examination of all the interests of the People, of the Government, & even of yourselves, I have arrived at the conclusion that I cannot grant your request."[23] He claimed that he had received a petition from sixty men in the neighborhood who would have to use that gin, asking that the government retain control of it. There is no record of such a document either among the letters received or in the registry of letters to the Freedmen's Bureau in Vicksburg. He further stated that the "officers & Superintendents on duty on the Bend unite in saying, that it would not be best for the interest of all, for you to have the Gin." According to the record, Captain Norton had written to Thomas the day before saying that he thought the petitioners were not capable of running the gin because it would take men of means and education to satisfy everyone.[24] Unfortunately, that letter was not preserved and there is no evidence of any other from officials on the Bend.

Thomas asserted that the government would have a large quantity of cotton that year, and therefore he must keep complete control of the gin. If the blacks ran it as poorly as they had the sawmill assigned to them the previous spring, the gin would be a complete failure. Thomas accused them of neglecting needed repairs on the mill and charging such high prices that he had to ship lumber from Vicksburg. He denied that they had been treated unfairly by the gin agent the previous year and assured them that he would see that they got everything they had earned during the present year.

Thomas particularly criticized the leaders of the group.

I have many reasons for believing that the men who have been the prime movers in getting up this petition, are actuated by the desire to make money: they want to get their own cotton ginned, and care but little for the hundreds of poor people around them, whose cotton should receive attention first.

Later he narrowed his attack still further, obviously referring to Benjamin Montgomery: "I recognize among the signers of your petition, the name of a colored man who has speculated more on Davis Bend, & made more money than any other man on it: One who has repeatedly sold whiskey in direct violation of my orders." Apparently Ben and the assistant commissioner had had prior difficulties. Thomas went on to criticize speculators in general, and black ones in particular, who located on the Bend to make money "off of the ignorance of their former fellow servants." Then, implying that all who signed the petition were victims of Montgomery's cunning, he added, "I am aware of how easy it is for a designing colored man to ingratiate himself into the good feelings of his race & get them to sign a petition which will result in profit to him."[25]

This overlong, disorganized reply seemed to carry an undertone of bitterness out of proportion to the subject discussed. The assistant commissioner obviously doubted both the ability and the purpose of the black leaders. When compared with the articulate epistles that Thomas regularly directed to Washington, this letter sounded petty and waspish. However, there was no mistaking the message, and the subject should have been closed.

But the leaders of the black lessees were so unhappy that they decided to try one last communication, probably more to satisfy themselves than to reverse the decision. After a false start late in August, the Committee of Five, including both Thornton and Benjamin Montgomery as well as Bland, Broadwater, and Gla, sent a reply to Thomas on September 3. They acknowledged that his letter did not require a reply but added, "we would remain silent were it not evident from the tenor of your communication that you have been grossly misinformed in regard to our position, & the unity of sentiment existing among the colored planters." There had been no impartial investigation "to ascertain the general wish of the planters." Instead, there was a meeting at the Home Farm where only "one side was offered." There Thomas's agent claimed that he had been selected as the only one capable of running the gin and insisted that the blacks sign a petition endorsing him. Through misrepresentation the agent secured the signatures of about one-fourth of those present, but only one was from Hurricane Plantation.[26]

The letter reiterated their claims to competency and their desire to gin cotton for Davis Bend planters at the lowest possible rate, "furnishing bagging rope, twine, etc., & delivering the Bales ready for shipping at $7.50." They denied Thomas's charges that they had mismanaged the sawmill and questioned his claim that he had been forced by their high prices to ship lumber to the Bend. Finally, they said, "We are accused of speculation. We beg of you Colonel for the sake of Justice and truth, to call an impartial investigation into that matter & thereby ascertain who are the real speculators." Dropping the usual deferential closing, they signed the letter, "Your obt. Servts, The Committee of Five."

This very firm letter was not calculated to win the sympathy or support of an already hostile white official; it is unlikely that the Montgomerys and their associates expected that it would. Rather, they sounded like any group of indignant businessmen who felt that a gross injustice had been done, one that hurt both their pride and their pocketbook. Thomas could not have missed the implication of equality in this direct and very competently expressed protest. At any rate he did not dignify it with a reply. No doubt he thought he had dealt firmly with a threatened grab at power by some arrogant blacks on his model plantation, and that would be the last of it.

But Samuel Thomas, the intelligent and dedicated administrator of freedmen in Mississippi, made the mistake of underestimating Benjamin Montgomery, one of his 400,000 charges. Montgomery was an experienced black businessman. Whenever men of affairs had discounted him because of his color or position, he had always had recourse to his powerful ally and friend, Joseph Davis. Under new postwar conditions he may have had doubts about the efficacy of this solution, but he turned to it as a last resort.

Joseph Davis had fled to Tuscaloosa, Alabama, in 1863 after the Union army seized his inland sanctuary behind Vicksburg. There he managed to set up a makeshift household for his surviving dependents, including a handful of slaves; his beloved wife, Eliza, had died en route. When the war ended, Joseph was still providing for his granddaughter Lise and other scattered members of his extended family as soon as they could reach him. Unfortunately, Davis's finances no longer made this generosity easy. He had lost all of his cotton income since 1861. Much of his other wealth had been converted into worthless Confederate money, and all of his household goods had been destroyed. The only assets he could claim in 1865 to meet his urgent need for funds were some isolated pieces of property and the fertile lands at Davis Bend. This frail but still handsome eighty-year-old who had created a life of elegance and luxury for himself, and who had been described as dominant and imperious, had now lost everything except his strong will.

Early in October 1865 Davis returned to Mississippi, and Montgomery immediately informed him in detail about the gin controversy. On October 14 he sent Davis copies of all the correspondence between Colonel Thomas and the black planters regarding the lease of the gin. Montgomery gave a minute account of their losses of tools and animals as a result of army confiscation and reported new abuses that they were suffering at the hands of the Freedmen's Bureau.[27] Evidently Montgomery had already agreed to manage the leasing of the plantations for his former master the next year, assuming that they would be restored to Davis promptly. Both men seemed to be eagerly planning for the time when the Bend would be free of Yankee supervision. Montgomery sent Davis some writing paper and cigars as well as $400 in payment of a debt. The interdependence between these two men, which had been so important to both before the war, seemed to have been resumed very quickly.

No sooner had Davis heard Ben's story of mistreatment by the Freedmen's Bureau than he joined in the battle. He sent John T. Donaly, an experienced machinist, to inspect the Hurricane gin to determine the extent of repairs that Thomas's agent had made. After two visits, the second accompanied by Ben Montgomery, Donaly wrote a long, certified report of his findings. He concluded that "the business at the Gin House and Mill is now not carried on in a proper and workmanlike manner nor the Machinery run with proper care and attention, all owing to a lack of sufficient knowledge on the part of the Parties carrying on the business of Ginning and Baling." Only minor repairs had been made, worth less than fifty dollars. The freedmen who were operating both the gin and press told Donaly that the whites knew nothing about the way either worked.[28] Donaly's statement strongly indicted the management that Thomas had been so anxious to select carefully for its efficient operation. Judging from this report, there was ample justification for the dissatisfaction of the black planters.

On October 21, in Vicksburg, where he and his family had found lodging in a large boardinghouse, Joseph Davis drew up a legal contract with Benjamin Montgomery for the leasing and cultivation of Hurricane and Brierfield plantations for the next year. It was signed by both parties and notarized by the clerk of the Circuit Court of Warren County.[29] That same day Davis forwarded the contract and Donaly's report to Colonel Thomas with a letter detailing the abuses Davis's former slaves claimed they had endured at the hands of the Freedman's Bureau. He began by objecting to the confiscation of their houses and went on to complain about the seizure of horses, mules, and oxen which greatly hampered their ability to cultivate the plantations. "Is it asking too much that this stock with the wagons be returned to them?" He requested that two of the freedmen be authorized to locate and reclaim any of the animals they could identify.

Without mentioning Bedford's reduced charge of twelve dollars per bale, Davis lectured Thomas on the costs of ginning cotton, including an itemized account that claimed to show the true cost to be about seventy-five cents a bale. He deplored the bureau's practice of forcing impecunious freedmen to settle their ration accounts with seed cotton at well below the market price. He also complained about damage to his property and requested compensation. This was not an angry letter; rather, it expressed Davis's deep concern about reported abuse of "his people" and his property. There was no mention of the long letter he had written to President Andrew Johnson from Alabama requesting the return of his plantations. He seemed to assume that official compliance was imminent, and he spoke as an aggrieved landowner.

However, Davis did not wait for a reply before seeking a wider audience for his complaints in the *Vicksburg Journal.* On October 25 T. B. Manlove, the editor of that pro-Union newspaper, wrote to Colonel Thomas that he had been requested to publish "the correspondence between you and the Colored Planters at Davis Bend."[30] Thomas thanked Manlove for consulting his wishes before publishing his correspondence with "the two Montgomery colored men of Davis Bend." The assistant commissioner obviously did not consider the petitions the work of the freedmen in general. Nor did he regard his denial of their request as quite so fair as he had indicated to them. He confessed to Manlove, "If I am not mistaken my answer to Mr. Montgomery reflects upon the colored people more than I am willing to make public, although true." He asserted that Montgomery wanted to undertake a ginning business "that I did not think that he had the means or capacity to conduct." Thomas said he refused the request for good reason and did not think the public would have an interest in the correspondence.[31] Needless to say, it remained unpublished.

Meanwhile, Davis was sending a messenger to Thomas's office every day impatiently seeking a reply to his October 21 letter. Finally, on the twenty-sixth, Joseph went in person to see the bureau chief and was told bluntly that he might receive a reply to his letter "soon." This cool rejection infuriated Davis and prompted him to compose a letter to Thomas's superior in Washington that contained, in addition to the usual recital of alleged grievances, a personal attack on the assistant commissioner. Saying that he and "the poor negroes" were in the power of Colonel Thomas, he added that he tried "to preserve the respect due his rank and position, but it is difficult to preserve respect for one who has none for himself, or the rights of others."[32]

Apparently determined to give Thomas one more chance to answer before complaining to his superior, Davis held his letter to O. O. Howard while he wrote again to the assistant commissioner. He solicited a reply to his earlier letter and detailed new reported abuses against individual freedmen at Davis Bend.[33] When he still had no response two days later, Davis resumed his letter to Howard in an even more vituperative vein. "It is evident that if steps are not immediately taken to check the robbery and fraud of the officers & agents, the negroes will be deprived of everything, and left without the power to procure teams, and other supplies to cultivate next year." Returning to his personal attack on Samuel Thomas, Joseph said, "It is painful to speak harshly of any one, but I have seldom seen in any condition—never in his condition, one so regardless of truth." But Davis had an explanation for Thomas's alleged acts of duplicity. "Col. Thomas expects to raise this year by the labor of the negroes 3000 Bales Cotton, the profits of which must go to him & his officers & agents. It is not surprising then that he is unwilling to quit."[34] Davis asked Howard to order an investigation so that he could prove his charges. Although the elderly Mississippian was unaware of it, this suggestion was unnecessary, for that very day Thomas had issued an order establishing a board of officers to hear and adjust complaints of a list of people, white and black, "and such other parties as may have complaints of abuse, detention of property, or dishonesty on the part of officers or citizens on Davis Bend."[35]

As the board swung into action, Davis fired off a second letter to President Johnson. The seven-page appeal he had sent while still in Alabama gave an account of the mistreatment he had suffered as an innocent nonparticipant in the war; as a result of these trying experiences he claimed to deserve speedy restoration of his property.[36] In the new letter he bitterly attacked the bureau for using "every device that *fraud avarice* and *falsehood* can bring to their aid to continue their possession" of his plantations. Davis reiterated his usual complaints about stolen animals and tools, the army selling diseased horses to the freedmen and driving them from their homes. He denied that he was scheming to seize the plantation: "Could anything be more absurd than that an Old Man, entering his 82nd year without power, without means, without a home and might almost say without a country, should threaten to expel a military force."[37] By this time it was clear that Davis was engaged in a bitter struggle with the bureau, and he hoped to enlist the chief executive on his side. Always sensitive to political trends, Joseph thought he might benefit by the growing rift between Johnson and the Radicals. At least he could supply specific cases of abuse to aid the president's campaign against the Freedmen's Bureau. As a prominent, lifelong Democrat and a member of the wealthy planter class whom Johnson envied but respected, Davis might hope for a sympathetic hearing.

Meanwhile, the board of investigation began its work. On November 10, Ben Montgomery reported to Davis, "There was a committee of investigation on the Bend a few days ago inquiring into the various complaints, but they proved to be nothing mort than members of the same clan and may approve of the acts of those here." Already Montgomery had recognized the weakness of the board: it was set up to investigate alleged acts of injustice and fraud by bureau officials, but it was composed of members of the very group it was supposed to examine. The main target of criticism was Samuel Thomas, the commanding officer under whom all three members served. From the beginning it was clear that their purpose was to provide a report that would satisfy headquarters in Washington that the criticism was unjustified. In their investigation at Davis Bend, Ben reported that E. S. Bedford, the gin agent, claimed under oath that he spent $1,200 on gin repairs (though Donaly had appraised repairs at less than $50). The agent also testified that he had to hire two white men at $100 per month each to operate the Hurricane gin. Montgomery noted that "such expensive arrangements. . . were never necessary before."[38]

The board moved to Vicksburg to hear further testimony. Alerted to their activities by now, Joseph Davis mobilized his forces to make a legally correct and persuasive case for gross abuse of "his people" and himself. He retained the services of four prominent lawyers and prepared statements of grievances and lists of witnesses. He submitted a formal complaint to the board in which he detailed chronologically all the alleged evil acts perpetrated either by or under the orders of Colonel Thomas from December 18, 1863, when he and his troops first occupied the Bend, to the fall of 1865. In consideration of all the damage his people and property had suffered, Davis expected to be granted an indemnity "such . . . as the nature of the case may require," so he added an itemized list of claims which amounted to the startling sum of $176,800.[39] The army officers, already irritated by the insistence of Davis's demands, must have been incensed at this impertinent request for a total reconstruction of "the nest of the Confederacy."

Davis prepared a list of "questions to be asked of Bedford and Captain Norton." The eight questions for the gin agent were designed to reveal all the details of his operations, including costs and profits, his means of rendering accounts to freedmen, and the identities of those involved with him in the gin concession. The Davis forces also drew up lists of witnesses, including bureau personnel and former Davis slaves.[40]

Colonel Thomas, too, gave some thought to guiding the hearings; he authorized a letter to the board containing probing questions to be asked of B. T. Montgomery. They included the details of his contract with Joseph Davis for 1866, and such telling questions as "Whether the Joe Davis people will be less oppressed when they pay one-third of what they raise [to Davis for the use of the land] than they are now, paying nothing?" and "What he has been required to pay to the Government?"[41] This is the only recorded instance of direct intervention by Thomas in the investigation, and it seems to indicate that he considered Benjamin Montgomery the true source of the troubles at Davis Bend.

Meanwhile, Joseph Davis retained the services of a fifth attorney, Armistead Burwell, an established Vicksburg lawyer whose mansion and fortune had been destroyed by the war. He had opposed secession and remained loyal to the Union at the cost of painful social and professional ostracism. Perhaps Davis hoped to increase his chances of a favorable decision of the board by adding to his team a man with more acceptable political credentials. If so, he was doomed to disappointment, because Burwell attended only one session of the hearings before withdrawing from the case. Joseph was angry at this abandonment and wrote to the pro-Union attorney accusing him of unethical behavior. He declared, "The obligations of counsel and client are the most sacred in social life. After a long experience, you are the first that I have known, after possessing himself of the facts, and circumstances at the hour of trial has desserted his trust." Davis exercised some restraint by omitting a final sentence that he had included in the first draft of the letter, saying, "I hope your remorse may be less than that of Judas Iscariot."[42]

However, even the milder version stung Burwell. He was so angry that he printed and circulated a long response, claiming that Davis had misrepresented the case and failed to provide all the facts to his new attorney. When Burwell reached the court, he found four lawyers present but no Negroes, although Joseph had pretended that he was "acting for and on behalf of some sixty freedmen." Burwell decided that it would be "a great diminution of my self-respect to take the fifth of a frivolous case, which had been progressing for more than a week." He had agreed to serve without fee on behalf of aggrieved freedmen, but after seeing that there were no real clients present and learning the nature of the proceedings, he realized that Davis was using the freedmen "for your own seditious purposes, to make a petty war of litigation and strife, against an odious Department of an odious Government, which you have done all in your power to destroy." Burwell continued, "You have all the venom of the poisonous adder, but without its power to strike." This vituperation went on for two closely printed pages, in the course of which Burwell revealed that he had been the victim of much "sly and secret insinuation and slander" from those who remained "as bitter in their hatred to the Union and Government in their secret hearts, as they were six months ago, when they had armies in the field." He insisted that Davis's attack on him was false and motivated by the worst kind of treason.[43] The intensity of Burwell's reaction to his fellow Mississippian shows the deep divisions that wracked postwar society in the South.

Although this response provided telling criticism of Joseph Davis, the withdrawal of Burwell as attorney had no effect on the hearings of the board. Unfortunately, the official minutes were not preserved, but the Davis forces took notes on at least part of the testimony, providing a glimpse of the proceedings. They reported that Colonel Thomas was called before the board twice and under oath gave an account of his occupation of Davis Bend. He admitted that some of the Davis Negroes were evicted from their houses but claimed that inconvenience was unavoidable in order to provide for the mass of refugees. Their animals and tools were confiscated under a general military order, and he denied that the freedmen had been deprived of any part of their cotton. He claimed that the high charge for ginning was in lieu of the authorized two-cents-per-pound tax for use of the land. The assistant commissioner's testimony seemed to provide reasonable explanations for the complaints against him, and Dr. Foster, the surgeon in charge of the hospital at Hurricane from March 1864 to April 1865, corroborated many of Thomas's statements.[44]

The notes recorded the testimony of nine freedmen, all of them from the Davis plantations, who related their particular grievances concerning loss of animals and living quarters or lack of payment for their cotton. Ben Montgomery complained that when he fled to Ohio, army officers appropriated all his household goods and store merchandise. He claimed that currently the people were doing well as a result of his assistance; he had "paid out for them . . . in order for them to raise crops, about $4,000." However, he was not sure that the people at the Bend were any better off "in a pecuniary sense" than they had been in 1863, because now many were deeply in debt. This account makes Montgomery's testimony sound arrogant and self-righteous, but it is difficult to judge from such scanty records.

At least one complainant left no doubt about his attitude toward the proceedings. In disgust, Joseph Davis presented a formal protest to the board. First, he said, "Most of the time of the Board is taken up by Chaplain Jas. A. Hawley President of the Board in lecturing and insulting witnesses." Furthermore, Davis was forbidden to question witnesses and therefore prevented from developing his case. He was told "by the Prest of the Board that if there was anything he wanted to know he could tell him and if he thought it was necessary he would enquire of the witness." Joseph asked that his protest be entered in the record of their proceedings, "feeling the impossibility of getting the evidence through the authority of the Board."[45] It must have been infuriating for this meticulous lawyer to see legal custom and procedure flouted by an arrogant Yankee army chaplain, and Davis was not accustomed to suffering in silence.

The proceedings continued, however, and on November 24 the board submitted its findings to Colonel Thomas in a fourteen-page report. It stated that ample notice of its hearings was circulated around Davis Bend but "no complaints were offered from any parties except those on Joe Davis plantations." It added "these all seemed to belong to a clique who were kept in communication with Mr. D. thro one of his former servants Benjamin F. [sic] Montgomery a very shrewd and intelligent Negro."[46] Thus the target for blame was established early in the report.

The board considered the cases of ten different freedmen and found small justification for their complaints. Since slaves could not own property, the horses, mules, and oxen at Davis Bend had been properly confiscated as abandoned or captured goods. In several instances, the freedman first said that he was satisfied with his crop settlement for the previous year but then changed his story under the prompting of his old master and claimed that he had received only a small part of his earnings. However, in each case, when his store account was read to him, the man acknowledged receipt of every item. The report concluded that most claimants exhibited "a disposition to get everything [they] could of Government with very little regard to justice." The officials found this especially irritating since these freedmen "had been living at Government expense when all the return that any rendered was a small portion of labor indispensible to the support of multitudes otherwise utterly dependent & helpless." This was a theme repeatedly expressed by Freedmen's Bureau officers: that each freedman was responsible for the welfare of all his fellow blacks and should think of their good before his own. Such a collective consciousness was certainly alien to the individualistic work ethic that inspired many of these same white officials to strive to become capitalist tycoons. Evidently they did not, and perhaps could not, regard a former slave as properly having similar personal ambitions.

The board praised the army officers for making no distinction between the Davis blacks and the refugees in the distribution of houses and concluded that, as Thomas had testified, the freedmen were fairly compensated for their cotton in 1864. They conceded that Bedford's evidence indicated that in 1865 the people were not getting the benefit of the difference between the prices of seed and ginned cotton. However, they concluded cryptically, "There is not sufficient evidence to show what becomes of these profits, nor if there are interested parties, who they are." It does seem odd that so important a part of their investigation was left incomplete.

The board complained of Davis's behavior during the hearings, which they described as "incomprehensible and unbecoming . . . querrelous [sic] and unfair" and his language "often so severe and ungentlemanly as to require that he should be rebuked and silenced." They concluded that "his conduct . . . was evidently intended as a covert assault on the Government we represent."

As had been hinted at the outset, the board reserved its most severe censure for "Benjamin F. Montgomery." He had every reason to be satisfied.

> He farmed land given by the Bureau without rent, has kept a store at large profits, doing a business worth about $2500.00 a year, nett, and paying no taxes, and when refused the gin, in addition to both his other branches of business, has stirred up dissatisfaction among his former fellow servants.

They found his behavior especially inexcusable because Montgomery was "a man of great shrewdness & intelligence & considerable education." They added that "his influence is very considerable." His dissatisfaction was attributed to "his disappointment in not getting the Gins this year and his wish to please his Old Master J. E. Davis from whom he has endeavored to get what he evidently regards as a valuable lease." The board concluded, "It is apparent that most of the disturbance with Mr. Davis & with the Negroes spring from him." So a long investigation had uncovered the true cause of the Davis Bend trouble—it was Benjamin Montgomery. Even Joseph Davis was viewed as a mere pawn in the hands of this skillful black man.

Evidently the tenor of the board's conclusions was apparent to Montgomery even before their report was written, and he became increasingly apprehensive of the results of alienating these important men. About this time Colonel Thomas happened to go downriver on the same boat with Montgomery, and in the course of the journey told him that he had received orders from General Howard to arrest and imprison Ben for entering into a contract with Davis, a person disloyal to the United States. Montgomery pled for clemency, and Thomas said that he would grant him two days before putting him in jail. Actually, Thomas merely kept him under surveillance for several days. Montgomery concluded that Thomas hoped he would flee so that the bureau could confiscate the large quantity of cotton the Montgomerys had raised or received from others in payment of ration bills.[47] However accurate Montgomery's interpretation of the motives of the assistant commissioner, this incident must have frightened the able and ambitious freedman. Thomas's display of power coupled with his evident hostility boded ill for the future of the Montgomerys.

On the night of November 18, while in Vicksburg, perhaps to testify at the hearings, Ben wrote a careful letter to his former master, attempting to call a halt to the conflict. He said:

> After much reflection upon the nature and circumstances connected with the case now agitating your mind . . . I would, with all regard for your superior judgement, beg leave to suggest that the matter be not pressed further at present if your feelings in the case can possibly allow you to do so.[48]

When he laid the matter before Davis, Ben said, he had not realized that it would be so disturbing to him. He continued:

> In view of the much suffering and loss that has been caused by the war, I am unwilling to press our complaints too far, which might prove a great loss and much inconvenience to you and yours, without any benefit to us more than be considered, more restless and dissatisfied than others of our color and condition.

Here was a heartfelt plea to stop the conflict with Thomas and the bureau. Clearly, Ben wished that he had accepted the gin decision without further protest, but he could not put the genie back in the bottle. There was no stopping old Joe now that he had gotten a taste of battle.

The other side showed no sign of weakening its campaign. The subordinates of Colonel Thomas, with his approval, drew up a statement of support for him and persuaded more than a hundred freedmen at Davis Bend to sign it. They swore that "we have never been oppressed in any way by Col. Thomas; but acknowledge that we have received simple justice in all matters, while he has had our affairs under his charge."[49] The signers included Gla, Broadwater, and Bland, who had joined the Montgomerys in the gin request. In fact, the last fifteen signatures were procured by Judge Gla after the meeting, from persons who had not been present. So not only had Ben's former partners endorsed a document supporting his adversary, but the ringleader had persuaded other literate freedmen to sign it too. Thomas later identified those who signed the statement as all the colored planters of Davis Bend "who have occupied any position worthy of consideration."[50] This document was intended not only to bolster Thomas's claim to the freedmen's support, but also to isolate the Montgomerys as the only troublemakers on the Bend. No wonder Ben felt increasing apprehension.

Just before Christmas Colonel Thomas forwarded to General Howard the report of the board of investigation along with the endorsement by the Davis Bend planters. He wrote a long cover letter responding to all the criticism and justifying his policies for the model colony. Without mentioning the Montgomerys by name, he said that he had not let "the colored people" have the gin lease; he feared they lacked the money to repair and run it, and he had been right. He insisted that his judgment had been based purely on what he thought was best for the people.[51]

Evidently Thomas did not care to reveal to his superior in Washington his personal antagonism toward Montgomery. He was not so reticent about his feelings for Joseph Davis. He said he had not answered Davis's letters because they were "incoherent, querulous & full of misstatements & therefore beneath my notice." He had only appointed the board in order to see whether the blacks had any complaints; he knew that Davis would use any means to regain his plantations, so his charges were not worth considering. Furthermore, Davis "refused to take the oath of allegiance before the board, & declared that he would never ask for a pardon." This traitor had no right to his property, and therefore Thomas would lease it again. At their last interview he had ordered Davis out of his office and would take no further notice of him.

This was not a difficult vow to keep, for Joseph Davis neither visited nor wrote to Colonel Thomas again. However, he continued his campaign to recover his property and relieve his former slaves from what he believed to be the curse of the bureau. While continuing to write to the president, Davis broadened his efforts to include appeals to former political allies, such as Senator James Guthrie of Kentucky, a Democrat, and Burton Harrison, former private secretary to Jefferson Davis.[52] He even tried to enlist the support of a Radical Republican and former abolitionist, Senator Henry Wilson of Massachusetts.[53] Although there were no immediate responses to these letters, it would be incorrect to assume that they accomplished nothing. Each time that Davis addressed the chief executive or some other influential person in Washington, his letter was read and forwarded to General Howard, who was forced to take action on it; usually he referred it to Mississippi for investigation and comment. For example, the Wilson letter was returned to the senator after four months of circulation and inquiry within the government.[54] Although the conclusions reached by bureau and army investigators exonerated Colonel Thomas, the commissioner of the bureau was still forced to defend the honesty of its operations in Mississippi to a critical senator. Each time an investigation was made or a review conducted, even though the bulk of the evidence was favorable to Thomas, there must have been some erosion in the confidence placed in him by his superiors.

The assistant commissioner did all that he could through letters to Howard to refute the charges against him and discredit their author.[55] In his year-end report for 1865 Thomas proudly presented a detailed statement of the successful Davis Bend colony, where 181 independent companies had produced 1,736 bales of cotton, 12,000 bushels of corn, and enough vegetables to total a crop value of $397,700. After the deduction of all expenses, the Davis Bend planters realized a profit of $159,200, for an average of almost $880 per company or $122.46 per adult. Of course, this was distributed unequally, with the large planters receiving the major share while many hired hands had little or no cash at year's end. The Home Farm made a profit of almost $26,000, and the bureau netted close to $45,000 from the Bend. No wonder Colonel Thomas called the experiment "a grand success" and claimed it proved how well the freedmen could operate as independent farmers. There was no mention of any discontent among them. Thomas expressed regret only that, with the return to their owners of all but the Davis plantations, the promising experiment must end.[56]

On New Year's Day 1866 Thomas drafted a long letter opposing the restoration of Hurricane and Brierfield to Joseph Davis. He assured Howard that Davis's charges were made in a desperate effort to regain his lands by discrediting Thomas and the bureau. No respectable Southerner approved of his tactics; even Governor Sharkey failed to endorse Davis's petition to the president. Furthermore, Thomas contended with some exaggeration, "not a negro on Davis Bend will say that he has been wronged, but on the contrary will acknowledge his obligations to the Bureau."[57] Undoubtedly the Montgomerys would have contradicted that assertion. Thomas offered the contract between Montgomery and Davis as proof that the latter was not genuinely concerned about the freedmen; Davis's terms required one-third of the crop, a higher rent than was charged anywhere else in the South and far more than the two cents per pound stipulated by the bureau in 1865. Finally, the assistant commissioner requested permission to lease the Davis place to freedmen again in 1866 with the understanding that if the property was restored during the year, they could pay the government's rent to the owner. Thomas urged a speedy decision because "the time has arrived when arrangements must be made for planting, if a crop is to be made next year."

Thomas was not the only one concerned about lease arrangements for Hurricane and Brierfield. More than a month earlier Ben Montgomery had written to tell Thomas that he had instructed the freedmen to discontinue cutting cordwood "until it is known what disposition will be made of the place the ensuing year."[58] He ended the letter curtly: "If I have acted amiss advise me." Perhaps because of the strained relationship between them, Thomas failed to inform Ben that Washington headquarters was delaying a decision on the Davis property, and Thomas himself did not know what to do with it. When Thomas visited the Bend in January and explained land arrangements for all except the Davis places, Ben threatened to take matters into his own hands and begin dividing fields among the freedmen as though they were legally restored to Davis. E. S. Bedford, the gin agent and, since Captain Norton's transfer, part-time bureau representative, also pressed Thomas for a decision. Without any authority he had been telling people that the lands would again be leased by the government; so many freedmen were drifting away to sign contracts elsewhere that Bedford was afraid he would be unable to find enough lessees if he waited any longer.[59]

Montgomery described the same disturbing situation a few days later, noting that Bedford was beginning to parcel out the land but would not say on what terms it would be leased. Ben asserted to Davis that "the Party controlling affairs" had delayed a decision for so long while circulating "discouraging reports respecting this place" that many workers had been induced to leave. He was certain that the bureau's purpose was "to frighten & squander the Hurricane & Brierfield people." However, he reported with a confidence that bordered on bravado: "I am satisfied that none of our people will leave unless I do and I have no idea of doing so, although it was currently rumored that I could not stay, which reported threat only created a determination to test their power to drive me off."[60] It was no longer solely a question of a mere gin lease but rather a threat of permanent exile. All of Ben's dreams and plans were centered on these plantations, and he would fight with all his strength to remain there.

In his challenge to the authority of Thomas, a respected officer in the victorious Union army, Montgomery won handily, although it is not clear how he accomplished it. Early in February he cryptically reported to Davis, "I think we shall have no further trouble with those controlling matters here, as the extent of their power is known to more persons than themselves."[61] He and his sons had leased about 200 acres of Brierfield and were busy repairing the levees. If Samuel Thomas had indeed plotted to drive the Montgomerys off the Bend, he had failed. Perhaps it was Bedford and the other resident carpetbaggers who resented both the influence and the mercantile profits Ben enjoyed, and had schemed with Thomas to get rid of him.

In any case, the assistant commissioner had more important things to worry about in the first quarter of 1866 than the fate of one family of freedmen. The restoration of most of the plantations to their owners cut bureau revenues so drastically that in Mississippi it was no longer self-sustaining. As more army units were mustered out, it became increasingly difficult to keep bureau staff or to enforce bureau orders. In addition to the frustrating task of acting as next friend of the freedmen in the often hostile civil courts, bureau agents frequently found themselves caught in the middle between demanding planters and recalcitrant workers. Ever since the state legislature passed the stringent Black Code the previous November, Thomas had complained about their difficult position, "charged by the whites with inciting insurrection & inflating the hopes of the negroes, & by the blacks with failing to secure their rights."[62] The resumption of jurisdiction by local governments as well as the restoration of the land to former owners left the bureau in a primarily advisory role. With these changes, Thomas seemed to undergo a subtle shift of attitude; from his former crusading support for blacks, he gradually moved toward greater approval of white Southerners, noting what he termed "the favorable change in feelings of the white people towards the freedmen."[63] By March he reported that the shortage of labor had forced planters to treat workers well; when he visited the county court at Natchez he found that "the freedmen were allowed every privilege granted white men."[64] Despite this purported change in attitude, however, he faced mounting criticism of his actions from local whites, from some of his colleagues, and even received a scurrilous attack on his personal conduct from a newspaper in Cincinnati.[65] Although Thomas denied the charges in letters that bristled with indignation, it was apparent that his reputation was indelibly besmirched.

In January, when General Howard had asked his assistant commissioner in Mississippi whether or not he wanted to remain in his job, Thomas replied, "It is my desire to hold the position as long as I can retain the confidence of my superiors." He had every reason to believe that he had their confidence. In his official report for 1865 Howard had said that Colonel Thomas "since the organization of the Bureau has discharged his duties with zeal and ability."[66] But on April 10, 1866, an order from headquarters stated that "Col. Saml Thomas has been relieved from duty as Asst Comr for the Bureau for Miss . . . and directed to report in person to the Commissioner, in order to be placed on other important duty." Howard thanked him "for the energy, fidelity and ability he has displayed in the discharge of his delicate and difficult duties while laboring for the freedmen of the Mississippi Valley." The military commander for the state praised Thomas for his "enlightened, humane, just, and impartial course," which won him "the esteem and approbation of his professional brethren" as well as "the vast mass of the population of the State, both white and black." By May 15 Thomas was at work in bureau headquarters in Washington.[67]

If Samuel Thomas was as valuable an officer as his superiors claimed, why then was he removed from his position in Mississippi? The gin controversy at Davis Bend may not have been the only cause of his downfall, but there seems little doubt that the repeated complaints of Joseph Davis, made directly to the president and other influential public officials, contributed a great deal to his removal. Some years later, O. O. Howard reported that at this time:

> Any agent who took the part of the freedmen against a Southern planter . . . was traduced, and often, I am sorry to say, his discharge was brought about. The President was very anxious to be rid of every prominent officer who was reported to have been long the freedmen's friend. In his eyes assistant commissioners such as . . . Samuel Thomas . . . were too pronounced in behalf of those assailed; they seemed to be friends of the so-called carpet-baggers . . . and of Southern Unionists and negroes.[68]

Although Howard deplored the loss of these dedicated men, he was "obliged to execute the law under the direction of his Excellency." Thomas's shift of attitude toward white Southerners had come too late. The message had already reached the White House, largely through the efforts of Joseph Davis and Benjamin Montgomery, that the bureau under Thomas was destroying the utopia it claimed to be creating.

By mid-1866 Samuel Thomas and the entire gin controversy were fading memories at Davis Bend, but the puzzle remains as to why these three intelligent men became embroiled in such a bitter dispute. Normally one would expect to find the Freedmen's Bureau agent and the freedman united against the native white planter. Twentieth-century revisionists might predict a split along racial lines, combining the venal agent and the powerful planter against the exploited black man. However, the freedman-planter combination in opposition to the bureau representative seems most unlikely. What accounts for this strange division in the Davis Bend gin controversy?

Perhaps the behavior of Joseph Davis is the most readily understood. His hostility toward Samuel Thomas was perfectly natural; Davis must have seen Thomas as the symbol of the Yankee conqueror who had usurped his domain and destroyed his former way of life. Furthermore, before the war Davis had had a monopoly on paternalistic benevolence toward the blacks there; Thomas's arrogant assumption of this role, despite his ignorance of the people or previous conditions, must have been unbearably galling to the former master of Hurricane. There seems little doubt that Joseph Davis felt a genuine concern for "his people," which the war did not alter. In addition, Davis's self-interest decreed swift repossession of his plantations if he were ever to regain a measure of his former prosperity and continue to meet his assumed obligations as father figure to his extended family. Naturally, this frail octogenarian was quick to join in the attack on the bureau when such action might advance his efforts toward reclaiming his property. His alliance with Ben Montgomery meant only a resumption of a thirty-year partnership that had been based on mutual respect and dependence. Davis believed that he could rely on Montgomery's skill and ambition to help him cope with monumental postwar problems.

The aggressive, vituperative style with which Davis attacked Thomas and the bureau reflected Joseph's cumulative frustrations; his age, health, and refugee status were justification enough for his choleric outbursts. To these were added acute worry about the future of his beloved younger brother who was both a protégé and a surrogate son to him. As long as the former president of the Confederacy languished in prison while federal officials debated his fate, Joseph was likely to be waspish toward minor agents of that same government. Perhaps it was not that difficult for Davis to abandon the soft-spoken planter gentility and resume the rough manners of his youth; his intemperate outbursts were among the few forms of recreation still available to him. His son-in-law said, "I am glad you are inclined to annoy them, as *that* I think is as much satisfaction as you are likely to have."[69] Joseph Davis's behavior in the controversy stemmed from complex but generally comprehensible motives.

Samuel Thomas's hostility to Davis is equally logical. As the brother of Jeff Davis and the master of "the nest of the Confederacy," Joseph undoubtedly symbolized the Rebel enemy to Thomas. Moreover, in his previous two years of service to the freedmen, he had come to expect resistance to his policies from recalcitrant southern planters. He was predisposed to dislike Joseph even before receiving his impudent letters. Furthermore, Davis's goal, the restoration of his plantations, posed the ultimate threat to Thomas's model project, which had been the greatest accomplishment of his administration in Mississippi. If Davis Bend were lost, Thomas would have no orderly achievement to show inquisitive inspectors, reporters, and other visitors from the North. The irascible old Rebel, Davis, who was a minor irritant to Thomas at first, became a major problem for the assistant commissioner, and his hostility grew apace. There was never the possibility of amicable relations between these two men.

The real puzzle in the behavior of Samuel Thomas is his hostility toward Benjamin Montgomery. Thomas frequently exhorted the freedmen to work hard and become self-sufficient, for he deplored ignorance, laziness, or any other deviation from the universally accepted, nineteenth-century white standards of hard work and entrepreneurship. He believed in self-help and decreed that "if there is a freedman able to carry on business for himself, so construct the rules as to assist him, and let him work his way up." [70] Montgomery was precisely this—an industrious black entrepreneur seeking to expedite the transition to prosperous freedom in association with his fellow freedmen. He was intelligent, articulate, and ambitious, displaying the determination and initiative that Thomas so much admired. In short, Benjamin Montgomery personified what should have been Thomas's ideal freedman; yet Samuel Thomas hated him. Was Montgomery too different from the helpless, ignorant objects of pity whom Thomas had come to expect after two years in the field? Did this black success story disturb his own deep-seated racial preconceptions? Was his paternalistic benevolence challenged by the equality implicit in Montgomery's business ability? Did Ben's cool competence and air of command threaten the shaky authority of the Ohioan, who was still in his mid-twenties and whose unwieldy territory was only marginally organized? Or did Thomas honestly fear that Ben planned to exploit his fellow freedmen? All of these factors may have figured in Thomas's attitude. Although the assistant commissioner seemed to be a sincere champion of his black charges, he was also a product of his times, which presumed a reality of white superiority. He came from a state that had produced many abolitionists, but his family had migrated from Virginia, and Samuel grew up just across the river from slave territory. His recruitment into the Freedmen's Department may have resulted more from his ambition to advance in the

army than from a desire to serve an oppressed race; he was neither a clergyman nor missionary, as were many of his colleagues.
His subsequent career reveals Thomas as a very ambitious, pragmatic man whose philanthropy was reserved primarily for his
later years, when he had become a millionaire mining and
railroad tycoon moving in prominent New York social circles.[71]
There is nothing in the biography of Samuel Thomas that would
indicate that he would be charitably indulgent toward the
Montgomerys, but neither is there any explanation for his special
hostility.

How valid were the accusations against Thomas made by Davis
and the Montgomerys? Did he oppose any change because he
was personally profiting from the gin concession? Bedford's
operation of the gin was certainly inefficient, and his charges
seem to have been exorbitant even considering wartime inflation.
At least one white lessee of a plantation on the Bend implied that
Bedford and Thomas charged more than necessary, and later investigations did cast doubt on Bedford's honesty.[72] Since he was
granted the gin concession by Thomas and maintained in that
position for a second year, it seems that the assistant commissioner at least condoned his questionable performance.

None of the reasons that Thomas gave the black petitioners for
his refusal of the gin lease is valid. The amount of money needed
to repair the machinery was small, well within the Montgomerys'
means. Neither the ability nor the industriousness of the blacks
could be honestly faulted. As for the contention that they would
gin their own cotton and neglect the needs of poorer freedmen,
Ben later testified that Bedford did exactly that, with no objection
from Thomas.[73] Although he honestly may have doubted the ability of the blacks to run the gin and feared they would jeopardize
the success of his model project, Thomas displayed a surprising
loyalty to an agent of doubtful integrity, whose own unfamiliarity
with the process also threatened that success.

Thomas may have winked at Bedford's shady dealing, but there
is no evidence that he profited personally from his position. Repeated investigations after he left office in Mississippi failed to
turn up any proof of dishonesty; had this not been the case, men
such as John Eaton and O. O. Howard would not have given him
such high praise in their subsequent memoirs. One New York re-

porter summed up the consensus concerning Thomas: "Charges have been made against him personally for peculation; but I have failed to find any grounds for them, and it is the opinion of all the officers here [in Vicksburg] that he was the victim of misrepresentation, if not willful malice."[74] In the face of such testimony it is difficult to believe the charge Joseph Davis made privately to members of his family that Thomas had demanded a bribe from Davis for the return of his land. Some minor bureau representative might have suggested it, but had Thomas really tried to blackmail Davis, the latter would have broadcast the information to his many contacts around the nation; it was just the sort of ammunition he sought for his campaign.[75]

Samuel Thomas, then, like Joseph Davis, seems to have been motivated by a number of factors: the protection of his model project on Davis Bend; suspicion of a black man who, contrary to the stereotype, possessed skills equal to his own; distrust of a white planter who had been part of the "slave power" before the war and brother of the president of the rebel nation during it. However, all of these motives together still fall short of providing a satisfactory explanation for Thomas's aggressive hostility. Perhaps the tremendous pressures of his difficult job irritated and exhausted him to the point where he responded negatively to any unusual request. Perhaps he did not give sufficient thought to the black planters' request and then found himself wedded to a casually made decision. At any rate, he had no inkling when he turned down the petition that the repercussions would reach so far. Once his decision had been challenged, his anger at his own haste in making his decision and at Ben Montgomery for organizing a challenge to it both worked to engender an irrational antipathy to the man he saw as a scheming ingrate.

Even more surprising than Thomas's hostility toward Montgomery was Ben's direct attack upon the assistant commissioner. A black man who had been economically successful in the antebellum South could not have often allowed himself the luxury of expressing open hostility toward any white man, yet here he took on the highest ranking bureau officer in the state. The key to Ben's success was his unusual ability to win the patronage of important whites while maintaining a modest, self-effacing demeanor. He gained his ends by subtle persuasion rather than direct challenge, however righteous he believed his cause. He was more likely to appeal to benevolent self-interest than to an abstract sense of justice. Recognizing the extreme precariousness of his position as an ambitious black businessman in a racist white world, he did his best not to antagonize anyone. If Thomas's hostility toward Montgomery was irrational, Ben's toward Thomas seemed almost suicidal. Why did this intelligent former slave engage in open battle with an assistant commissioner appointed by the victorious occupying army?

In part, it may have been a power struggle between the two men for the leadership and control of the colony of freedmen at Davis Bend. If Montgomery were to recover his position as the de facto head of the blacks at the Bend, he had to show that he could wield sufficient influence to take care of their needs. The band of former Davis slaves was already predisposed to follow him, but the fluid mass of new refugees must be convinced of Ben's authority before he could reestablish order and insure an adequate labor supply for his ambitious plans. In the antebellum years, as Ben took on more and more of the responsibility for plantation operations, he must have seen many opportunities to make improvements in Davis's model community. For years he had probably been perfecting his own version of the utopian dream, with himself as leader. When freedom actually came, it must have been galling for him to find a brash, young Union officer with no knowledge of plantation operation and little understanding of the Davis blacks attempting to build a model colony under his own tutelage. If Joseph Davis became livid with anger just hearing about Thomas's clumsy usurpations, how much more intolerable it must have been for Montgomery actually to live on the old place under the new regime. Ben was desperate to regain his authority; however, in mid-1865 it was not at all clear that the tenure of Thomas and the bureau would be brief. Montgomery took a very great risk in challenging the assistant commissioner with only the questionable authority of his former master to back him up.

How valid were the charges made against him by Thomas and the other officials? Was he driven to this rash action by bureau interference with his attempts to fleece his fellow feedmen? Undoubtedly Montgomery was profiting from his store operation, just as he had before the war. He charged high markups, but he also took great risks in financing the penniless freedmen. Ben's customers, for the most part, knew him well; their trust in him was based on more than twenty years of experience with his business practices. Had his prices been grossly out of line, they would have traded elsewhere. The charge that Ben was a malcontent was obviously true. With his grand scheme for the colony, he could not remain content and docile under the bungling and, perhaps, fraudulence of the bureau agents. His personal ambition did not necessarily mean that he was unconcerned about the welfare of his fellows; in his ideal community each would prosper with the prosperity of the colony. By the same token, while Ben was using his former master to achieve his ends, he believed that their efforts would be mutually advantageous. He had real respect and even affection for Joseph Davis, born of their many shared experiences. In a sense, Montgomery was a part of the antebellum power structure and sought a return of its hegemony, although he certainly did not regret his new status as a free man. Perhaps this identification with the southern planters was the factor that made him so antagonistic to Thomas and precluded a cooperative relationship between them.

At any rate, the removal of Samuel Thomas in May 1866, while ending the personal clash, was only the most notable in a series of events marking the decline of federal power over the peninsula of Davis Bend. The army had closed the post there in October 1865, though five or six enlisted men in the colored infantry continued to be assigned to the Freedmen's Bureau representative until late February 1866, at which time they were mustered out of the service. Captain Gaylord Norton, who had headed freedmen's services there since the army occupation, was relieved of duty late in 1865. Thereafter, E. S. Bedford, the civilian gin agent, tried to handle bureau business on the Bend, though he lacked the authority of a full-time army officer.[76] The hospital was closed in April, and the patients, along with many inmates of the Home Farm, were transferred elsewhere. In May even the questionable authority of Bedford was withdrawn when he returned to New York State for reasons of health. Colonel Thomas's transfer removed the last federal official with an interest in creating an ideal colony on the Bend. He was not replaced; instead, the office of assistant commissioner was for the first time combined with that of military commander of the state, a post held by Major General T. J. Wood. Henceforth, the bureau would be more concerned with defending past actions than with initiating new projects.[77]

In June, sparked by the Davis complaints, two major investigations of the bureau's conduct at Davis Bend culminated in lengthy reports, one to the inspector general of the army and the other to the assistant commissioner of the Freedmen's Bureau. Although both reports exonerated Thomas and official acts of the bureau, they were critical of agents on the scene such as Bedford. This time there was no mention of Joseph Davis and his efforts to recover his property, nor was there any criticism of Benjamin Montgomery and his disruptive activities. Captain John F. Ritter informed Colonel M. P. Bestow, assistant adjutant general of the Department of Mississippi, that he found the Davis Bend freedmen healthy, generally contented and progressing favorably. He advised that "the less interference with their concerns that can possibly be made, the better they will succeed."[78]

Captain A. W. Preston reported to Lieutenant Stuart Eldridge, assistant attorney general for the Freedmen's Bureau in Mississippi, that he too found the blacks at Davis Bend prospering under government tutelage.

> Their crops are better than those generally surrounding them, their houses are more comfortable than the quarters occupied by Freedmen usually, and finally they appear contented and happy, industrious and energetic, possessing all the requirements, which properly tutored, will make the Freedmen useful citizens.[79]

Preston documented his report with nine affidavits or letters from residents of the Bend. Five of the freedmen swore that they knew of no cheating by Colonel Thomas or any bureau agents, although some admitted that they had heard complaints of gin overcharges and poor handling of the crop. A.D.W. Leavens and J. H. Leitch, physicians living at Brierfield, claimed that they thought well of Bedford and knew of no illegal acts committed by bureau officers. However, Benjamin Montgomery wrote a long letter reiterating the complaints he had made in his testimony before the board of investigation the previous year, and again in an affidavit in May. He was especially critical of the confiscation of tools and animals, as well as the high charges for ginning for the past two years. He claimed that the "colored planters" at Hurricane had "petitioned unanimously" for the gin concession, promising to gin properly all available cotton for $7.50 per bale; instead they were forced to pay $12 for a poor and discriminatory job. Bedford's defensive affidavit, sent from Chenango County, New York, claimed that $12 was "the uniform price for the year 1865."[80] However, the burden of official criticism had shifted; the culprit was no longer the unscrupulous Montgomery and his disloyal former master but rather the opportunistic Bedford and his cohorts.

These investigations may well have been part of the frantic efforts of the Vicksburg district to clean its own house in anticipation of a visit from the unfriendly inspectors appointed by President Andrew Johnson to seek scandal in the Freedmen's Bureau. News of the impending arrival of Generals Joseph S. Fullerton and James B. Steedman caused local panic; they had uncovered a major scandal in North Carolina, and their presence in the Mississippi Valley encouraged all dissident Southerners to come forth with complaints. General Wood and his staff hastily sought to remove all potential causes for criticism. On June 4 Captain W. L. Ryan was assigned to Davis Bend as full-time bureau subcommissioner "to promote the welfare of the people" and secure for them "all the blessings to which their newly attained situation entitles them." In his role as protector of freedmen, Ryan was cautioned to observe the order forbidding investment of his private funds there.

On June 20, just nine days before the generals' arrival in Vicksburg, Wood ordered the permanent closing of all stores on Davis Bend, "to prevent an indiscriminate and demoralizing traffic of luxuries and articles actually harmful to the Freedmen." Five days later Ben Montgomery wrote on behalf of Montgomery & Sons—as their two stores were now called—protesting the order, which they claimed had subjected their customers to great inconvenience and expense. "The senior member of our firm has conducted a similar business on the Bend for the past 24 years, and the present year we are [supplying] at least 4/5 of those cultivating the Davis plantations." They asserted that Captain Ryan could verify their good record. Since they had complied with all regulations and held federal, state, and county licenses, they requested permission to reopen their stores.[81]

The next day Wood issued another order, allowing the resumption of "trade in the necessaries of life" at reasonable profits. However, he warned that "any extortionate charges, or the sale of intoxicating liquors will subject the offenders to immediate expulsion from the colony." The same day this order was issued, Thornton Montgomery signed an affidavit at bureau headquarters in Vicksburg, swearing that he never knew of whiskey being sold on Davis Bend by order of Colonel Thomas; in fact, he had seen orders strictly forbidding such sales. Although there is no proof, it seems likely that bureau officials made this affidavit a condition for reopening the Montgomery stores. Captain Preston, who witnessed it, probably hoped to strengthen bureau defenses against attacks by temperance advocates without inciting those articulate Davis freedmen to further protest.

Ben was disgusted with Captain Ryan's nervous insistence that all "fancy articles" be concealed until after "the probable or expected visit of Genls F&S." Montgomery told Davis that his stores carried few luxury items and no brass jewelry, but, he added, "I am opposed to hiding as I expect to do, what I suppose to be lawful business." However, he hoped the order would discourage "those who settle only a few days, weeks or months . . . for the express purpose of swindling the ignorant."[82] After a generation in business Ben felt that his reputation was well established, and he resented petty interference by insecure government agents. As it happened, General Steedman and General Fullerton bypassed Davis Bend on their inspection tour, but while they were in Vicksburg, Joseph Davis briefed them thoroughly on the complaints he and the freedmen had made against the bureau.[83]

Montgomery & Sons continued to be annoyed by the presence of northern merchants who sold cheap goods on the Bend at high prices, preferably in exchange for unginned cotton. At Hurricane there were three stores, the Montgomerys' two, which, as Ben noted, provided credit for 80 percent of the freedmen, and a cash store operated by former army captain C. E. Furlong and R. B. Williams, both white Northerners. Two additional stores were opened at Brierfield later in the year, one by Stuart Glascott, whose brother was an officer in the Freedmen's Bureau, and the other by P. G. Carter, who, with his sister, also conducted Sunday school and church services for the freedmen. Although Montgomerys' markup of 20 to 25 percent allowed them a tidy profit, they resented the intrusion of cotton-hungry carpetbaggers. As Ben remarked to Davis, "In the commencement of the season when prospects were gloomy they were not to be seen, now [that the crop is secure] we have more than is necessary."[84] P. G. Carter was the target of most of the criticism from the freedmen and even from some neighboring white planters. In August he circulated a handbill in the Mississippi Valley soliciting consignments of goods to be sold to the freedmen on the Bend, whom he numbered at 4,000, double the estimate of the bureau agent. Carter asserted that "almost anything, even of an inferior quality, finds a ready market at enormous prices" among these people in exchange for a lien on their cotton. He added, "The crop is now out of danger and looks fine and promising." Carter also offered to act as agent for enterprising cotton brokers. Although he had told General Wood that he benevolently sacrificed profits to supply needy freedmen whose welfare was his prime concern, Carter continued to arouse angry protests from dissatisfied customers about his rotten flour and tainted hams. In June, as a result of his investigation, Captain Preston dismissed complaints of neighboring planters who claimed that Carter tried to entice away their hands with false promises. But by October Captain Ryan documented one case where the storekeeper supplied cheap goods for which he charged $170 and claimed in payment cotton worth $400. Since Carter was the only merchant against whom the freedmen had made "serious and repeated complaints for unfair dealings," Ryan recommended that his store be closed and he be banished from the Bend. However, Preston accused Ryan of judging Carter on scant evidence, perhaps because the bureau agent was "secretly working in the interest of one or both of the other merchants." The Vicksburg bureau was so demoralized that its officers attacked each other rather than take drastic action of any sort.[85]

The weakening of government control was demonstrated earlier in the year when Thomas again leased the gin to E. S. Bedford, but this time insisted that he take Thornton Montgomery as his partner. Ben did not inform Joseph Davis of this arrangement until late July, and then justified it as necessary "in order to prevent them from having the entire control as was the case last year." As partners in the $800 lease, the Montgomerys could make repairs themselves and supervise gin operations, recording "everything that is worth noting." Ben conceded it was a strange alliance, but thought they must make the best of it, "hoping that arrangements may be different another year." Although as late as June Ben had asserted that he could gin cotton on the Bend for $7.50 per bale, Bedford and Thornton charged $10.50 per bale that year. Captain Ryan reported some discontent among the freedmen, who, he said, expected to pay no more than $8 or $8.50 per bale. He claimed that the higher charge meant that the blacks were actually paying as much as $16 to $18 per acre land rent; many were threatening to set up gins for themselves to avoid these high costs.[86] When given a share of the power in this case, the Montgomerys seem to have made only a marginal improvement in objectionable government practices.

Nevertheless, Ben Montgomery and his sons were becoming the undisputed leaders of the black community on the Davis plantations. With a cooperative spirit that would have done credit to Robert Owen, they persuaded some fifteen or twenty lessees to join them in an effort to see how early they could produce a bale of cotton. By pooling all their ripe cotton, the group ginned two bales on August tenth. According to a New Orleans newspaper, the first bale of the season arrived at the market there on August 7, a week earlier than usual; under Montgomery leadership, the Davis Bend planters were among the first producers.

In September Ben took up the cause of some twenty freedmen who, with great effort, had cleared small plots of wooded land outside the levees, on which Bedford had told them they would not have to pay rent that year. However, when D. L. Glascott came to collect for the bureau, he insisted that they must pay five dollars per acre, the same as all who leased lands outside the levees. Ben drafted a strong letter of protest to General Wood for the illiterate freedmen, citing their improvement of the property as adequate substitute for rent. However, the bureau yielded to Bedford, who claimed that he had said the men would be exempt from rent only if their crop was flooded out; otherwise, all lands were subject to the same fee. Although unsuccessful in this instance, Ben was becoming more aggressive in his demands on behalf of the Davis Bend community.[87]

The Montgomerys also took the lead in continuing an independent court system there. The formal judiciary with elected judges and sheriffs was abandoned at the end of 1865, when all but the Davis lands were returned to their owners and Captain Norton was transferred. However, early in 1866, in response to local requests, Colonel Thomas authorized a panel of six judges chosen by the freedmen at Hurricane and Brierfield to sit as a board of arbitration for the settlement of disputes among them. From the first, this court was dominated by the Montgomerys and other large landholders. In May, when Thomas left Mississippi, these men became worried about the legality of their court, since it was based only on verbal authority from the former assistant commissioner. The killing of several head of cattle by some lessees while protecting their fields from trespass led three of the judges— Thornton Montgomery; his uncle, William Lewis, Jr.; and George W. Boyd, another large planter—to seek renewed authorization from the bureau. Thornton sent their request to Joseph D. Nicholson, Joseph Davis's protégé, who presented it to General Wood in Vicksburg. The bureau chief approved the court and said its decisions, "when in conformity with well-known principles of justice, will be respected and endorsed by the Bureau."[88] The system worked well, even arbitrating disputes between freedmen and whites, with the latter's consent. However, in June both Ritter and Preston recommended in their reports that it be abolished and the new subcommissioner be given authority to settle disagreements. The only reason given by either man for the change was the possibility that the prosperous judges might encounter some conflict of interest while enforcing contracts or settling disputes involving money. Their recommendations were so similar in wording they sounded as if they might have been dictated by Captain Ryan, the one whose power would be enhanced by abolition of the court. None of these officials had been on the scene the previous year or knew of the court tradition on the Davis places. However, their recommendation prevailed, and the board of arbitration was discontinued on June 16, 1866.[89]

Education was another area in which the freedmen at the

Bend asserted their independence. As they formed school boards, they assumed responsibility for financing their schools and choosing the teachers. By midsummer 1866, all the schools were self-supporting and all five teachers were black. In a report to Major Preston, Virginia C. Green, one of these teachers, noted that she opened a school on Wood's plantation on May 1 at the request of the four black trustees.[90] Soon she had enrolled 120 pupils and recruited her cousin—like Miss Green, a St. Louisan—to assist her. She claimed that the school, "supported by those alone who patronized it," provided basic education to eager, obedient pupils whose progress compared favorably "with children who have enjoyed superior advantages." The school was in session for four months before closing for cotton-picking recess, and she expected to reopen it when the pupils were free to return to their studies. This articulate young woman had been born "as far north as the lakes" and had never been a slave, but she identified completely with the freedmen. Although she expressed gratitude for the bureau's assistance, her black nationalist views contrasted sharply with the benevolent condescension of the white teachers. She asserted: "I trust that at no distant day we shall not need assistance from a Government we have labored to enrich without remuneration, and fought to preserve without citizenship, or a share in her glory if she has gained a victory." She looked forward to the time when her people would be educated and prosperous through their own efforts and would no longer have to endure racial insults. Perhaps then, she added bitterly, all their suffering would seem worthwhile, although "now we cannot feel so." It would be interesting to know what the Montgomerys thought of this militant black woman; even at his most indignant, Ben had never expressed such racial hostility.

Before the end of the year the Montgomerys engaged in one last contest with the Yankee interlopers. This time Ben did not use eloquent protests to higher authority but instead relied on his business expertise to outwit them in the economic arena. Of the twelve white men on the Davis places that fall, Ben described nine as "cotton hunters" who aimed to get possession of the freedmen's crops at a fraction of their market value. When the bureau insisted that their land rent be paid before any cotton was

Joseph E. Davis (Courtesy of
Mrs. Conrad M. Keubel)

Eliza Van Benthuysen Davis (Courtesy of Mrs. Conrad M. Keubel)

Jefferson and Varina Howell Davis (National Portrait
Gallery, Smithsonian Institution, Washington, D.C.)

Refugees and former Davis slaves at Davis Bend following surrender of Vicksburg, July 4, 1863 (J. Mack Moore Collection, Old Court House Museum, Vicksburg, Miss.)

The black community at Hurricane Garden Cottage, Davis Bend, 1863 (J. Mack Moore Collection, Old Court House Museum, Vicksburg, Miss.)

Benjamin Thornton Montgomery
(Reproduced from the Collections
of the Library of Congress)

Mary Lewis Montgomery (Reproduced from the Collections of the
Library of Congress)

The House Jeff Built. This photograph of the Brierfield Mansion was taken
on July 4, 1864, the first anniversary of the surrender of Vicksburg. An
Independence Day celebration was staged at Brierfield by Union Army
officers and Northern school teachers who worked with the Freedmen's
Bureau. (From the glass negative collection at the Old Court House
Museum—Eva W. Davis Memorial, Vicksburg)

The *Natchez*. Built in 1869 and famous for its race against the *Rob't. E. Lee* the following year, this was the sixth boat owned by Capt. T. P. Leathers and named for the Indian tribe. The *Natchez* made regular stops at Davis Bend. (From the glass negative collection, Old Court House Museum—Eva W. Davis Memorial, Vicksburg)

Isaiah T. Montgomery (Mississippi Department of Archives and History)

shipped to market, the black planters were in danger of forfeiting a large percentage of their profits. As early as September 10, Ben told Davis that he was determined to make it possible for them to pay their rent in cash, although he would have to borrow money to do so. He was already heavily indebted to the New Orleans merchants who had made it possible for him to supply most of the freedmen during the year. By October 3 Ben could report jubilantly that most of the rent was paid. He told Joseph Davis that, had the Montgomerys held their cotton and not secured cash to lend the black planters of Davis Bend, "there was no power to prevent [the cotton hunters] from seizing the peoples, and once allowed to commence, they would have soon controlled most of the cotton produced on the two places." He asserted that the whites had shipped a total of only some 30 bales instead of the 250 they would have procured without Montgomery intervention. He added proudly, "I have shipped 234 bales up to last night." Later that month he noted that the Yankees were actively soliciting the small amounts of seed cotton left in the hands of the freedmen, "now that they have failed to get control of the cotton by their first scheme." However, Ben was more concerned about future plans for the plantations. He had financed close to $20,000 worth of land rent in addition to several thousand in loans for freedmen's supplies. He had never engaged in such large-scale financial transactions on his own account before, and this successful venture must have stimulated his ambition. It was a heady lesson to learn that, as a free man, he could match wits with Northern whites and come out the victor.[91]

Joseph Davis was at least as concerned as the Montgomerys about the future of his lands and continued his efforts to regain them from the federal government. When his appeals to the president and other prominent officials brought no results, he turned to other means. He had steadfastly refused to ask for a pardon because he believed he had done no wrong, but in the spring he yielded to the urging of family and friends and took the amnesty oath. He had a copy of it, along with personal endorsements from more than twenty-five leading political figures, printed and circulated as a petition among his friends and acquaintances around the nation. By mid-May he sent his oath and six pages of additional signatures to the president, formally requesting a pardon.

On September 8, 1866, he was notified that he had been granted a pardon by the president as of last March 28, but the Freedmen's Bureau ruled that he could not reclaim his property until the expiration of the freedmen's leases at the end of the year. Davis was so upset at the delay that his friend, J.H.D. Bowmar, managed to get a private audience with President Johnson to plead for immediate restoration of the plantations. The embattled Johnson refused, fearing a Radical plot to compromise him; he claimed that he had already strained the point in granting a pardon to the brother of Jefferson Davis. Somehow Bowmar persuaded O. O. Howard to pay Davis all the rent from the date of his pardon in March, although the bureau would retain the plantations until the first of January.[92] In October the old man's disappointment at the delay was somewhat assuaged by the first rent payment of $8,000; this and the final remittance of about $7,000 eased his financial burden. In mid-November, since the Black Code outlawed the sale of property to blacks, Davis secretly agreed to sell Hurricane and Brierfield to Benjamin Montgomery and his two sons for $300,000 to be paid over a period of ten years. At the end of December he requested the Freedmen's Bureau to turn over his plantations to Montgomery, and Ben reported the departure of the last whites.[93] The tenure of the Northerners on Davis Bend had ended.

What was the condition of the black community there after almost four years of federal control? The year 1866 had not been a good one for the cotton crop in Mississippi: heavy rains in the spring prevented cultivation, allowing weeds to choke some of the young plants; many of those that survived were burned by a long summer drought or devoured by the army worm, which appeared in September. Planters' profits were further eroded by a complex system of heavy taxation. Many of the novice planters from the North went bankrupt, but the black lessees at Davis Bend fared comparatively well. Although Ben noted that the cotton produced on Hurricane and Brierfield would "not much exceed half a crop," the high market price enabled the freedmen to pay their debts with a small reserve to start the next year.[94]

From the government's point of view, the colony had been a success. As a pro-Union newspaper editor noted: "The freedmen have had a home, the army relieved of their presence, they have been encouraged to do and act for themselves, and learn the rudiments, at least, of self-responsible life; and the whole plan, so far as possible, made self-sustaining."[95] Undoubtedly the freedmen did gain experience in handling their own affairs. Shortly before bureau officials departed, Ryan reported that most of the blacks "manage their farm and business with considerable ability." Preston believed that they benefited from holding their plots of land independently, just like the New England farmers who had similar small acreage. He found that these freedmen had "a personal interest in the success of their undertakings," and each was "ambitious to excel in the condition of his crop." Furthermore, Preston thought that the allocation of field size according to the wealth of the freedmen taught them a useful lesson in the process of social stratification: an industrious hand might become an employer with larger holdings next year.[96]

On balance, the blacks at Davis Bend probably benefited from federal government supervision. Admiral Porter's independent colony suffered from too little protection, and, at times, the one sponsored by Colonel Thomas suffered too much interference. But the freedmen were able to live a more stable life with less fear for their personal safety than their fellow blacks in other areas. After the first year, they were not threatened by the roving bands of marauders who broke up plantations and either killed or kidnapped many workers. The people at Davis Bend enjoyed better housing and a more certain food supply than freedmen in the surrounding countryside. And, in spite of the predatory carpetbaggers, they were less exploited by whites because their business relationships were more closely regulated by the bureau. Furthermore, since this was a demonstration colony, the prevailing spirit was enthusiastic and hopeful. Most white supervisors and black workers were made to feel that they were engaged in a significant experiment to which they must give their best efforts. This pride and self-conscious sense of importance contributed to the freedmen's development of confidence in their own worth and ability to handle their own affairs. Some of those who participated in the Montgomerys' challenge to white authority may have developed an unrealistic estimate of their own power. But on the whole, despite some serious blunders, the federally sponsored colonies guided the black community through a chaotic period from which they emerged with new assurance to face a life of freedom. For many, this brief period of apprenticeship eased the often traumatic transition from slavery.

III

Benjamin Montgomery Seeks to Implement the Dream

4

A Difficult Beginning

Know all men by these presents: That I, Joseph E. Davis, of the County of Warren and State of Mississippi, . . . do agree to sell to Benjamin T. Montgomery [Wm. Thornton Montgomery, and Isaiah Montgomery] . . the plantations known as Hurricane and Brierfield . . . containing four thousand or more acres of land, with buildings, trees, timber and appurtenances, . . . for the sum of $300,000 . . . [payable on or before the first of January, 1876, with annual advance interest payments of 6 percent starting on January first, 1867]. And for the said amount of purchase money I, Joseph E. Davis, do reserve a mortgage. Given under our hands and seals this Nineteenth day of November A.D. One thousand eight hundred and sixty six.[1]

By the documents signed on November 19, 1866, Ben Montgomery and his sons committed themselves to pay $18,000 interest for each of the next nine years, and at the end of that time, the entire principal of $300,000. Was $75 per acre a fair price for the two estates on the Mississippi? In 1859 and 1860 similar fertile cotton lands just across the river in Tensas Parish, Louisiana, sold for $125 to $130 an acre. Assuming the same per acre value, Hurricane and Brierfield would have been worth $520,000 before the war. In 1866, as a result of wartime destruction and dislocation, the same Louisiana land was selling for only 75 percent of its prewar price, according to the U.S. commissioner of agriculture; on that basis, the Davis places would have been worth about $390,000.[2] Instead Davis sold the plantations to Montgomery for 57 percent of their estimated antebellum value, or 77 percent of their 1866 worth. That same year, George C. Benham, a novice planter from the North, bought a comparable place on the river for which he paid "seventy-five dollars per acre, one-third cash in hand, balance in one and two years, with interest at eight per cent per annum." Since Montgomery made no down payment, had nine years to repay the principal, and paid only 6 percent interest, he made a better bargain than this carpet-bagger. Furthermore, Joseph Davis told his family that a northern man had offered him $300,000 for the places, but "he had resented the proposition as an insult."[3] The price to Montgomery matched Davis's best offer, but the terms were far easier than he would have demanded from a stranger. The subsequent precipitous decline in land value made the Montgomery mortgage seem unreasonably burdensome, but, judged by 1866 values, the Davis-Montgomery agreement appears fair to both parties.

Because the Mississippi Black Code forbade sale of real property to freedmen, Davis and Montgomery had to keep their bargain secret; publicly Davis claimed to be leasing the places to his former slaves. This, too, was contrary to state law, but the Freedmen's Bureau had announced that it would not tolerate enforcement of the ban on black leasing, and General Wood gave his approval to the Davis-Montgomery deal. On February 21, 1867, the governor of Mississippi signed a bill giving freedmen the right to own real property, and within a few days Joseph Davis legally closed the sale contract with Ben and his sons.[4]

A number of considerations prompted Davis to sell his beloved estates to the Montgomerys. His protracted fight to regain possession had impressed upon him the intensity of northern hatred of his brother. J.H.D. Bowmar had been hard put to convince General Samuel Thomas, acting as O. O. Howard's agent in Washington, that Joseph and not Jefferson Davis held title to Brierfield as well as Hurricane; otherwise, the government would have retained possession. Although President Johnson finally restored the property, there was mounting evidence of his waning power. As the authority of the Radical Republicans increased, so did Davis's fears of confiscation of one or both of his plantations. What better way to guarantee their safety from seizure than by selling them to the Radicals' protégés, the freedmen? Joseph recognized that his own age and frailty prevented him from attempting to rebuild the flourishing planting venture that had been his principal interest for thirty-four years; although he was strong enough to travel to Jackson and New Orleans from time to time, he could not face even a brief visit to his old home. However, he continued to be acutely concerned about the welfare of his former slaves, and through the sale to Montgomery sought to permit them continued occupation of their homes as long as they chose to remain. He authorized Ben to supply necessities to the old folks who could not fend for themselves and continually encouraged the others to reestablish the cooperative community he had fostered before the war. Although he knew that he was no longer able to implement it, he still cherished the utopian dream.[5]

Montgomery and his sons assumed this gigantic financial responsibility with mixed emotions. Ben was passionately eager to gain control of the enterprise that had engaged all of his skill and attention since he had become an adult. He had come to share Davis's faith in the possibility of creating an ideal community and was convinced that he was uniquely qualified to lead it. However, as a shrewd businessman he recognized the potential pitfalls he now faced. A few weeks earlier, citing "the price of cotton together with high tax and other uncertainties," he had declined Joseph's offer to sell the property because, he said, "the price you value it at would I fear involve me for life." After further negotiation Ben agreed to the purchase; although still worried about future cotton prices, he expressed a firm determination "to try and get everything in good working order and then work industriously and systematically to make the most we can."

The shortage of agricultural workers, a major concern for most cotton planters, was only a minor worry for Montgomery. He realized that there was "a great competition for labor"; in fact, he had received many written and verbal requests for hands in the past year, and recruiters were even then trying to entice the freedmen away. However, he was confident that his projected community would automatically attract a sufficient amount of "the right kind of labor."[6] To ensure this, Ben set to work at once to publicize details of his planned utopian colony. On November 21, just two days after signing the mortgage, he inserted an advertisement in the *Vicksburg Daily Times* announcing his plan to organize "a community composed exclusively of colored people" to cultivate Hurricane and Brierfield plantations starting the first day of January 1867. He invited the participation of "such as are recommended by honesty, industry, sobriety, and intelligence." A governing council chosen by the members of the community would "adopt such rules and regulations as experience shall show to be necessary for its welfare." Montgomery had already decided that there must be an annual tax of fifty cents per acre to be "strictly applied to the building of levees to guard against overflows." The council would assess a suitable tax to provide for schools and "the comfortable maintenance of the aged and helpless." In addition, the governing body would continue the judicial tradition: "If, unfortunately, drunken, idle and evil-disposed persons find their way into the community, it will be the duty of the council to expel them, and if the laws permit, to remove them from the community."

Hoping to disarm potential white opposition, Montgomery hastened to show that his freedmen's colony would not become a hotbed of black political activity. He asserted that discussions of the suffrage question and other political topics would be discouraged "as more likely to produce contention and idleness than harmony." The members of the association would strive "to obey strictly the laws of the State so far as they can understand them" and through hard work "to attain as much prosperity and happiness as are consistent with human nature." In a further attempt to placate the whites, Ben concluded that they hoped "their humble efforts [would] be regarded with charity and generosity by those of superior knowledge and position, whose good opinion it will be their earnest endeavor to deserve." It was signed "B. T. MONTGOMERY, colored, formerly a slave and one of the business managers of Joseph E. Davis, Esq., (the owner of the Hurricane and Brierfield plantations,) ON THE PART OF THE ASSOCIATION."[7]

Evidently not trusting his blandishments to defuse white opposition, Ben took his article to the Freedmen's Bureau headquarters in Vicksburg and requested General T. J. Wood's endorsement. As a result, he was able to add, "The undersigned has received assurances of full protection from the Commanding

General of the District." Furthermore, Wood appended a letter, which was published with Montgomery's notice, explaining the legal steps that led to Davis's leasing his property to Montgomery. Wood asserted that both parties would be protected in the exercise of their "unquestionable and indefeasible constitutional rights." He hoped that Davis's "noble and wise charity, and judicious business arrangement" would serve as a model for others, thereby contributing to "the improvement of the interests of both the white and black races in the State." The general concluded by commending the enterprise of Montgomery and his association to the kindness of all the citizens, especially "their neighbors in this county." As soon as the two items appeared in print, Wood forwarded a copy to O. O. Howard, noting that Montgomery had brought him the article "in his own handwriting," asking for Wood's approval. Unlike Samuel Thomas, Wood seemed very favorably impressed with Ben and his utopian goals. There could be no doubt that this project had the bureau's blessing and would receive whatever protection it could provide.[8]

Such a revolutionary plan of community organization inevitably attracted some attention in both the South and North. The *Vicksburg Times* asked editorially what northern philanthropist had entrusted such a large share of his own property to the freedmen to assist them in becoming "self-supporting and self-directing." Northerners were always ready to commit other people's property to such a cause, but seldom their own. The *Hinds County Gazette* in Jackson feared that Davis's lease to his former slaves might suggest a "similar arrangement to holders of large tracts of land in other parts of the state." It gloomily concluded, "We would prefer not to be a planter adjoining or adjacent to one of these colonies." In fact, at least one planter across the river wrote the Freedmen's Bureau that he wanted to lease his two plantations on the same terms as had Davis; General Wood urged bureau headquarters in Washington to publicize and foster the proposal.[9]

The *New York Times* shared General Wood's enthusiasm for Montgomery's project. A long editorial praised Ben for the "common-sense style of his advertisement" and predicted that he was "practical and sagacious enough" to succeed in this enterprise, "provided only he gets fair play from his neighbors." In their view, positive aspects of his venture included the fact that Montgomery had secured military approval in advance, had previous long experience in plantation management, and was working with people "with whose habits and aspirations, and with whose faults and foibles he [was] entirely familiar." The *Times* particularly praised his eschewing all political activity for his community. Intelligent freedmen such as Montgomery sought social and political advancement not through gifts of land or enfranchisement, the editor claimed, but rather by "making themselves an indispensable industrial power." This practical approach might well provide a lesson for all freedmen and their white friends. The editorial also singled out Joseph Davis as a potential model for other southern property owners. This aristocratic "Southerner of the Southerners" would never be guilty of "hastening any new social upheaval." The *Times* deemed his contract "in every sense conservative," containing convincing "elements of commercial strength." Though admitting that the project was "one of so purely an experimental character . . . that its success must be left to time to determine," the *Times* clearly believed that it had a bright future.[10]

The Davis family was not so sanguine about Joseph's risky venture. When Jefferson's wife, Varina, visited her brother-in-law in Vicksburg, Joseph told her of his tentative plan and asked her to consult her husband as soon as she was able to visit him in prison at Fortress Monroe. She objected to the scheme and soon a secret memorandum revealed that her husband shared her doubts. As the putative owner of Brierfield, Jefferson had a vital interest in the fate of the plantations. In his present situation he had no immediate prospects of managing the place himself, and there was a very real possibility that hardening Republican policy might lead to confiscation. He suggested that the agreement with the Montgomerys "having been made public it [would] be advisable to close soon and tightly, lest the desire for plunder & the active malignaty [sic] toward you as my Brother should prompt to some Congressional movement to interfere with it." He displayed a surprisingly low opinion of the Montgomerys' ability considering that he had repeatedly benefited from Ben's managerial skills before the war. Now he asserted, "Unless the negroes exceed my expectations they will never complete the payments." He conceded that their training had "elevated them to the grade of useful laborers" but predicted that "made lords of themselves I think they will rapidly lapse to the ignorance & vagrancy characteristic of the race." When this happened, he hoped that the Davis family's circumstances would have improved so that they could reclaim their property.[11] Like most of his contemporaries', Jefferson's firm belief in the innate inferiority of the black race had survived the war intact.

However, Joseph Davis pursued his plans undeterred. He had more confidence in Ben's ability than that of any white manager or potential buyer he knew. He admitted to his brother that "few expect the contract will be complied with," but added, "I trust it will if Ben lives, he is ambitious to be a rich man, and will control the labor." Some years later Isaiah Montgomery reported that Joseph Davis probably had not expected them to pay the full price for the plantations but considered the sale wise because "he knew that if anybody could make the place pay we could."[12]

The Montgomerys immediately set to work to justify Joseph's confidence in them. Ben realized that they had assumed a very heavy burden in view of their small capital reserve, and he was eager to work their way to a more secure position. He knew that many of his tenants would depend upon him for supplies until harvesttime, and there would be numerous other expenses of operating the plantations. Davis would need at least a part of the $18,000 interest payment due the first of January, but Montgomery proposed to borrow back $16,000 of it at 6 percent interest until November in order to have some working capital. As in all their business dealings, Davis was as cooperative as his financial condition permitted, without being too lenient. With this bit of relief, the Montgomerys applied themselves to the pressing tasks of repairing wartime destruction at Hurricane and Brierfield. They especially wanted to rebuild the fences separating their land from their white neighbors to minimize the danger of friction as a result of stray cattle or boundary disputes. There was also urgent need for routine maintenance of the living quarters and outbuildings as well as the cisterns, all of which had been neglected during the unsettled years of Yankee occupation.[13]

However, the first concern of the new owners was restoration of flood protection, which was so vital in that river bottom land.

By early December 1866 they had cleaned out and deepened more than two miles of ditches and were clearing the undergrowth from the levees so that they could begin necessary repairs. Adequate flood protection was not only a costly business, it required the cooperation of all the planters on the Bend. No matter how strong and high the Montgomerys built their levees, if even one of their neighbors left his in disrepair, all the fields might be inundated. Shortly before the war the four principal planters at Davis Bend had built across the neck of the peninsula a levee a mile and a half long and from eight to sixteen feet high. They divided the total cost of $27,000 among them according to acreage protected; Henry Turner paid one-half the cost, Joseph Davis one-fourth, and Jefferson Davis and R. Y. Wood each paid one-eighth. This levee was located entirely on the Turner and Wood plantations, but was equally essential for the protection of the Davis places. Floods in 1862 and 1865 had weakened this and all other levees on the Bend, and there had been no concerted effort to rebuild them. In early 1867 Ben Montgomery attempted to organize some form of cooperation to restore adequate protection for all. He visited Palmyra, where the Lovell brothers had taken over the Turner-Quitman plantation. Joseph Lovell agreed that prompt action was required and suggested that the planters appoint a levee inspector to determine the needs. Since Wood's levees were in the worst condition, it did not seem prudent to choose him, so Lovell recommended that his own brother be selected. Although the Montgomerys now owned two of the four largest plantations, Lovell did not consider Ben for the appointment; perhaps he thought it would be more difficult for a freedman to gain the essential participation of the whites.[14] In any case, although all the planters promised cooperation, they were slow in getting the work done and their efforts proved inadequate.

Unfortunately for Montgomery's utopian community, the spring of 1867 brought a major flood to the lower Mississippi Valley. The previous winter there had been unusually heavy rain and snow in the Ohio Valley; in early spring, a widespread series of intense rainstorms occurred throughout the Mississippi watershed, overtaxing that already swollen river. By the end of February Ben reported that the Mississippi was rising at the rate of four or five inches a day and stood only three feet below the bank at Hurricane. Joseph Davis wrote Ben detailed advice for bolstering all the levees on the Bend; armed with this authority, the latter made the rounds of the neighbors and found them all working frantically, if belatedly, toward the same end. The major concern was the frail levee at Ursino; R. Y. Wood's lessee, Captain Mitchell, was absent, but his superintendent had some twenty-five hands filling up the cut at one end. Although the rate of rise slowed, the river continued to edge upward. By March 21 Montgomery reported that, in spite of drenching rains, he had more than one hundred hands at work on Wood's portion of the levee. A week later almost all the able-bodied males on the Bend were at work there in a race with the rising river. According to Ben, Wood's levee had an inadequate base and "seemed to be a den of crayfish & filled with rotten roots, &c. which allows a free passage of water through it." Some 250 men from Hurricane and Brierfield were working on a mile and a half of it, while men from other plantations shored up other sections. Ben was proud of the fact that all the men from his community gave their services without charge, although he provided twenty-five or thirty dollars worth of whiskey per day for them. These men had also made about 150 handbarrows for the use of the entire work force. In criticism of the absent R. Y. Wood, Ben commented: "If the party owning the land had as much generosity as the men who are laboring to protect it, they certainly would not accept so much work for nothing: especially when by far the largest portion of them are dependent upon their daily labor for bread."[15]

All their efforts proved futile, however, and by the middle of April much of Davis Bend was under water. According to Montgomery, many of the freedmen had found refuge in a twenty-by-sixty foot church near the graveyard, or in the hospital at Hurricane. Some had raised their floors or removed their belongings to the upper stories of their dwellings. At Brierfield many found shelter in the Davis mansion, where missionary teachers had lived the previous year. A number of the tenants became discouraged and left the Bend to start anew on other places. Ben reported that labor recruiters enticed some away by predicting that "they might expect 10 feet more water which would float many of their houses." All of this boded ill for the success of Montgomery's fledgling black community, and he became deeply discouraged. As the flood crested, prospects looked extremely gloomy, with the need for expensive repairs to flood-damaged buildings, equipment, and levees complicated by the impossibility of producing a large crop when replanting began so late in the year. Ben assured Davis that he believed in "the possibility of our ultimate success in this enterprise . . . but to accomplish it in the time specified requires an attendance of circumstances far more favorable than there is now any possibility to expect." Davis wrote a very encouraging reply, promising leniency in the terms of their bargain and urging Montgomery to continue the effort.[16] This momentary fit of depression at the height of the 1867 flood was uncharacteristic of Montgomery. It evidently impressed Davis so much that he took pains to rebuild the confidence and hope of the man upon whose success his own livelihood now depended. Had he taken a less supportive stance, Montgomery might have abandoned the entire enterprise before it had gotten well started.

With this encouragement and the prospect of some debt relief, Ben recovered his optimism within a few days and was again busy making the best of the situation. Since the roads were impassable, he set the hands to work making simple boats on which they could float rails for repairing badly damaged fences. As the water slowly receded, they began planting cotton on the uncovered ridges, adding rows as new land appeared. By early May Ben was able to assess the damage and found that the flood had "added material injury to the already dilapidated buildings." In the quarters, some houses were tilted because their foundations had settled unevenly; many chimneys had fallen, and some of the smaller work buildings were gone entirely. Parts of the sawmill and gin were undermined, and the furnace there had lost its flue. Not only were the cisterns flooded, but the cement previously bought for their repair had been ruined by the water. Furthermore, the levees had all suffered some damage from the swirling river and would require extensive additional repair. Many cattle had been lost and those that survived were lean and sickly, suffering from a meager diet of "young cottonwood branches, cane & moss, with a limited quantity of corn, oats & hay." By the end of May the people were still replanting as the water fell, but they had very little to show for five months of strenuous effort.[17]

However, the most serious permanent damage did not become apparent until later in the year. The ditch across the neck of the peninsula always filled with water during a flood. This situation had worried Joseph Davis since the clandestine antebellum attempt of General Quitman's hirelings, incited by steamboat captains and upriver planters, to dig a canal across this neck that would change the course of the river. Only through legal action, armed intervention, and legislative proscription had Davis managed to halt this effort. Union troops had deepened the ditch in order to aid in protecting the freedmen from guerrilla raids during federal occupation, and Davis had unsuccessfully requested the government to fill in that depression. The moderate flood in 1866 had sent the Mississippi across it at a depth of 15 feet for a short time, but the river returned to its former channel as the water fell. However, the much more severe flood of 1867 sent the river through the depression with such velocity that it cut a permanent new channel some 500 yards across the peninsula, thus shortening the Mississippi River by more than 20 miles.[18]

Ben noted that steamers were trying to use the shortened route as the waters rose late in February, and by the third week in March all but the largest were passing through it. The Montgomerys immediately felt the inconvenience of being off the highway, such as infrequent mail deliveries and misdirected freight shipments. However, in the flood crisis these seemed of relatively minor concern, for everyone assumed that they were temporary. Indeed, as the water receded many boats resumed their former route around the Bend, and a map sketched by the Montgomerys in June showed both waterways. But the cutoff remained the main channel of the river, and by fall the Bend was too shallow to accommodate commercial vessels. Since both Hurricane and Brierfield were now on Palmyra Lake instead of what was Palmyra or Davis Bend, the Montgomerys were forced to ship and receive freight via their neighbors' landings. The closest dock was at Ursino on R. Y. Wood's plantation, but its use required hauling supplies over roads that were frequently little better than swamps. The landing on the Bank plantation, operated by a northern corporation, was still farther away but proved a bit more accessible and, at least for most of the year, offered an alternative. Still, Ben was deeply worried by the fact that his success might now depend upon the whim of Wood, an impoverished white landowner whose failure to maintain his levees had contributed to the general flood loss that year. Wood was only minimally cooperative with his white neighbors; now Ben must have felt real alarm to have this man, reputed to have been a slave exploiter, as the arbiter of his fate. Furthermore, the value of the Montgomery estates was diminished substantially by the disaster, which removed them from their river access. No matter how fertile the fields, there could be no profit unless the crops could inexpensively reach the riverboats and, thus, the markets. The destruction of buildings and fences paled in comparison to this permanent new handicap.[19]

The Montgomerys were reminded of the latent suspicion and potential hostility of their white neighbors when they sought to reopen the post office at Hurricane store. Joseph Davis had managed to get it established there in 1855, although there was frequent difficulty in maintaining regular mail deliveries; young slaves such as Isaiah Montgomery often rowed across the river to Ashwood, Louisiana, to fetch it when reluctant steamboat captains neglected to stop at Davis Bend.[20] All mail service in the South had ceased during the war and was only slowly resumed, even in the cities. The greatest obstacle was the federal requirement that all postmasters and mail contractors take the Ironclad Oath, swearing that they had not held office in, or served in the armed forces of, or given aid and comfort to the Confederacy. Ben Montgomery was especially eager to regain the post office at Hurricane after November 1866, when the postmaster at Vicksburg refused to allow Jack Raily, Joseph Davis's servant, to continue to pick up their mail and send it down as freight on the first available boat. Instead, someone then resident at the Bend had to call for it in person at the Vicksburg post office, incurring an added expense of eight to sixteen dollars per week for steamboat passage.

Montgomery drew up a petition to the postmaster general of the United States on behalf of the 1,500 residents of Davis Bend, requesting the reestablishment of the post office at Hurricane, leaving blank the name of the postmaster so that the signers could recommend someone. In January, when he went to see Joseph Lovell about cooperative levee repairs, Ben broached the subject of reopening the post office and showed him the petition. Lovell was very discouraging, noting that neither he nor his brother could sign the Ironclad Oath and that the white lessees on the other plantations were not sufficiently permanent. Moreover, he considered Hurricane an undesirable location, because large boats had difficulty landing there in low water. Since this was before the flood, he did not include the crippling effect of the permanent cutoff. Ben suggested that he or one of his sons could take on the postmastership, as they had handled the work unofficially before the war. Lovell scoffed at this idea, asserting, "to recommend a colored man would be the first of the kind in any of the southern states, and would have a significant bearing and probably produce some excitement."[21] Ben certainly did not want to cause any excitement, but, as he would tell Davis, the freedmen received 75 percent of the letters and newspapers that came to the Bend and thus were the ones most inconvenienced by the lack of service. However, since Lovell was so adamant, Ben merely sent a copy of the petition to Davis and did not circulate it immediately.[22]

A few weeks later Montgomery learned that Joseph Lovell had gone to the white residents with a petition of his own to have a post office set up at the Bank plantation, naming Huntington and Pitkin, the managers there, as postmasters. Lovell had secured the endorsement of the postmaster at Natchez as well as most of the resident whites on the Bend; however, Captain Mitchell at Ursino told Ben that his signature had been added without his knowledge. This underhanded move by Lovell spurred the Montgomerys to action. In less than a week they had circulated their petition and sent it to Joseph Davis, asking him to get the approval of the Vicksburg postmaster and forward it to Washington. The people, undoubtedly with Ben's approval, had recommended Thornton Montgomery as a suitable postmaster for Hurricane. Perhaps because of the power of Radical Republicans in Washington that spring, the freedmen's petition was successful; on May 6 "William T. Montgomery" was appointed postmaster of the reestablished office at Hurricane, and by June 4 he had filed the required papers and map making his tenure legal. This did not ensure regular mail delivery at Davis Bend any more than it had before the war, but at least the post office was safely returned to Montgomery's store, where it provided one more reason for potential customers to gather at this community center.[23]

Ben Montgomery demonstrated his new assertiveness with whites in other ways besides the successful scheme to regain the mail franchise. In December 1865 he had bought two mules valued at $150 each from Dr. J. N. Leitch, one of the resident physicians at Brierfield. Leitch had previously bought the mules from O. K. Hawley, another Northerner. Almost a year after Montgomery's purchase, Hawley's former partner, Irvin Ward, claimed that he was entitled to the mules as part of their partnership, and had them confiscated from Ben. The freedman immediately took legal action, retaining a white lawyer who had been a business associate of both Hawley and Ward. By June 1867 Montgomery claimed that, in addition to his original $300 investment, he had lost $1.50 per day in foregone services of the mules, steamboat passage to Vicksburg twice for himself and once for a witness at $8 each, and attorney's fees of $50—or total damages of at least $546, not counting the value of his lost time. The case was eventually settled in Ben's favor, and Irvin Ward returned the mules; however, they were by then afflicted with farsy, a disease that claimed the life of one of them within a week and rendered the other unfit for service.[24] Although not receiving complete satisfaction in this instance, Ben had dared to sue a white man and retain a white lawyer just as any other large planter would have done. Of course, his action did not seem so serious an offense to southern whites since he was dealing exclusively with carpetbaggers.

In another episode, Montgomery challenged the authority of the county government, but this time he relied on Joseph Davis to help him gain the assistance of prominent state officials. On June 5 he received a notice from the sheriff of Warren County that he owed taxes on Hurricane and Brierfield for 1866. He was not the owner of these plantations until January 1, 1867, but he wisely decided not to resist local authorities directly. He instructed Scharff Brothers, his agent in Vicksburg, to pay the taxes and then, with the assistance of Joseph Davis, appealed the case all the way to the state legislature, the governor, and the federal commander of the Fourth Military District. Although everyone agreed that the taxes had been collected erroneously, Montgomery and Davis had to present the official endorsements to the Warren County Board of Police before the sheriff would refund the money.[25] In this instance, spurred on by his precarious financial condition, Montgomery managed to manipulate both the antebellum white elite and the new military authority in order to save needless expense.

Montgomery eagerly noted the national political trend that replaced the comparatively pro-white, presidential Reconstruction policies with the more stringent military rule mandated by the Radical Republicans. He welcomed the newly appointed registrars to Hurricane, where they enrolled over 300 freedmen and any whites who could swear to the required oath. He was pleased to have his store serve as registration headquarters for men from all parts of the Bend. However, Ben failed to share Joseph Davis's rather optimistic view of the benefits the freedmen might expect from political participation. When the editor of the *Vicksburg Weekly Times* asked Davis to enlist Montgomery's services as the political correspondent from his area, Ben quickly refused, saying, "had I the capacity to contribute anything, existing circumstances render it entirely out of my power to accede." Referring to his published disavowal of politics for himself and his new black community, he asserted that "any participation in political affairs would be inconsistent with my established programme." Furthermore, he expressed personal doubts about the probable benefits of black political activity. He reminded Davis of "the bitter opposition heretofore manifested to the extension of suffrage to the colored people, by many of the South," and suggested that such prejudice would prevent the favorable results northern Radicals expected. He pointed out that "the feeling that you have manifested for the welfare of the colored people generally is very different from that of many others, both North & South. Your view of their general capabilities is also different."[26] Montgomery was far more sensitive to the depth of white prejudice than was Joseph Davis, and the former slave did not want to jeopardize his utopian dream by venturing into politics, even when the power of freedmen seemed to be in the ascendant. He mistrusted the durability of white concern and feared that eventual removal of federal troops and national control would return to power the white Southerners who were most enraged by black political activity. Although better qualified to hold office than the majority of Mississippians of whatever color, Montgomery cherished no political ambitions. His goals were confined to the perfection of his dual role as prosperous planter-merchant and patriarchal leader of his model colony.

However, in the best interests of this community, Montgomery soon felt compelled to accept a political appointment in spite of his qualms. The maintenance of law and order was a serious problem throughout the South after the war, and violence-prone Mississippi was no exception. One Vicksburg newspaper noted, "Lawlessness is the order of the day, and reports of outrages upon persons and property of unoffending citizens are constantly reaching us from all quarters." A storekeeper in Woodville, Mississippi, complained that "low pilfering and stealing are quite common and there is but little safety for life or property." As Captain Norton stated in his "Rules and Regulations," Davis Bend had suffered from petty thievery during the tenure of the Freedmen's Bureau, and the freedmen's court continued to deal with such cases throughout its existence. Whitelaw Reid, the northern journalist, commented on the propensity of some newly freed slaves at Davis Bend to embrace religion enthusiastically at church services and then go out and steal food or a mule from their neighbors. In 1866 Captain W. L. Ryan reported that some freedmen were stealing small quantities of cotton and selling it at stores on the Bend; and as late as that fall Ryan's office was burglarized and all his clothing and personal effects stolen.[27]

The departure of the Freedmen's Bureau left Davis Bend without any law enforcement officials. The shaky civil government and the uncertain military regime were occupied in petty contests of strength and concentrated their feeble law enforcement efforts on population centers such as Vicksburg. Montgomery's new community council lacked the supporting authority that Joseph Davis had given to the slave court or that Samuel Thomas and his federal troops had provided for the freedmen's board of arbitration. Furthermore, unsettled conditions on the Bend in 1867 added to the difficulties of maintaining a law-abiding community. Ben noted that "our unfinished organization [is] scattered asunder by the overflow," and those who remained were subjected to "the persuasion of various parties anxious to secure labor elsewhere," whose inflated offers met with "some success too among the unstable minds." Some of the former black soldiers had kept their arms, and others had obtained guns as their proudest badge of freedom. At a time when maximum cooperation was required of every resident if the community project was to survive, the Montgomerys lacked the means even to ensure the citizens' safety from assault and robbery.[28]

In the oppressive heat of August some defiant residents revealed the weakness of the proprietors to the entire community. One day, outside the Montgomerys' store, two men had a disagreement that resulted in a fist fight. Ben intervened and sent the protagonists away, anticipating no further trouble. However, a few hours later one of the men, a frequent troublemaker named Bryant Wood, returned to the Hurricane store accompanied by some twenty friends, "two-thirds of whom were armed with Guns & Revolvers." Wood sent a challenge to his opponent to come out and fight, but Montgomery persuaded the latter to refuse the challenge. When Ben remonstrated with Wood he was advised to keep out of a matter that was none of his business. Although the trouble blew over without bodily harm to anyone, this armed defiance seemed to demonstrate the impotence of the Montgomerys and raised the specter of true anarchy. Deeply disturbed, Ben and his sons reluctantly decided that they must seek help from outside authority, even though it entailed tacit admission that the black community had not yet achieved the self-sufficiency it sought. They decided to appeal by letter to General Ord, the highest-ranking federal officer in the region, one of whose avowed duties was the maintenance of peace and order.[29]

Ben immediately followed up this letter with a personal interview with the general in Vicksburg, who claimed his limited troop strength precluded direct police action in rural areas. However, Ord was so favorably impressed that he suggested Montgomery should be appointed Freedmen's Bureau agent for the Bend and its vicinity. He sent the freedman to see General A. C. Gillem, who had replaced General Wood as commander of the District of Mississippi, and hence as assistant commissioner of the Freedmen's Bureau. In a private note, Ord advised Gillem that "Mr. M. is well qualified [for the agent's assignment] and would do justice to his own color and race." However, before appointing him, Ord suggested that Gillem "write to prominent union citizens or gentlemen and ask for his character." The commander was not going to succumb to Ben's charms without investigating his reputation among important whites.[30]

General Gillem was not overwhelmed by Montgomery's evident capacity but shifted the decision back to his superior, General Ord. Gillem informed Ben of the straitened condition of the Freedmen's Bureau and suggested that law enforcement could best be provided for Davis Bend by General Ord's appointment of "a Police." He recommended that Ben volunteer for that assignment and so inform the general. Montgomery reported this conversation to Ord in a letter that heartily endorsed Gillem's suggestion, asserting that a resident law officer would "be of much service in protecting the good against the encroachments of the bad." He humbly agreed to undertake the task and promised to fulfill the duties impartially if Ord should appoint him. Montgomery added that he would not accept the assignment "without the consent of the majority of the people," but maintained that, as Ord could ascertain, they had demonstrated their choice on previous occasions.[31]

Ord referred Montgomery's second letter to Gillem, asking whether he had "sufficient data in his office in regard to B. T. Montgomery's character to warrant his appointment as Magistrate," and if so, to what office should he be named. A few days earlier, in response to Montgomery's first letter, Gillem had assigned Lieutenant H. R. Williams to investigate and report on Montgomery's reputation. However, before Williams' report was completed, further difficulties compelled Ord to act in the matter.[32]

The precipitating cause was again Bryant Wood, the pugnacious freedman from Hurricane. Perhaps because of his anger at the Montgomerys, Wood went upriver to buy supplies in Vicksburg. On the return trip aboard the steamboat *Grey Eagle,* he had a disagreement with one of the deckhands. According to Wood, he asked the boatman to retrieve his hat, which had blown off as Wood chatted with a white man on an upper deck. The deckhand rudely refused, saying he did not catch hats for "niggers." Later, as he left the boat at the Hurricane landing, Wood claimed that the man jumped him without a word and started beating him. The freedman retaliated with his walking stick and, when that broke, with his fists. Soon other deckhands joined the fight, and in the ensuing brawl, Wood claimed that he was stabbed in the shoulder and robbed of his purse containing $370. A few days later, he took four freedmen with him to Vicksburg where he swore to his version of the encounter; his friends could corroborate only his story of the fight on the landing.[33]

Captain Platt asked C. P. Huntington, white manager of the Bank plantation, to investigate the affair, but he could find no one to confirm Wood's testimony. Ben Ousley, who had been aboard the *Grey Eagle* when Wood returned from Vicksburg, asserted that the latter had quarreled with the deckhand over a card game, and only the intervention of the boat's captain saved the freedman's life. At Huntington's request Ben Montgomery added a letter declaring that he had been occupied in the store and saw only that there was a fight in progress; he knew nothing about its cause or Wood's alleged loss of money. However, Montgomery labeled Wood a troublemaker "of an overbearing and turbulent disposition" who had threatened him with an armed band of men just the week before. Ben recounted the circumstances and said that he had reported the affair to General Ord. In conclusion, Ben stated emphatically, "It is not my wish to retain such persons in our community."[34]

When Gillem learned of the incident, he sent a guard to the levee to arrest the men Wood accused, but by then the *Grey Eagle* was gone and Gillem let the matter drop. However, Wood was determined to exercise his new rights as a citizen, so he retained two white attorneys and brought suit against the boatmen in the civil courts. Upon the *Grey Eagle*'s return, the lawyers sought a warrant for the arrest of the accused, but the mayor of Vicksburg refused, claiming it would violate quarantine restrictions to bring the men into the city. The lawyers requested General Gillem's assistance, suggesting that the men might be arrested but not brought into the city until their quarantine expired. When there was no action taken either by city authorities or the Freedmen's Bureau, Wood's attorneys appealed to

General Ord for justice. Finally, three months after the altercation, a deputy marshal accompanied by Bryant Wood arrested three of the deckhands from the *Grey Eagle*.[35]

Meanwhile, the second Bryant Wood affair prompted Ben Montgomery to try another means of gaining a law enforcement officer for Davis Bend. This time he tried the old method of appealing through Joseph Davis, even though federal policy seemed hostile to un-Reconstructed Southerners. Ben knew that Davis had interviews with Ord from time to time, so he asked him to remind the general that they still lacked any authority to punish serious offenses on the Bend. He told of a freedman from the Lovells' plantation who savagely beat a woman field hand there and threatened to shoot her employer when he tried to intervene. Ben feared that if they went unpunished the number and seriousness of such acts might increase. Davis gave Ben's letter to General Ord, who referred it to Gillem with orders to punish the gun-wielding freedman if investigation proved him guilty as charged. Ord pointed out to Gillem that the author of the letter was "himself a colored man."[36]

Shortly after this, General Ord discussed the question of law enforcement on the Bend with C. P. Huntington, who may have come to his attention as a result of his service to the bureau in the Bryant Wood affair. By this time Ord had decided that there must be a justice of the peace appointed to keep order on the Bend, and he sought suggestions for a candidate. Huntington, a busy plantation manager from the North who was having a great deal of trouble disciplining his workers, recommended the appointment of Ben Montgomery. However, on August 27 Ord issued an order naming Huntington himself justice of the peace and Thornton Montgomery as constable. Perhaps Ben's clash with Colonel Thomas two years earlier had left negative assessments of him in bureau files or in agents' memories, which Gillem or Ord uncovered and held against him. Or perhaps General Ord, like Colonel Thomas, merely found Montgomery's cool competence too alien to his preconceptions of black men. At any rate, despite his very positive first impression, Ord passed over Ben in favor of the white carpetbagger, although he made a concession to the freedmen by naming Thornton as constable.[37]

The problem of selecting a peace officer for the Bend was not

yet solved, however. The order of appointment stated that Thornton Montgomery must post bond as required by Mississippi law
before assuming his office, but it failed to stipulate any such
requirement for Huntington, nor had Ord mentioned it in their
conversation. The Northerner immediately swore in his constable
and began an investigation of the fracas reported by Ben Montgomery. A couple of days later Huntington received notice from
General Ord that he too must post the required $2,000 bond. He
promptly sent all his official papers back to the general asserting
that he could not comply and was "consequently incapacitated
for the highly responsible office so kindly offered to me a
stranger." He claimed that Ben and Thornton Montgomery were
the only permanent residents "of sufficient intelligence" to receive the appointments and again urged the commander to name
Ben the new justice of the peace. He stressed "the importance of
enforcing law in this community of over 1800 souls, so long left
unbridled by law or its representatives."[38]

By this time both Ord and Gillem recognized the urgent need
for a policeman at the Bend. As though to reenforce this conviction, Huntington wrote Platt beseeching his aid in solving the
dilemma of the large lessees. His company, with thirty-two
squads of freedmen at work on plantations in the state, had a
great deal of money invested and must have some return as soon
as possible. Their need to get the crop picked and ginned expedi-
tiously was increased by the fact that their leases expired at the
end of the year. Nevertheless, some of their workers refused to
gin their cotton, giving various implausible excuses. In despera-
tion, Huntington asserted, "I dare not resort to force for I am
afraid of you & there is no civil officer here—What shall I do? not
only with this case but others where we have difficulty with our
hands." He begged Platt to give him either official or friendly advice to "relieve a poor fellow in trouble."[39]

General Ord finally yielded to this pressure and asked Ben
Montgomery if he could qualify for and would accept the office of
justice of the peace at Davis Bend. Upon receipt of Ben's affirma-
tive reply, Ord issued the required order on September 10.
Montgomery told Davis that he had been pleased with the appointment of Huntington and regretted that the white man could
not qualify. As for his own appointment, Ben stated, "Though

quite unfit for the position, I deem it prudent, under existing circumstances, to accept." Neither Ben nor Thornton had the least difficulty qualifying for these civil offices; they could truthfully swear that they had not served in the armed forces, held an office, or given aid and comfort to the Confederacy, and each could post $2,000 bond based on their own real-estate holdings. Such a combination was rare among white Southerners, and almost nonexistent among blacks. There seems little doubt that the Montgomerys were the first Negroes to hold public office in Mississippi, and perhaps in the entire South. Nineteen months later, in April 1869, John Roy Lynch was named justice of the peace at Natchez. This ambitious young freedman went on to the state and eventually the national legislature. Referring to his appointment as justice of the peace, Lynch claimed that it was "the first time in the history of the state that a colored man had been commissioned to fill such an office." Later Governor Adelbert Ames claimed that there was "not a single colored man in office" when he appointed Lynch in 1869. These erroneous claims from people who lived so near Davis Bend show how successful the Montgomerys were at avoiding publicity. Apparently the Vicksburg papers ignored Ben's appointment, and the Jackson *Weekly Clarion* gave it only brief, but favorable, notice, concluding: "Montgomery was the former slave of Mr. Davis, and his confidential business manager, and discharged his duties with fidelity and rectitude. Like all who were faithful as slaves, Montgomery now possesses the confidence and respect of the white people."[40]

A justice of the peace in Mississippi wielded considerable power: he had original jurisdiction in all civil cases involving no more than $300; he had jurisdiction concurrent with the county courts in criminal cases below the grade of felony; and in more serious cases involving felonies or capital offenses, he had to examine witnesses and decide whether or not to bind the accused over to the next grand jury. If he did so bind someone over, he was obliged to decide whether to free the accused on bail, to fix the amount of bail, if any, and to determine the acceptability of bondsmen. If the evidence seemed insufficient, he could discharge the accused from further custody. One observer of the Davis Bend scene said, "The Mississippi justice of the peace has more authority than any magistrate in any other state in the Union."[41] In this office, Benjamin Montgomery had enough power to enforce the law and protect the security of his colonists, which was so essential to the fulfillment of his dream. He had hoped to avoid any form of political involvement, but circumstances had forced him to accept this public office. Now he was determined to use his power discreetly; fortunately, the overwhelming majority of his constituents were his fellow freedmen. He invoked his position to assist law-abiding people on all parts of the Bend. For example, when the freedmen at Ursino failed to raise enough cotton to satisfy the claims of their white creditors, Montgomery appealed to the Freedmen's Bureau to permit the blacks to keep the last third of their crop as part payment for their labor. Although this was not one of his duties, he used his title to add weight to his request.[42]

Having accepted their first official assignment without serious adverse reaction, the Montgomerys continued to take on other minor political assignments whenever it seemed to serve the best interests of the community. In November, when a state election was held to determine whether the people wanted to convene a constitutional convention, the registrar of Davis Bend precinct was E. W. Raymond, one of the white lessees of Ursino. But all the other posts were filled by members of the Montgomery family: Ben was appointed judge, Thornton served as clerk, and Ben's brother-in-law, William Lewis, Jr., was sworn in as deputy sheriff for election day. The commissioners of election, Raymond and the two Montgomerys, reported that all 381 votes in their precinct were cast in favor of the convention. Ben's policy of nonparticipation was modified to permit these noncontroversial acts of good citizenship.[43]

In addition to flood damage and lawlessness, the fledgling black colony at Davis Bend had to endure still another affliction in 1867: massive invasions of insect pests. Flood-soaked fields and frequent rains during the growing season provided a favorable environment for all sorts of insects. By the end of May, while the workers were planting behind receding floodwaters, cutworms began preying on the tender new cotton plants along the ridges. These pests appeared at night, ate the plants at any stage of their development, and disappeared into the ground during daylight, precluding efforts to trap them. By early summer some of the Hurricane fields were so denuded by these pests that they required replanting. Cutworms and locusts continued to plague the black planters throughout the summer, but the appearance of the dreaded army worm in mid-July caused even greater alarm. The destructive potential of this pest in both the larva and moth stages had been demonstrated forcefully the previous year, and all hands rallied in a cooperative attempt to prevent its spread. As in the leveeing efforts during that year's flood, Ben Montgomery led the planters in planning and organizing the attack on the insects. They tried to trap the moths by setting fires at night, and when this proved ineffective they set cups and other small containers baited with molasses and vinegar on stakes scattered throughout the fields. The great number of moths captured by this method—as many as a hundred per trap in one night—encouraged Montgomery to believe for a time that the battle would be won. He persuaded the Lovell brothers on Palmyra and Huntington at the Bank place to follow the same course, but the lessees at Ursino were slow to follow suit. In spite of all the moths destroyed, the worms continued to spread, and Montgomery mobilized all available hands to catch them as well as the moths. He encouraged budding entrepreneurs among the small children by paying them five cents per hundred for moths and twenty cents per pint for worms. One August morning they caught one peck of worms on Hurricane alone. Ben realized that many people scoffed at such efforts to destroy the pests, but he insisted that the residents must use every possible means to check their progress. He firmly believed, as he told the colonists, that the ultimate success of the community depended upon their willingness to work hard. He could not encourage idle hand-wringing in the face of disaster if he could devise any action which might help even a little. For a while he thought that they were keeping pace with the worms' increase, but daily showers in September allowed the pests to wreak havoc on cotton that was already several weeks behind in development. The resulting damage was much worse than that of 1866. A planter across the river noted, "In a few days the fields were blackened like fire had swept over them." A storekeeper in Woodville reported that the worms worked so swiftly that "where yesterday the fields looked green

and promising, by the morrow they had only the cotton stalks."
Ben suggested that "the abundance of destructive insects may be
attributable to the scarcity of birds" in recent years. He had observed that "the small portion of the fields that are subject to the
range of chickens are not troubled by the insects," and, presaging
modern environmentalists, recommended that steps be taken to
protect the birds.[44] But the 1867 crop had suffered still another
blow.

When all the cotton was baled and all accounts settled, there
was ample proof that it was, indeed, a very bad year. As Montgomery pointed out to Davis, the yield of cotton from the fertile
fields on the Bend was very high considering flood and insect
losses—well in excess of the 1866 crop—but "still a pressing
want attends the planter, merchant & laborer, and much suffering is anticipated among the latter class." Ben attributed this to
the high cost of provisions, the disorganized state of labor, heavy
federal and state taxes, and especially the rapid decline in the
price of cotton. Although they shipped 620 bales from Hurricane
and Brierfield, the Montgomerys did not earn enough to meet
their liabilities for the year. Shortly after the flood it became apparent to Ben that they could never save the $18,000 interest due
the first of January in addition to the $16,000 note payable in
November. When he suggested perhaps their contract of sale
should be rescinded, Davis encouraged him to persevere and
agreed to forgive the interest for 1867, which lifted more than
half their immediate burden. Ben regained his optimistic outlook
and remained hopeful until fall, when the bales of cotton he sent
to New Orleans produced such disappointing returns. Payne and
Huntington, his factors there, were having financial difficulties
too, and in mid-November they were unable to cover a $2,000
overdraft that Montgomery had given Davis. They asserted that
Montgomery always "kept a very good account and has shown
more ability to manage his business and has taken better care of
his credit than almost any country merchant who ships to us."
However, their reduced reserves would not permit them to advance the money before Ben's cotton reached them, as was their
custom before the war. Montgomery was chagrined and
apologized profusely to Davis for the inconvenience, making the
draft good as quickly as possible. He had always maintained his

credit especially carefully because he knew that, as a black man, he was continually under suspicion.[45]

The Montgomerys were certainly not alone in their financial distress. Their yield of 620 bales was almost double that of the Lovells, who, without the necessity of paying rent, still lost about $2,000 for the year. Huntington and Pitkin shipped 604 bales from their company's lands at Bank, Lake, and Upper Palmyra Island, paying all of their expenses except rent. At Ursino, the lessees shipped only 119 bales, continuing the heavy losses the owner claimed to have suffered for the past seven years. Across the river, one large planter spent $25,000 and produced only 20 bales, while others reported similar complete failures. For most it was, as one northern neophyte titled his account of it, *A Year of Wreck*.[46]

The losses fell especially heavily on the black planters who had rented plots large enough to require additional hands. The combined discouragements of flood and army worms dispersed many laborers, and, at harvesttime, still others were induced to defect to plantations across the river by the promise of $1 or $1.50 per day for their labor. Ben estimated that he and others in the community lost about 300 bales of cotton as a result of this crucial labor shortage. Ben was extremely critical of such disloyalty within the ranks of the association. He told Davis, "If so fortunate as to ever get organized, I shall propose the dismemberment of any who may leave to work elsewhere when their services are needed here, either in their own or associate neighbor's field." There would be no objection to them working for others when the community did not need their services, but he believed that loyalty to the community was essential, and defectors should be banished from membership.[47]

Montgomery did not consider the experiences of the year entirely wasted. He admitted that it was especially hard on "the working classes" but thought those who escaped starvation might learn "valuable lessons of economy that could be learned no other way." Although this judgment sounds harsh in our twentieth-century welfare state, Ben reflected the prevailing attitude toward the benefits of poverty. He saw another advantage of the difficulties: "This year enables us . . . to form some idea of the capacity of different parties planting, which may be of some service in aportioning [sic] the land another season."[48]

Montgomery believed hope to be an essential stimulus to perseverance, and he was hopeful of the eventual realization of his utopian dream. After all the vicissitudes of their first year, he asserted, "Although we have a tight time of it, in common with almost every body else, I am inclined to think the community system will work well." He admitted that it would take time for it to become "properly systematized," but he was eager to get on with the task. When he announced that he would rent the fields at Hurricane and Brierfield for four to six dollars per acre in 1868, some old residents complained, although that was less than the Lovells planned to charge. Ben thought his rate was fair and stood by it. He told Davis, "Feeling satisfied of having made just offers and dealt fairly with the people, I entertain no fears of the results." Within a few days the dissidents had changed their minds about moving elsewhere, and no more muttering was heard.[49] As the leader of a potentially ideal community, Montgomery cherished hopes of instituting government by calm consensus as the residents demonstrated their responsibility. However, as the proprietor, whose responsibility it was to meet heavy financial commitments, he felt no need to establish an economic democracy, which required majority approval to fix rents. In his first year as leader of the community, he demonstrated the same sort of pragmatic idealism that had characterized his former master.

In many ways 1868 was a modified replay of the previous disastrous year. The new lessees of Wood's plantation proved as feckless as their predecessors at repairing the Ursino levees; a few men with handbarrows made so little progress that Montgomery and Lovell had to step in and run seven or eight teams with scrapers daily for some weeks. Ben resented the diversion of men and animals sorely needed for plowing their own fields, but flood memories were too fresh to allow neglect of any of the levees. This time their efforts proved worthwhile; although there was another flood, with the river rising throughout the spring and into June, it never reached the peak of 1867, and the levees saved the Bend from overflow.[50]

A long dry spell from mid-May till late July damaged the corn, slowed development of the cotton, and required the workers to pull fodder for the livestock earlier than usual. When the rains finally came, they were so heavy they knocked off some of the forms from the cotton plants and again fostered the spread of the army worm. By late September the blight was widespread, and Ben exclaimed that "It exceeds anything of the kind I have ever seen." He estimated that the worm damage would cut their cotton yield almost in half.[51]

As a result of their losses in 1867, the Montgomerys were without reserves and had to buy all supplies for their hands and themselves on credit. Since many planters had failed to pay their debts the previous year, factors such as Payne and Huntington in New Orleans were again hard pressed and unable to make the usual loans. In March Ben began to worry about maintaining a line of credit with them, and in May Payne and Huntington informed him that they could no longer furnish the necessary supplies but would try to help the Montgomerys find another agent. Despite difficulties, Ben managed to establish a connection with a firm in St. Louis, although on much less favorable terms. In early June he made a trip downriver to New Orleans to confer with Payne and Huntington in person and persuaded them to continue to supply him as far as they were able, thus avoiding a major change for Montgomery & Sons.[52]

Meanwhile, Joseph Davis was forced to live in straitened circumstances, and Montgomery expressed "a very deep concern for the present and future welfare of you and yours." He sent Davis's granddaughter a coop containing a dozen chickens and a box of eight dozen eggs, with a promise of more to come, in order, as he said, to "save some cash purchases during the crippled state of affairs." From time to time during the spring and summer Ben sent Davis small sums of money, but only after he sold the first bales of cotton in mid-September was he able to remit drafts in $500 and $1,000 amounts. During this time of tight money, the Montgomerys received their tax bill, and there was no doubt that they had to pay it this year. Ben delayed payment as long as possible, hoping the assessment would be reduced to correspond with the great decline in real-estate values over the last two years. When in late May he received a last warning and was threatened with a tax sale of the property, Ben finally went to pay the taxes and was pleased to find that they amounted to little more than $300; this was considerably less than had been demanded by the previous sheriff. It was a relief to Montgomery to be able to buy warrants and settle this obligation.[53]

This year even the expense of routine maintenance proved burdensome. In June Ben began repairs on the gin and its steam engine in preparation for the impending ginning season. One gin stand was in especially bad shape, but Montgomery decided to order new parts rather than replace it. He sent his order to the manufacturer's agent in New Orleans and was told he must supply the model number and precise dimensions to the factory in Massachusetts. When this was done, Ben was notified that the old gin stand, built in 1851, was so outdated that they no longer made parts for it, and he would have to ship them the old parts so that the factory could fashion new ones exactly the right size. By this time it was so late in the season that Montgomery could not wait longer, so he was forced to buy a costly, if more efficient, new gin stand. Before he could ship his cotton, he also had to finance extensive repairs on the road and bridges between his plantations and Ursino; a bar that had formed near the cutoff and prevented boats from going around the Bend made the landing at the Bank plantation as useless as the one at Hurricane. Now all of the freight sent or received on the south end of Davis Bend had to use the landing owned by the impoverished absentee, Robert Y. Wood.[54]

Yet all of these difficulties failed to destroy Montgomery's enthusiasm for the planting venture. When the army worm munched its way through their cotton fields, Ben said philosophically, "We shall only have to try again." And the drastic drop in land values only whetted his appetite for more cotton acreage. In October the Montgomerys were offered a fine plantation called Balmoral near Lake St. Joseph in Louisiana, containing 2,900 acres, 600 of which were above the high-water level. With all the necessary buildings, including a large steam gin and press, the plantation was selling for a mere $25,000—or less than ten dollars an acre. This sounded very tempting to men who had paid seventy-five dollars per acre for Hurricane and Brierfield. The

Montgomerys seriously considered buying Balmoral and leasing it to desirable tenants. When Ben broached the subject to Davis, the latter grew very worried, fearing the Montgomerys would overextend their financial and managerial resources to the detriment of Davis's interests. Ben hastened to assure Joseph that he would take no action without consulting him and concluded, "Having on hand about as much as I can manage there is no just reason why I should hasten to involve myself further unless with the most perfect safety." Both men knew that there was no guarantee of such safety, and Montgomery eventually abandoned the plan with some reluctance. Perhaps he had no serious intention of buying another plantation when he was having such difficulties maintaining the ones he had. But at least the suggestion showed Davis that Montgomery was aware of the burden imposed upon them by the unrealistically high mortgage they were obligated to service each year. This may have added weight to Ben's year-end request that Davis forgive the $3,000 note that had been due the previous January.[55]

Although 1868 was another poor crop year, by mid-December the community at Hurricane and Brierfield had ginned 790 bales, compared with 554 at Lovells' and only 153 at Wood's place. Ben assured Joseph that "the past year was generally disastrous, we lost money, and our services." He remitted to Davis the entire sum of rent collected from the tenants—some $9,600—and implied that their purchase agreement was in abeyance for the present. Montgomery stated: "Until the time arrives when we can see our ability to fulfill the agreement heretofore made with you, we hope to make the property you have so kindly committed to our charge pay you as fully as any other property of similar extent."[56] Since they had lost money for the last two years, the Montgomerys were again unable to meet the $18,000 interest payment due January 1, 1869. Ben was quite willing to cancel the sale contract if he could do so without penalty. However, Joseph Davis was accustomed to cycles of agricultural disaster and believed the plantations would prove profitable again under Montgomery's management when conditions improved. Therefore, he agreed to forgive another interest payment and urged Ben to continue in the attempt to create their model community.

Once again Joseph's faith in his former slaves was not shared by the rest of the family. Brother Jefferson, now freed from custody and traveling in England, grew indignant when he learned of the disappointing yield from the plantations and of Montgomery's reluctance to continue. "The proposition [of] Ben & his son to abandon their contract was preposterous after having had all its benefits, & without having met its obligations," he asserted rather inaccurately considering there had been no benefits, only losses, for the two years of Montgomery ownership. Jefferson reminded Joseph that when he sold the places to Ben there had been other offers from people with enough capital to insure a forfeit if they defaulted on their contract. The Montgomerys not only failed to provide this but had also missed interest payments, which should now be regarded as unpaid obligations. As he had before, the younger Davis disparaged Montgomery because of his race:

> It is no doubt true that the property is too large for the administrative capacity of a negro, & that he must ultimately fail. . . . Free negroes may work partially under a white man of character, . . . by themselves, I have not expected them to effect anything permanent or important.

Jefferson went on to impugn Ben's honesty and integrity, saying he had expected the former slave eventually to transfer the profits from the plantations to his small store, "but supposed it would be done secretly, by covert agents, rather than by direct proposition."[57] The bitter antagonism of the former president of the Confederacy toward the Montgomerys seemed to exceed mere race prejudice. Although Ben had served him well, Jefferson may have resented the authority he wielded and the competence he displayed. Perhaps there had always been a bit of rivalry between them for the attention and approval of the father figure, Joseph Davis. Or perhaps in 1868 Jefferson was merely reflecting the exasperation of a former national leader trying to survive after his world had collapsed. The Davis family finances desperately needed the profits from Hurricane and Brierfield.

There is no evidence that the Montgomerys learned of Jefferson's jaundiced appraisal of their integrity and potential; with Joseph's encouragement, Ben continued to believe in the possibility of ultimate success. Undaunted by recent disasters, in November he reasserted his credo: "I believe that by associating ourselves together and exercising industry and economy—with due regard for law and order—we can succeed. And there will perhaps never be a better time to start than now." He thought that many freedmen were recognizing the disadvantages of moving about "in search of an easier way to make a living," and would probably be "more reliable associates" as a result of their experiences.[58]

Unfortunately, a couple of weeks after this optimistic assessment, Montgomery was faced with another violent incident that challenged the cohesion of his infant association. This time the instigators were not "strangers," as Ben called freedmen from off the Bend, but younger members of prominent black families in the community. One moonlit night three men and two women, led by Jordan Green and Matilda McKinney, broke into the gin house and were about to steal some cotton when the watchman awoke and challenged them. They fled as he opened fire, leaving their sacks and Matilda's shoes behind. Although readily identified by the guard, who saw them clearly in the moonlight, the five denied their guilt. Montgomery had intended to bring the matter before "the most thinking men of the place," as he termed their judicial council, and let them render justice and fix the penalty. However, two nights later, four of the five accused attacked the guard, and Jordan Green tried to kill him with an axe. Other residents prevented bloodshed, but Ben felt compelled to take official action against the perpetrators, presumably in his role as justice of the peace. In his account to Davis it is obvious that Montgomery was reluctant to resort to the machinery of white civil law; he cited the expense and loss of time, but probably also considered it an indication of the failure of the association. Nevertheless, he insisted that "the rights of the community must be respected."[59]

Such evidence of the baser side of human nature saddened but never permanently discouraged Montgomery or dimmed his hope of creating a "community of cooperation." He was as pragmatic in his social as in his financial or agricultural appraisals. Even after two years of almost constant disappointment, he was still able to say on the last day of the year 1868 that he thought their chances had never looked better, if only they could "secure the levee against overflow" and make improvements that would "render the place more attracting to the right kind of labor."[60] A small increase in rent would be entirely applied to major levee repairs. Although he still sought advice from his former master and kept him informed of the details of plantation operation, it was clear that Benjamin Montgomery had survived the first two arduous years as an independent planter with renewed faith in his own ability and the potential of his fellow freedmen. He was not burdened with the dead weight of pessimism, which often immobilized his white counterparts in those years. While the southern whites wasted time in corrosive hatred of their Yankee conquerors or sank into the crippling lethargy of defeat, Ben could only rejoice that, indeed, the old life was gone forever. However large the obstacles to his postwar success, they could never seem as formidable as the strictures that had so recently circumscribed his chances. This delight in his incredible good fortune gave Montgomery the momentum of optimism his white neighbors lacked. Perhaps he sensed that, at the age of fifty and less than five years from slavery, he was on the threshold of the most challenging and satisfying years of his remarkable career.

5

Prosperity
and Independence

The year 1869 ushered in a half decade of comparative prosperity and independence for the black community at Hurricane and Brierfield. Favorable weather, with only minor floods and insect blights, permitted abundant crops that yielded adequate rewards even in a declining market. The heavy burden of debt service for both tenants and proprietors hindered, but did not prevent, progress toward economic security. Reconstruction politicians and their white southern opponents impinged relatively little upon the Davis Bend community; even inflated tax bills were manageable irritants. With white attention largely centered elsewhere, the freedmen of the infant colony were left as free from outside interference as was possible in an interdependent world.

Perhaps the greatest single liberating force was the death of Joseph Davis on September 18, 1870. Although the eighty-five-year-old former master had not set foot on the Bend since 1862, he had remained the ultimate authority for many of his old charges. Davis had survived the rigors of life as a war refugee and a ruined aristocrat in remarkably good health; while avoiding his former home, he continued to travel, making an extended visit to relatives in Kentucky and Pennsylvania in August and September of 1869. Late that year he suffered an accident while alighting from his carriage and never completely recovered from his injuries. Perhaps the fact that the freedmen on the Bend were doing well and no longer desperately needed his aid contributed to a diminution of his will to live. At any rate, by spring he had commissioned Ben to construct tombs for himself and his wife, Eliza, whose body had been returned to the Hurricane graveyard from Lauderdale Springs. Joseph continued to dictate indignant letters castigating importunate creditors or Union sympathizers, but the joy seemed to be gone from this favorite pastime. With no acute illness to foretell it, he quietly died in the early hours of a Sunday morning in September 1870. In an important sense, his death cut the cord of a latent paternalism that had delayed complete independence for the colony at Davis Bend.[1]

Nevertheless, the freedmen's demonstrations of grief during Davis's funeral at Hurricane were not mere rituals performed to please the whites present; many of the former slaves genuinely regretted the demise of the strong man who had dealt more fairly with them than had any other white for as long as they could remember. The remaining Davis blacks were a select group; the dissidents and those whose memories of slavery were too bitter had not returned to Hurricane after the war. Other freedmen with a strong drive for independence had moved on and had no further contact with the Davis family. However, the old folks, the more dependent middle-aged and young people, and those, like the Montgomerys, who held prominent positions in the colony, probably were sincerely grieved at the loss of "old Marse Joe."[2] Many had sought his assistance in adjusting to their new lives. As in the following letter, some had requested money in order to make a beginning.[3]

Hurricane Jan 24th 1867

Dear Master

I wish to know if you will loan me fifty dollars to give me a start in raising a crop of cotton, to be returned through B. T. Montgomery at the end of the year. I should have gone up to you, but thought you would be better satisfied with me if I should send this letter instead. This is the first year I have had a piece of land to cultivate, and I am anxious to do well.

If you see fit, please send to me through B. T. Montgomery, or his care.

Your ob't Servant

Henderson Newton

Warren Watt had asked for $150 to buy a horse; William Kannigan had needed Davis to guarantee his loan for a mule; George

Green had requested him to advance "any reasonable amt of funds" that Green's agent might need while trading a mule for him; and Simon Gaiter, who earlier lost his own animal, had wanted his former master to reclaim a Davis mule that the freedman had seen on the street in Vicksburg and send it to the Bend so that he could cultivate his crop. The Montgomerys were not the only ones who sought Joseph's intercession with government authorities; Henderson Newton's appeal for the collection of almost $70 in bills due him from some Northerners for blacksmith work was piloted through the Freedmen's Bureau bureaucracy by the sympathetic Davis. And he seldom refused their pleas for small sums as long as he had any available cash.[4] Although not resident on the Bend, old Joe represented a form of security to many as a court of last resort. No matter how much wealth Ben Montgomery achieved, he seemed unlikely to fill completely Davis's paternalistic role.

Montgomery himself must have learned of Davis's death with mixed feelings. No one had benefited more from the white planter's generosity and confidence or relied on him more for day-to-day advice and support. Ben was quite aware of his debt and expressed his gratitude several times in the months preceding Davis's death. For example, in one letter he said, "Your valuable instruction and unwavering concern for our success and comfort is appreciated. And we sincerely hope that you and yours will never have cause to regret the indulgence you have so kindly extended to us." However, as Montgomery's experience and confidence grew, and as Davis's strength and grasp of details weakened, the former slave seemed almost imperceptibly to move away from his tutelage and assume an independent position. This process had been under way for a long time; by mid-1866 Ben had abandoned the salutation "Dear Master" for the less subservient "Kind Sir" or "Very Kind Sir." By 1869 evidences of this evolution were multiplying. Although it is impossible to determine how often Montgomery wrote to Davis, since all of the letters probably were not preserved, the occasions appeared to be declining. In March 1869 Ben wrote a hasty note concluding with the guilty promise of weekly reports from then on. Many of his letters became mere notes, furnishing only the scantiest information about plantation affairs. And although occasionally, in the longer epistles, he discussed some new seed or machine, Ben usually failed to ask for the older man's opinion of it. The letters could have been written by any large, successful planter to another who was his friend and equal. They frequently closed with phrases such as "Mary and the children ask to be remembered to yourself and Miss Leize." There were references to visits by the rest of the Montgomery family to Joseph Davis where news was exchanged, but increasingly Ben made excuses for not getting up to see the old gentleman—reasons such as the need to supervise the ginning personally because reliable help was unavailable. Once Montgomery devoted most of a page to explaining why he had made a brief visit to Vicksburg without calling on Davis.[5] Hence, when Davis's death, expected for the past twenty years, finally occurred, Ben Montgomery had already moved beyond the dependence of earlier years. Still, it must have given him pause to realize that his benefactor, counselor, and friend was gone, for theirs had been no ordinary master-slave relationship. The sensitive and intelligent black man probably felt both liberated and saddened by the event.

Montgomery's first concern was with the disposition of Davis's estate, of which the Davis Bend plantations constituted the major portion. Although Davis owned land in Arkansas and in Claiborne and Washington counties in Mississippi, it was of comparatively little value. The heirs' only hope for a substantial inheritance rested with the proceeds of the sale of Hurricane and Brierfield. When Joseph's will was probated just three days after his death, Ben must have been gratified at the provision relating to their contract:

> It is my wish and desire that my executors shall extend a liberal indulgence to B. T. Montgomery, Wm. Thornton Montgomery, and Isaiah Montgomery, or their survivors, the purchasers of the Hurricane and Brierfield plantations, by extending the time for the payment, so long as they pay the interest thereon, or show a disposition to act fairly by making the proper exertions to meet their engagements, or to remit such portions of the interest as in their judgement may appear proper [but not exceeding one half]. . . .[6]

By the time he dictated this will in March 1869, Davis had realized that the Montgomerys were unlikely to be able to meet the 1876 deadline for repayment of the principal; nor, as experience had shown, could they always pay the interest. But he wanted his executors to give the blacks every opportunity to succeed, just as he would have done. Although somewhat reassured by these generous instructions, Ben and his sons probably still felt some concern. They knew all three executors: J.H.D. Bowmar, the prominent Vicksburg physician who had persuaded President Johnson and General Howard to return the confiscated plantations to Davis; Joseph D. Smith, a Davis nephew; and, most significantly, Jefferson Davis. These men shared neither Joseph's dream of a "community of cooperation" nor his confidence in the ability of the blacks to create it. When the younger Davis and his wife visited the Bend in early 1868, his disappointment with plantation operations was all too apparent, although he graciously received the warm greetings of his former bondsmen. In 1869 Jefferson had advised his brother from England, "If Montgomery & Sons will not, or can not comply with their contract, could not some one with capital be found to take the lands & secure to you a revenue free from any vexatious attention on your part?"[7] Ben must have wondered how lenient such a person would be in implementing the will of his late brother.

As though to allay such fears, in December, when Jefferson was in Vicksburg, the executors summoned Ben and Thornton to meet with them. The Montgomerys requested mitigation of the terms of their contract, alleging that the $18,000 annual interest payments "prevented them from making the necessary improvements to increase the productiveness of the places," which would help secure a permanent labor supply. The executors agreed to postpone the interest due January 1, 1871, if the Montgomerys paid the 1870 interest by that time. Furthermore, they "generally gave assurance of the purpose to execute the intent of the Testator" and promised the Montgomerys that they would "exercise all proper clemency towards [them], upon proof of their continued and faithful effort to discharge the obligations they had assumed." It is not clear whether these prominent white men achieved their purpose of relieving "the impression that [the Montgomerys] would be treated more harshly by the executors than by the Testator," but Ben must have felt at least a bit encouraged.[8]

Back on the Bend, the Montgomerys immediately took steps that tested the degree of their autonomy under the new circumstances. The perennial levee problem had continued to plague them. Each new lessee at Wood's place was as reluctant as his predecessor to incur any expense for flood control. Each winter Ben spearheaded a joint project for mutual security, and each spring he faced disappointment when the Ursino residents failed to live up to their promises. For example, one December he noted pessimistically, "The season for levying is at hand and we have not yet been able to ascertain what the proprietor of the Wood's place can be induced to do. They seem to lack energy and under present circumstances I do not know how they can be forced." By the next month Ben was resigned to the fact that "Palmyra & Hurricane will have to help repair the Wood's levee." He acknowledged that the lessees there "have been so long indulged that in the present state of affairs it seems almost impossible to force them to their duty." [9] After nearly complete neglect of the work in 1869, Montgomery and Lovell hired a contractor for $2,400 to repair the crucial levee, but, in addition to the difficulty in getting the lessees to pay their third of the cost, Ben felt that the protection thus afforded was inadequate. The temporary managers at Ursino were interested only in quick profits and therefore were willing to gamble on a weak levee rather than make a major investment in repair. As a resident landowner, Montgomery sought long-range protection, but he had no leverage with the carpetbaggers. On the contrary, he had to court their favor, because he frequently needed to use the Ursino landing. [10]

On January 20, 1871, the Montgomerys took action they hoped would solve this continuing problem once and for all: they bought the Ursino plantation from the bankrupt owner, Robert Y. Wood, for $100,000. This added 1,557 acres of fertile bottom land to their holdings and gave them undisputed control of the levee and the landing. The executors were not slow in reacting to this bold move, which threatened to overextend the financial and managerial resources of the Montgomerys. They feared that the purchase "would materially conflict with the interests of the Estate of J. E. Davis, unless some check was put on the purchasers that would prevent their appropriating the money derived from the Hurricane and Brierfield to the payment, and use of Ursino plantation." Since the Montgomerys were unhappy with their contract for Hurricane and Brierfield now that land prices had fallen so sharply, might they not default on it while draining the resources of the plantations to the benefit of Ursino? This would not be incompatible with Ben's well-known purpose of establishing a black community; after all, a number of former Davis slaves were already residing at Ursino, and it would be easy gradually to shift the best of the others there. Although there is no evidence that this was Montgomery's intention, the executors' concern seemed plausible.[11]

Although Ben assured them that "we consider our existing obligations sacred," J. H. D. Bowmar and Jefferson Davis made a special trip to Davis Bend in April 1871 to force the Montgomerys to give them a mortgage on Ursino, in order to guarantee the fulfillment of their contract for Hurricane and Brierfield. The executors later noted that "the mortgage was given by the Montgomerys with reluctance." It was obvious that they had no choice but to comply with the demand; there was good reason to question how independent the freedmen were in their large planting venture at this point. However, they soon demonstrated that they were as able to maneuver these whites as they had their recent opponents in government and business. In December Ben persuaded the influential Bowmar to renegotiate the Montgomerys' agreement with R. Y. Wood; as a result, the sale price of Ursino was reduced to a more equitable $75,000, or $48 per acre. Still, the Montgomerys worried about the encumbrance and in a series of meetings with the executors in January, by cleverly manipulating offers and counteroffers, they managed to get the mortgage canceled. Bowmar, Smith, and Davis obviously were annoyed when the blacks, pleading great need, wrung from them substantial interest concessions, only to trade them immediately for the removal of the Ursino mortgage. Although they may have felt manipulated and used, the executors kept reminding each other that the concessions were mandated by Joseph Davis's will and were in line with his wishes.[12] These white men continued to express discontent with the tardiness of the Montgomerys in meeting their heavy financial obligations to the estate and constantly suspected the freedmen of concealing from them the full extent of their assets. However, the executors, while giving the Montgomerys much unsolicited advice, made small reductions and postponements in the interest payments year by year.

In October 1874 they candidly admitted that the proceeds from the plantations under Montgomery tenure were as satisfactory "as could be obtained from a change in the condition of the property."[13] Thus, although these white Southerners were uneasy in their role as patrons of the black colony, circumstances and Davis's will prevented them from interfering materially in its development.

As in any agricultural community, the rhythm of life at Davis Bend was set by the demands of the cotton crop and varied only slightly from year to year. Winter clearing and plowing were followed by spring planting of both cotton and corn. Careful cultivation with hoe and plow was completed by midsummer, when the first cotton bolls began to open. From August through November all hands were recruited to reap the snowy harvest. These busy days brought the excitement of competition between individuals and farms to see who could pick the most in a day, and which planter had produced the largest quantity or highest quality of cotton that year. Before Christmas the fevered pace of the harvest had slowed, as bad weather permitted only sporadic gleaning of the last remnants of the crop. The Hurricane gin did not process the final bale of the 1871 crop until March 5, 1872, by which time the entire cycle was in full swing again. No matter how small his individual share in the crop production, every person on the Bend found his life regulated by the rhythm of the seasons.[14]

Hoping to make their black colony a model agriculturally as well as socially, the Montgomerys gave careful attention to the variety of cotton seed they planted. Frequently discussing the matter with Davis, Ben discovered a decade earlier than most Mississippi planters that while the Peeler variety produced a longer, finer staple, Dixon's seed of Georgia was much more prolific. Although quantity was important—and Ben admitted that they planted Dixon's seed extensively—the black planters were always eager to compete for recognition of the quality of their product. Some fields were planted early with the hope of producing the first cotton bloom or boll, and as Ben noted in 1868, "We hope to be among the first to ship a bale of new cotton from the river land."[15] Proof of the quality of their crop came on October 9, 1870, when "Montgomery & Sons, Hurricane, Miss." won first prize of $500 for the best single bale of long staple cotton at the famous St. Louis Fair. The reactions of Mississippi newspapers give some insight into racial attitudes of the time. Editor George W. Harper of the *Hinds County Gazette* was the first to report the story, referring proudly to "Mr. Montgomery" of Warren County. In the same issue, he revealed his color bias.

All the negroes in this vicinity were in town again on Saturday—to the utter neglect of their cotton picking—for the purpose of going through the nonsense of militia drill. Notwithstanding all the very bad prospects ahead, poor Sambo still permits himself to be led about, a puppet in the hands of those who control him. He cannot possibly pay out this year, yet he loses no occasion to drop his work to participate in every fool thing that comes along.

Obviously, Harper was not aware that "Mr. Montgomery" was a "poor Sambo." The next week, when he listed the eight prizewinners from Mississippi, the editor noted that Montgomery & Sons were "colored." Their unusual success elicited no further comment from Harper, although he devoted two long paragraphs to Mr. McShan, the white recipient of the prize for the best short staple variety, noting that Mrs. McShan picked "nearly every ounce of the cotton" in the prize bale with her own "fair fingers." Other local papers greeted the news of the Montgomerys' success with the same restraint, usually noting that they were black but never commenting further. In fact, the St. Louis agents who exhibited the prize cotton did not suspect that their Davis Bend customers were Negroes. Perhaps that premium bale of long staple cotton would never have been presented for judgment by J. J. Roe & Co. had they been fully informed.[16]

Six years later Benjamin Montgomery's short staple cotton won an award in an even more impressive forum, the international exposition in Philadelphia marking the Centenary of American Independence. Here, in competition with cotton from Egypt, Brazil, the Fiji Islands, and the United States, Montgomery's was judged "about the best bale of cotton on exhibition" and one of three entrees deemed worthy of a medal. The judges included men from Great Britain and Portugal, in addition to "a Providence mill-owner," "a Savannah cotton expert," and "the largest planter in the United States," Col. Edmund Richardson of Jackson, Mississippi. A *New York Times* reporter, inspecting the prizewinning bale, "made by a colored man from Mississippi," noted, "It's staple was long and fine, and the preparation was exceedingly beautiful. It was soft, and with that faint creaminess of color which showed that the cotton bolls had been picked just at the right time, and that wonderful care had been taken in ginning it." This time Ben Montgomery's honor seemed to have escaped notice by local newspapers, perhaps because the list of centennial awards gave his address as "Philadelphia, Penn." Ironically, the *Vicksburg Herald* heaped extravagant praise on Adam Kellogg, a carpetbag planter from Vermont, whose successful plantation in Madison Parish, Louisiana, just twenty miles below Vicksburg, was deemed a credit to the region.[17]

Not only was the quality of the Montgomery cotton impressive in 1870, its quantity, too, reached an unprecedented level. The 1869 crop had totaled 1,900 bales, more than double the previous year. But the next year's ideal growing season and industrious cultivation on the part of the black planters produced a healthy increase to 2,500 bales. Although the price of cotton had fallen to twelve to fifteen cents per pound at New Orleans, the Montgomerys must have grossed about $165,000 on their crop. If, as the experts agreed, the cost of producing a pound of cotton "on the best alluvial soils, in a good season, and with close management" was at least ten cents, the Montgomerys could have netted more than $50,000. However, their heavy interest payments probably increased production costs above the optimum and reduced their profit proportionately. Whatever the return, their cotton output had been impressive; the whites on the former Quitman lands, which had nearly the same acreage, had produced only 1,228 bales, or half the Montgomery crop. The black owners must have felt very optimistic as they began the 1871 season, for they had added to their holdings the Ursino plantation, from which Dr. Bowmar predicted they could expect another 1,000 bales. Since all black landowners in twenty Mississippi cotton counties produced a total of only 6,141 bales in 1870, the Montgomerys, who would produce more than half that quantity the next year, were indeed unique.[18] Their risky venture seemed to be succeeding; they were rumored to be the third largest planters in the state.

While continuing to rely primarily upon cotton, Ben sought to diversify his crops. In 1870 the two plantations produced some 2,000 bushels of corn, all of which was probably consumed on the place. In addition, sweet potatoes and orchard and garden crops added another $27,000 to farm productivity. Ben was always interested in planting improved strains of these crops and had often discussed their relative merits with Joseph Davis. Early in 1868 Montgomery wanted to try raising barley, because he had read that it was especially recommended for horses, but Davis located and sent him the seed too late for planting that year. The next season, Montgomery decided to try still another innovation. He wrote his former master:

> We have a circular from a Broom factory at N. Orleans, the encouraging tenor of which inclines us to try the planting of a few acres of broom corn. They are at present offering 22¢ per lb. or $220 per ton, which prices cannot continue long if the supply is increased. We shall probably plant 25 or 30 acres, if we obtain the seed in time, have sent for some.

Four months later they were well pleased with the growth of the broom corn even though they had not had time to give it proper attention.[19]

Ben's mechanical interests, combined with his keen analysis of worldwide markets, led him to suggest a novel improvement that is compatible with modern economic theory. The first year after the war he forecast a continuing downward trend in cotton prices and announced that, if he remained on the Bend, he expected to "introduce the Loom and encourage mechanical industry as well as agricultural." In twentieth-century economic terms, he proposed by expanding vertically to capture the added value of manufacturing cloth as well as producing cotton. Unfortunately, Montgomery never amassed enough capital to implement this experiment.[20]

In 1868 he had another idea, which, when later implemented by others, contributed to the rise of rural marketing centers for cotton. Up to that time, plantation cotton presses produced bales so loosely packed they required recompressing at the shipping port. This added operation increased costs and wasted considerable cotton. When the Hurricane press needed extensive repairs, Ben proposed, "If found practicable and likely to pay, I may attempt to put up a press that will reduce the bales to a size that will obviate repressing." He asked if Davis knew of any such devices then in use, adding, "If not, such a press, if simple and durable, might be worth something." Within five years powerful steam compresses began to appear in the South in conjunction with rural ginneries and cotton warehouses, allowing the crop to be prepared and shipped to distant markets without reprocessing. Since the Hurricane gin and press had been steam-driven for many years, and hence had the requisite power, Ben may have installed one of the new compresses. At any rate, the store, the gin, and the press on Hurricane soon qualified as a rural marketing center.[21]

In another case, Montgomery modified an existing device and thereby added cropland to the plantations. In the spring of 1870, after failing to get R. Y. Wood's cooperation in the project, Ben ordered an elaborate machine with which he proposed to drain a large area of sloughland. These swamps always filled with water in the spring and after heavy rains, but they contained very fertile soil that could be made productive if kept drained. Montgomery installed a ponderous steam engine and boiler on the site in preparation for the large new pump, supposed to have a capacity of 2,600,000 gallons per hour. Everyone who heard about the scheme, including Joseph Davis, predicted that it would fail, and, indeed, there were frequent malfunctions in the first few weeks after its inauguration. Unwilling to accept defeat, Montgomery applied all of his engineering skill to the problem and soon devised modifications of the pump mechanism, which he sent to the manufacturers in Aurora, Indiana. Delighted with the improvements in their product, the company made the new parts and sent them to Montgomery free of charge. By early June the black planter could proudly display his successful contraption beside the newly reclaimed fields of late corn to visitors whom he termed "favorably disappointed" with his success. Two years later the pump was still an object of curiosity as it continued to function effectively, although it required frequent attention from Montgomery and his apprentice mechanic, Nephew Joshua.[22]

During a protracted spring drought in 1872 Ben spent several days building a temporary sprinkler that saved some ridgeland fields of cotton. That August a water shortage at Ursino prevented the operation of the gin; Ben and Thornton finally managed to drive a well and set up a pump adequate for their needs. Each year Ben overhauled the entire gin apparatus and remained on call throughout the ginning season to keep the unreliable machinery operating. In October 1873, as the cotton harvest reached its peak, disaster threatened when the Hurricane gin was destroyed by fire. Within a month, however, Ben had constructed a new, improved gin of his own design, powered temporarily by the draining-machine engine and financed by the $6,000 insurance compensation.[23] Clearly the elder Montgomery's mechanical genius as well as his managerial skill were significant factors in the success at Davis Bend.

However, when the census taker asked his occupation, Ben replied "Merchant & Farmer." Obviously he regarded his engineering and even his planting activities as secondary to his mercantile venture. The complex operations of Montgomery & Sons in the 1870s bore little resemblance to the tiny retail outlet Ben had first opened at Hurricane in 1841, but his twenty-two years of experience gave Montgomery some significant advantages in the expanded market of the postwar era. He already knew what sorts of goods would appeal to the new freedmen, so his first purchases from the merchants in Cincinnati were eminently salable. His prior claim to the store and house near the landing gave him a desirable, rent-free location and allowed him to use all his small accumulated capital for inventory. Thornton's return even before the last gun was fired also gave them a head start on the swarm of carpetbag traders who followed the refugee masses to the Bend. As freedmen themselves, the Montgomerys not only understood the needs and wants of the black tenants and hands, but they knew the trustworthiness of many of them from long acquaintanceship. These advantages allowed the firm to develop a credit base and a clientele that put them in an ideal position for later expansion under the postwar crop-lien system.[24]

Montgomery & Sons reaped the benefits of Ben's excellent credit rating with his suppliers. As we have seen, Payne and Huntington, their New Orleans factors, praised Ben's credit record and management ability, highly recommending him to J. J. Roe & Co. in St. Louis. More significantly, the black firm achieved the distinction of an excellent rating from the R. G. Dun Mercantile Agency, whose confidential reference books provided essential credit information on firms throughout the United States. The brief ratings that appeared in the semiannual *Mercantile Reference Book* were based on rather detailed reports from observers in each county, which were carefully copied into Credit Ledgers at Dun's headquarters in New York. At their first appearance in the ledgers in 1869 the Montgomerys reportedly had a good credit reputation in Vicksburg and were considered "very reliable and safe," with an estimated net worth of about $75,000; however, because of their heavy indebtedness for the plantations, they were given only an "E" rating, which meant a pecuniary strength of $25,000 to $50,000. After the bumper crop of 1870, the Dun reporter predicted that the Montgomerys would soon be able to pay for the Davis estates, because they were "doing a large & profitable business" and had the ability to "make money fast." The next year they were listed as owning a large, prosperous business and paying all their bills promptly. By 1872 they had been awarded the coveted rating of "A No 1," which meant that they were entitled to unlimited general credit; that enviable assessment was repeated the next year. The reporters usually noted that their subjects were freedmen, but nonetheless creditworthy. For example, the November 30, 1869, entry stated, "They are negroes, but negroes of unusual intelligence & extraordinary bus[iness] qualifications." In late 1871 a Dun reporter claimed that they were "in high standing in Vicksburg, and regarded rich for the county." In July 1873 another Dun reporter estimated their net worth at $230,000. Since only about 7 percent of southern merchants in this period received ratings of $50,000 or above, the Montgomerys were among the wealthiest merchant-planters in the South.[25]

By 1869 their letterhead read: "Montgomery & Sons, Commission Merchants and Dealers in Plantation Supplies, Hurricane, Miss." Unlike their antebellum operation, which had stocked primarily luxury items for slaves whose basic subsistence was supplied by their master, the postwar Hurricane store provided most of the freedmen's needs, usually on long-term credit. Since the

Montgomerys now stocked a much larger inventory of goods and performed credit and banking functions as well, they needed to keep more elaborate records than in the past. With characteristic efficiency Ben turned to his family to obtain the necessary manpower. When he resumed operations in 1865, the elder Montgomery gave twenty-two-year-old Thornton increasingly important public responsibilities: he was the first to return to the Bend with new merchandise and the original lessee of some of the Davis lands; he signed the gin petitions along with Ben and the other community leaders; he was chosen to be postmaster in May 1867, and constable in August. Though Ben's hand was still firmly at the helm, it seemed that Thornton was being groomed as his successor.

The elder Montgomery also enlisted the talents of his younger son, Isaiah, whose intelligence and charm had won the patronage of such discerning men as Joseph Davis and Admiral Porter. In 1866, when he established the firm of Montgomery & Sons, Ben gave the nineteen-year-old full responsibility for keeping the records of the family's expanding business ventures. As Isaiah later recalled, this proved to be a chastening experience: "I thought I was pretty well educated but found I couldn't keep books. Although I had read widely in the Hurricane library— chiefly history—I had never been beyond long division in arithmetic." He remedied this deficiency first by riding to a neighboring plantation two nights a week for private lessons in basic arithmetic from Miss Lou Smith, one of the northern teachers. Then he found some experienced instructors for the practical application of his new knowledge. "My work for father threw me in contact with the clerks on the river steamboats. Those men were almost always good bookkeepers."[26] By 1872 Isaiah was manager of an office staff that included a professional bookkeeper and a clerk.

Ben had divided planting operations on the three places among family members. Isaiah was responsible for the cultivation of all of the Hurricane acreage not rented to tenants. Thornton lived at Ursino and supervised its operation as well as making frequent business trips to Vicksburg and New Orleans. Ben lived with his wife and two daughters in the only mansion that had survived the war, Jefferson Davis's home at Brierfield, but he shared responsibility for the cultivation of that plantation with his wife, Mary. With hired hands and a group of dependent children she worked the fields of the Home Farm. Thus, Ben was freed to oversee agricultural and mercantile operations on all three plantations, experimenting with new techniques, entertaining frequent visitors who came on plantation, store, or political business, and seeing that all the machines and people were working properly.

Just as the enlarged Hurricane store was the social center of the black community, so the offices above it were the nerve center of its management. There B. L. Hickman, the full-time bookkeeper, and Virginia, the eldest Montgomery daughter, toiled daily amid a vast library of ledgers. They posted the daily "blotter" of store sales both in ledgers containing individual accounts and in the journal of the firm's business. They kept the "Gin Book," the "Shop Books" for the blacksmith and the wheelwright, the "Mill Book," and the drayage accounts. They recorded standing and special orders from suppliers as well as keeping the "Invoice Book," the "Bill of Lading Book," and the "Receipts Book." They kept one "Bale List" of cotton purchased from individuals and another for cotton shipped and sold on consignment; each steamboat up from New Orleans brought a stack of "CoSales" or statements of these transactions, which had to be credited to the appropriate accounts. Every three months the quarterly reports had to be filled out and balanced, and in March of each year, when most tenants' accounts had been settled, an inventory was taken and all the books subjected to a "trial balance." In 1872 it took Hickman almost a week of searching ledgers page by page to find the errors and tally the trial balance. The problem was even greater when the books from the small branch store at Ursino were audited; it took Hickman and Virginia from May 15 to June 3 to correct and balance them. In addition to their work with ledgers, the two clerks often had to deal with an office full of freedmen requesting special orders for goods unavailable in the store or cash on account to pay a doctor's bill, buy a steamboat ticket, or even to spend at a neighboring store.[27]

From his adjoining office, while handling most of the correspondence, Isaiah supervised the clerical staff, often assisting in posting when work was heavy and always inspecting the trial balances. However, Isaiah's multiple responsibilities frequently took him away from the office. As the manager, he thought it important to deal personally with the officers of steamboats that stopped to unload freight and pick up plantation produce. Unfortunately, these boats followed very loose schedules, so it was impossible to know precisely when to expect them. As a result, Isaiah spent many hours, often all through the night, waiting for a tardy vessel. In 1871 he married and moved into the Montgomery quarters near the landing, but during much of the year he shipped from the Ursino landing several miles away. No wonder his sister noted that frequently he looked "somewhat restbroken."

As soon as he entered the office in the morning, the younger Montgomery son was "surrounded by many persons each of whom had his little business to settle." He handled all the major year-end settlements with tenants and hands, carefully explaining debits and credits and advising them about disposal of the balance. He enjoyed these duties when the customers prospered, but hated to have to attach the cotton of unsuccessful ones. Isaiah also did most of the surveying at the beginning of the year to establish field boundaries, and spent part of each spring day supervising the plowing and planting of his Hurricane fields. At age twenty-five he carried his full share of the management burden of the Montgomery firm.[28]

Supervision of the store itself was assigned to William Lewis, Jr., Mary Montgomery's thirty-nine-year-old brother, who managed the salesclerks, arranged merchandise displays, and made many inventory decisions. He was assisted by his and Mary Montgomery's nephew, Benjamin T. Green, who had gone to live with the Montgomerys when his father, James, died in 1867. He served as a field hand for three years until Ben Montgomery noticed his interest in the store and set him to work as a clerk. The industrious lad did well, and by 1872 he was promoted to assistant manager. Both Virginia and Rebecca Montgomery worked in the store at times, and, during peak periods, such as the third of July or Christmas holidays, Uncle William might recruit Titus and Mary Lewis as well. The extended Montgomery-Lewis family provided a vast pool of able and loyal young people to meet the management needs of the community.[29]

The general store at Hurricane, like others of its genre, stocked an amazing variety of goods, from staples such as meal, flour, salt pork, sugar, and coffee to nails, hoes, plows, and plow irons for the farm and crockery, tin, and glassware for the kitchen. There were bolts of cloth in many patterns and textures, with thread, pins, and needles for seamstresses; but there were also ready-made dresses and suits, which were increasingly popular despite their questionable quality and style. There were boxes of sturdy shoes for men and women as well as fancy ones for dress-up occasions, all devilishly uncomfortable until broken in, because they were all made for one width and had no right or left differentiation. The hapless customer merely selected one shoe of about the right length, found its identical mate, then hoped they would shape to his feet before the blisters became unbearable. No wonder the children went barefoot eight months of the year![30]

One corner of the store was devoted to colorful displays of patent medicines. These included remedies for headaches, toothaches, neuralgia and rheumatism, dyspepsia and various stomach complaints, as well as general debility and female ailments. No family escaped ill health for an entire year; some members were sure to contract malaria during the summer even if they were robust in other seasons. On July 26 Virginia noted in her diary, "Many persons are complaining of fever and ague. . . . The season is not a healthy one." When her grandparents were ill with fever, she sent them "some Wilhofts Tonic"; in September she mixed up some tonic for her father, who had chills; and in October she herself took some "composition tea" for the same ailment.[31] Although the tonics were probably mostly alcohol, which temporarily relieved the symptoms but did nothing to cure the illness, they were very popular where physicians were scarce and the knowledge of medicine was limited. It would be more than a quarter century before the Pure Food and Drug Act required manufacturers to substantiate their claims and reveal the ingredients in their nostrums.

The Hurricane store also carried boxes of cheese, caddies of tobacco and barrels of whiskey from Cincinnati; looms from St. Louis for those who chose to weave their own cotton cloth; and fancy net and lace from New Orleans for trimming ladies' hats. With all this variety there were times after a bumper harvest, such as the one in 1872, when the store could not supply the demand for "dry goods and fancies." More seriously, in July there was a temporary shortage of staples for rations; in September meat was so scarce that the residents were forced to substitute fish; and in November Hickman took the steamboat *R. E. Lee* down to Natchez to buy beef for the store. From time to time shortages occurred in all sorts of items. During the busy season, small denominations of paper currency and change were scarce, and one of Virginia's regular duties was to "patch up the money" so that torn and worn bills could be returned to circulation.

Daily store receipts in both cash and credit varied from below $125 on a dull day to over $200 when trade was brisk, probably averaging around $165. This meant that the Hurricane store had an unusually large annual volume of more than $50,000. Two recent historians of the southern general store in this period have found that "an annual business in excess of $10,000 was considered quite substantial, and a volume of $4,000 to $5,000 seems typical." [32]

The first thing that an entering patron was likely to notice when his eyes became adjusted to the dim interior was not the tangle of harness and rope hanging from the ceiling or the patent medicine posters on the wall but the heavy metal grill of the post office window, the tangible symbol of the United States government and the community's link to the outside world. Although most residents had little occasion to use it, this window was the focus of attention whenever a passing steamboat put off a sack of mail containing newspapers from Vicksburg, Natchez, Cincinnati, or New York. Then William Lewis, Jr., Isaiah, or Virginia would read snatches of the news aloud to the assembled group while sorting the letters, circulars, magazines, and parcels for the few lucky recipients. The schedule of mail arrivals, supposed to be twice a week each way, up- and downriver, was subject to frequent interruption just as in the days before the war. For example, in early February 1872 Virginia reported that the boats had lost their mail contract, so Davis Bend received no deliveries. Two weeks later she complained that "no mail whatever has reached us so our knowledge of public affairs is meager." The next day sporadic service was resumed, and on March 2 she happily noted that "our boats are again carrying the mail." However, two days later the *Natchez* stopped deliveries, cutting the Davis Bend service in half for more than two months. The steamboat company finally negotiated a satisfactory contract directly with the postmaster general, and Virginia remarked, "I am glad to have two mails again."[33]

Even with all boats in service, it was not always easy to send and receive mail. Often, when she heard a boat whistle earlier than expected, Virginia would rush to the Hurricane store, make up the outgoing mailbag and dispatch it to the landing, only to have the steamboat's arrival delayed for several hours. Then again, sometimes without even a warning toot, the boat would arrive early, before the Davis Bend mail sack was ready. In the latter case, the unobliging captain might refuse to leave the incoming mail he had brought. When the deposit point was the Ursino landing instead of Hurricane, the problem became even more acute. Since Thornton Montgomery, the official postmaster, was seldom at Hurricane, primary responsibility for the post office operation was delegated to his sister Virginia, whose clerical duties required her regular presence at the store and office anyway. This was a time-consuming task; once she noted, "Our office cancelled 46 letters today, besides sending a bundle of missent letters and papers—we also sent off Dead Letters and 2 or 3 Registered." Since much of the postal business involved credit transactions, she had to keep records for the firm as well as the post office department. However, she took pride in the increasing volume of mail she handled, because it was an indication of progress in literacy among the members of the association. She commented, "We must have more readers, as we have [more] subscribers." Even the increase of the postmaster's salary to forty-nine dollars a month in mid-1872 was not as significant as this proof of community improvement.[34]

Were the Montgomerys wise to maintain and expand their mercantile firm after the war? Most observers, both contemporary and modern, would agree that they were. A Mississippian noted in 1868, "The negroes, since they have become producers on their own account, keep a large amount of money in circulation in the country, and consume on a much larger scale than formerly, which makes the business of supplying them as lucrative, if not more so, than planting or renting." A modern scholar asserted, "As landlord, storekeeper, and creditor, the country merchant became the most important economic power" in the postwar South; and when he also became local justice of the peace, he added political authority to his economic preeminence.[35]

These powerful furnishing merchants have received much of the blame for the debt peonage that afflicted the South for half a century after the Civil War. Were the Montgomerys merely unusually successful black versions of the new oppressors? Was the association just a clever cover for the exploitation of their fellow freedmen through the crop-lien system? The evidence available, scanty though it is, seems to indicate that they were not exploiting their tenants and hands. Although the effective interest rate they charged for credit was not recorded, it is clear that they used differing cash and credit prices. Their credit markup, like that of other furnishing merchants, may well have ranged from 30 to 100 percent. However, as a Jewish merchant told an English traveler in 1871, "It ish profit in de books, not profit in de pocket," for the risks of default were very great. Even if, as historians Roger Ransom and Richard Sutch assert, the merchants paid no more than 6 to 10 percent to the wholesalers for trade credit, they were still not assured of huge profits. Ransom and Sutch claim that to justify an interest rate of 100 percent, the merchant would have needed a default rate of at least 60 percent annually. They further argue that, in such cases, he would have taken steps to reduce his credit losses such as "discriminating against poor credit risks" or "employing supervisory personnel to oversee the debtors' farms."[36] Neither of these moves would have had significant value to the Montgomerys. In the close-knit colony, they could not be as ruthless as some white storekeepers who denied food and other necessities to their defaulters. In addition to his own sensitivities, Ben had a mandate from Joseph Davis to provide for the old and unproductive former Davis slaves. Furthermore, he had no need to employ supervisory personnel; he and his large family were in close daily contact with community members, making suggestions, giving encouragement, and offering the cooperation of the group where needed. And yet, with all these advantages, one of the major reasons observers gave for subsequent troubles of the Montgomery planter-merchant enterprise was the tremendous credit losses suffered during bad years. Had their interest charges to their clients been truly exorbitant, they would have made enough profit in the good years to carry them through. Skillful businessman that he was and, as his former master noted, "ambitious to be a rich man," it still seems that Ben Montgomery did not fully seize his opportunities to exploit his fellow freedmen. Although they had an effective credit monopoly, Montgomery & Sons wielded their power with restraint; most of the family seemed to share Ben's dream of fostering an ideal black community where all would prosper together.

What was daily life like in this potential utopia? Mary Virginia's diary provides a detailed picture of the Montgomery family's routine. As previously noted, Ben and Mary and their two daughters, Virginia and Rebecca, lived in the Jefferson Davis mansion at Brierfield. This rambling, one-story house, set back a mile and a quarter from the river, lacked the pretentiousness of the huge Hurricane mansion the Yankees had destroyed, but it provided ample room for comfortable living. All eight rooms in the main section were spacious, with sixteen-foot ceilings and windows twelve feet tall that opened out on front and back porches, providing easy access for cooling breezes. These rooms and the adjacent kitchen, pantry, and storeroom contained more than 4000 square feet of living space, while the ample verandas added another 3500 feet. The main gallery and those on the two recessed wings were lined with tall white columns, giving a broken-colonnade effect to the front of the gracious house. By 1872 the Montgomerys had repaired most of the damage done by vandals and souvenir seekers and were able to live in surroundings that differed little from those enjoyed by the prewar occupants.[37]

The Montgomerys were a close but not an exclusive family. In 1870 the Brierfield household contained some twenty-seven persons, including servants, hands, and wards. Three young relatives—Benjamin and Chlote Green and Charles Henry—lived there and attended school. The cook, Martha Brooks, had four children and a grandson with her; Lucy, her eighteen-year-old daughter, assisted her with kitchen and household tasks. Jennie Hattes was also listed as a domestic servant, while three young men worked as farmhands. An old couple, Jack and Betsey Mitchell, aged ninety-seven and seventy-one, continued to live in their old quarters, helping with light tasks. The rest of the household were children ranging in age from the five-year-old McKinney twins to Sampson Hattes, who was eleven; these young wards worked in Mary Montgomery's fields in exchange for food, lodging, clothing, and instruction of various sorts. They were more than servants but less than full members of the family. Either orphans or children from impoverished homes, they probably felt fortunate to be able to live with the Montgomerys and share their affluence. They received some schooling and much training in good work habits while being petted and given frequent opportunity for fun and frolic. Joseph Davis's family often included poor relatives, but it seems likely that the Montgomery wards, as heirs of the African and the slave-family tradition, benefited from a warmer and more total acceptance with little or no discrimination because of their dependency.[38]

In many ways the Montgomerys, less than ten years from slavery, enjoyed the same life-style as wealthy white planters had before the war. In early 1872 Virginia's consuming interest was in restoring and developing a spectacular flower garden at Brierfield. Although she consulted her father about the design of the new garden and the location of walks and fences, Virginia was responsible for directing the daily tasks of the three or four workers she was authorized to hire. She ordered seeds, bulbs, young trees, and shrubs from their agents in Vicksburg and New Orleans. Her mother and sister joined in planting and transplanting them, delighting in working the names of family members into some of the flower beds. Although rosebushes constituted the primary attraction, Virginia's garden also contained beds of jasmine, lilies, pinks, sweet peas, zinnias, primroses, marigolds, portulaca, poppies, bachelor buttons, and cockscombs. Flowers deemed less attractive, such as iris, were replanted in the flower yard, out of sight of the house but available for table bouquets. Virginia ordered the hands to fill numerous large flowerpots with special soil so that she could cultivate an artistic flower assortment on the galleries, but the destructive antics of the ever-present kittens doomed this project to failure. One May Sunday, after proudly conducting some guests around, this typical planter's daughter could say, "The garden is already a source of indefinite pleasure to me. In years to come I expect to make it my chief entertainment."[39] Although by fall she was engrossed in other activities, Virginia's horticultural interests seemed very similar to those of the previous mistress of Brierfield, Varina Davis.

Also like their white counterparts, the Montgomery girls were fashion conscious and spent a great deal of time planning their wardrobes. Unlike antebellum women, however, they did most of the dressmaking themselves, with only occasional assistance from a hired seamstress or from their mother, who had sewn previously for the mistress of Hurricane. Virginia and Rebecca made skirts, waists, overskirts, and basques of linen, calico, wool, Chinese silk, or velvet. Virginia was delighted when she found that Beck, as she called her sister, had started to make her a new gabrielle because, she said, "it will be so long and fashionable." They learned of the latest styles from *Demorest's Monthly Magazine,* which, for three dollars per year, not only brought them serial stories, poetry, music, and sketches but colored fashion plates and, stapled into each issue, a tissue-paper dress pattern. Davis Bend seemed even less isolated from the world of haute couture when Mrs. Green at Ursino subscribed to the relatively new *Harper's Bazar,* "a Weekly Illustrated Family Journal, devoted to Fashion and Home Literature." Modeled on *Der Bazar* in Berlin, this first American fashion weekly boasted that it had arranged with "the Fashion Papers of Europe, so that henceforth the fashions will appear in *Harper's Bazar* simultaneously with their appearance in Paris." This magazine too contained patterns and woodcuts of the new styles. Virginia and Rebecca borrowed the magazine before making a new Dolly Varden or remodeling a velvet overskirt. They sewed on their own machine and were in demand in the community to instruct new owners in sewing-machine techniques such as threading the bobbin.[40]

In still another way the Montgomery daughters seemed typical young ladies of the planter class: both sought to become accomplished pianists. Virginia spent some time practicing almost every day before or after work. If she missed a day or two, she made up for it by spending two hours or more at the keyboard. She ordered sheet music from as far away as Boston and received it as a gift from visitors or returning travelers; she labeled Mr. Hickman's gift selections "both pretty and popular." The songs she mentioned were all in the latter mode, such pieces as "Kiss Me Good-night, Mama," "Willie Dear," "Maggie May," "Caroline," and, during the political campaign, "a little Grant song." She and Beck sometimes played and sang for young men callers, and they frequently entertained at social gatherings where there was a piano. Only Rebecca took music lessons from Mrs. Shadd, the schoolteacher. Perhaps Virginia, who was two years older, had progressed beyond that level, or Beck may have been more interested in music. Although she practiced faithfully, Virginia admitted one night that her ears were not musical and she turned to books for recreation.[41]

The entire Montgomery family seemed to have a passion for reading. The scope of their newspaper subscriptions rivaled that of the Davis's before them. In addition to the Vicksburg papers, they regularly read the *Cincinnati Times,* the *Chicago Tribune,* and three New York papers—the *Ledger,* the *Times,* and the *Tribune.* Furthermore, unlike the Davis family, they read and contributed to black newspapers such as the *New Orleans Tribune* immediately after the war, and the *Louisianian* and Frederick Douglass's *New National Era* in 1871. They delighted in political discussions at least as much as had their former masters; when the *New York Times* arrived on August 15, 1872, with a detailed political supplement, the whole family took turns reading and discussing it. Their Sunday family gatherings were occasions for exchanging and commenting upon articles they had read during the week, not only in newspapers but also in the several magazines to which they subscribed. Perhaps their favorite in 1872 was *Harper's Weekly,* whose Republican bias agreed with their own. One can imagine with what relish they greeted each Nast cartoon, with its cruel caricatures of Horace Greeley. They may have questioned the magazine's uncritical praise of the Freedmen's Bureau, but there is no evidence that Ben wrote to set the editor straight as he did to the *New York Times* on August 16. Although they chose not to seek political office, the Montgomerys were astute observers of government at all levels; their multiple subscriptions kept them as well informed as Joseph Davis had been in the antebellum years.[42]

Virginia probably took a more active part in the political discussions than most planters' daughters, but the rest of her reading was even farther from the norm for nineteenth-century young ladies. Evidently she had shown an aptitude for intellectual achievement at an early age. It is interesting to note that when Ben located and engaged a white tutor before the war, he sent Isaiah and Virginia to him; when Joseph Davis enlarged the class, he sent only male children from his household. It was not generally considered suitable for females to undertake the same rigorous course of study prescribed for men. But Ben firmly believed in developing the full potential of each of his children, and he himself delighted in traditional learning. Hence, Virginia was encouraged to pursue her own interests in any area of study. By 1872, in her early twenties, she had had very little formal schooling, but she prescribed for herself a rigorous, if eclectic, course of self-education. She spent some time each day reading such works as the poetry of Byron, Pope's essays, the life of Dryden, and each of Plutarch's *Lives*. She studied ancient and sacred history, with considerable emphasis on Bible stories. Since neither she nor her family attended church, and her father seemed to have a positive aversion for religion, she treated the Bible as any other literary classic rather than as divine revelation. For example, when she found conflicting versions of the Tower of Babel story, she sought to resolve them by further research. Darwin's *Origin of Species* seemed rather difficult and dull, and she spent only a short time reading chemistry, zoology, and geology, preferring to try the "chrystallizing" experiments described in her mineralogy book.

But Virginia reserved her greatest enthusiasm for the pseudo-science, phrenology. Introduced into the United States from Europe in the 1820s, it had become a popular cult by the 1840s, with practicing phrenologists, phrenological societies, and a phrenological magazine. It is not surprising that Virginia Montgomery did not discover phrenology until 1872. The South had remained comparatively isolated from intellectual movements that swept the rest of the country shortly before the war; the Davis library probably contained no works on the subject. If it had, Virginia, who was only twelve when the war started, would not have been interested in reading them. A decade later, however, she embraced the cult with all the enthusiasm of a convert. She not only subscribed to *Well's Phrenological Journal* and eagerly read each issue, but she bought charts and a model human head so that she could become an amateur phrenologist herself. This "science" provided Virginia with a pleasant party game to entertain her friends, and it also abetted her own drive for self-improvement. If she could only read her skull shape properly, she might learn to know her own weaknesses and work to eliminate them.[43]

S. G. Wells's contribution to Virginia's improvement was not limited to information on phrenology; in the course of the year 1872 she also ordered *Wells' Self Culture, Self Education,* and their *Self Instructor,* as well as *Weaver's Helps for the Young.* When office work was slow, she discussed her reading with Hickman, the bookkeeper, and encouraged him to send for *Wells' Mirror of the Mind.* She persuaded her father to read *Self Culture* and was delighted when he acknowledged that he was "highly pleased with it."

Both father and daughter were ardent devotees of the cult of self-improvement that had been a part of American thinking since Benjamin Franklin and had enjoyed increased popularity in the antebellum rise of Jacksonian democracy. The Unitarians and Transcendentalists of the 1830s taught that everyone must make the most of the powers God had given him; the drive for public schools and libraries furthered this purpose. Although it had enjoyed little popularity in the antebellum South, the cult struck fertile soil among ambitious freedmen a generation later. Ben Montgomery himself was a prime example of the rewards of self-improvement. Furthermore, his dream of a utopian community was based on a belief in the ability of his fellow freedmen to improve through their own efforts. His daughter's diary recorded a life so fully programmed with improving activities that it resembled the rigid regimen of the great female Transcendentalist, Margaret Fuller. Two years before the organization of the first Chautauqua Assembly, and two decades before the popularization of the cult of the self-made man, the Montgomerys were well ahead of the mainstream of American thought.[44] Although Virginia resembled a typical planter's daughter in her maidenly interests in gardening, piano playing, and fashionable clothes, her serious intellectual pursuits set her apart from most nineteenth-century women of whatever class or color.

The Montgomerys frequently displayed the traditional southern hospitality. Every Sunday the family gathered at one of the three plantations, most often at Brierfield, which not only boasted the finest house but was also midway between Hurricane and Ursino. Sundays usually began at Brierfield with leisurely reading and conversation on the gallery before breakfast. Then the tempo picked up as preparations for guests began. Frequently, Virginia supervised the straightening up and dusting while Rebecca saw to the kitchen. Aunt Martha, the cook, ably took care of dinner if she was present, but often she took the day off to visit elsewhere. Sometimes one of her daughters, either Lucy or Alice, assisted Beck in the all-morning task of preparing a large company dinner. The guests began arriving by noon, and dinner was served when all were present, between two and four in the afternoon. The food was always ample and, Virginia often noted, "very rich every bit of it." Sometimes there were delicacies such as squabs or opossum; and the first strawberries, figs, and watermelons were always saved for these occasions.

Sometimes the clan gathered at Hurricane, where Isaiah and his bride lived in the house near the landing where the younger Montgomerys had been born. Martha Robb Montgomery was an intelligent and personable young lady from Vicksburg, with very light skin. Since all of the Montgomerys were, as Jefferson Davis put it, "as black as the ten of spades," this was probably the first infusion of white blood into the family. However, in spite of, or perhaps partly because of her light complexion, Martha seems to have been readily accepted by her in-laws and the Davis Bend community. Her position was further secured when, on March 4, 1872, she gave birth to a son. The entire family was delighted with the first member of a new Montgomery generation. Mary doted on her grandson; Ben made him a "Go-Cart" as soon as he could sit up; Thornton insisted that he should be named William Thornton and was disappointed if on Sunday he did not get to see the baby. As for his two aunties, Virginia and Rebecca adored little Willie from the first and vied with each other for a chance to make his clothes or play with him. The Sunday gatherings were greatly enlivened by his infant antics.[45]

Dinner at Hurricane became even more attractive after the new kitchen and dining room were completed in September. The old building was in such disrepair that on one occasion Cousin Betsey fell through a hole in the floor and injured her leg. Isaiah had some difficulty finding able carpenters to construct the new one, but after four or five months it was completed to his satisfaction and the delight of his wife. He ordered a fine new stove, which arrived from Cincinnati slightly damaged but still able to cook food much faster than the old one. There was a celebration on September 15, when all the family drove through intense heat and dust to inaugurate the new building.

About once a month the family gathered at Ursino, where Thornton headed a household. Although he never married, the duties of hostess were capably provided for him by Mrs. Virginia Green. She was the free Negro from St. Louis who had come to the Bend in 1866 to teach freedmen at a school on Wood's place, and who had eloquently expressed her black nationalist views in a long letter to the Freedmen's Bureau. By 1870 she was listed as a clerk living at Ursino, probably in charge of the small branch store there. Although there is no evidence of it, she may have been the widow of one of the Greens from Davis Bend. At any rate, she was a highly respected lady and treated as one of the family. In 1872 she was thirty-seven years old, while Thornton was twenty-nine. There seems to have been no romantic link between them, although she was always included with Thornton in any social invitation. She was a worldly person who seemed to inspire Virginia Montgomery's awe and admiration. She gave splendid dinners, frequently adding something exotic such as Rhine wine or, on one occasion, champagne. She subscribed to the new *Harper's Bazar,* and regularly wore fashionable clothes. She had been born in northern Ohio and may have attended Oberlin College; at least she was well acquainted with the art teacher there. This sophisticated and strong-willed woman must have contributed a great deal to the Montgomerys' Sunday discussions of national affairs.

From time to time the Montgomerys also welcomed house guests. After she was "hospitably entertained" for several days at Brierfield, Frances E. W. Harper, a black poet and former antislavery activist, wrote a northern friend of the marvelous prosperity of the Montgomerys in 1871. A black plow inventor remained at Brierfield for almost a month, and both black and white politicians stayed overnight when campaigns brought them to the Bend. The white Scharff brothers, prominent wholesale merchants and the Montgomerys' agents in Vicksburg, visited the plantations frequently; on two occasions Lazarus Scharff brought his little son to stay for several days.[46]

A less socially compatible pair of white men visited the Montgomerys in May, but Virginia was uncharacteristically reticent in describing their stay. She had been preparing for two days for the visit of Vicksburg friends on a May Day "picnic excursion." That morning a messenger announced that Jefferson Davis and Dr. J.H.D. Bowmar were at Ursino and would come to Brierfield after breakfast. Having dispatched the best buggy for them, Virginia said, "I brushed around the house and donned my white dress, smoothed my hair and pinned on a rose or two." She gave no details of their stay, merely noting that "both gentlemen were polished in their manners and on the whole I have been pleased with their visit." Her excursionist friends did not come, so perhaps her brief comments about the Davis executors stemmed from disappointment. However, the nervous care with which she prepared the house and herself would seem to indicate that she felt some anxiety about their visit.

In a letter to a friend in Chicago, Dr. Bowmar gave a more detailed account of their Davis Bend visit of the previous year. Because it concerned the famous former president of the Confederacy, the *Chicago Tribune* printed it and the Jackson *Weekly Clarion* reprinted it. After describing the Davis plantations and the terms by which the Montgomerys held them, Bowmar said, "Ben, who is very black, but thoroughly educated before the war, met us [at Hurricane] and gave us breakfast, waiting on the table himself, but not offering to take a seat." They then took a carriage tour of the plantation and proceeded to Brierfield. Bowmar continued, "After dinner, at which our wealthy host again waited on us in elegant style, we passed on to a very large and valuable plantation [Ursino] which has been purchased by Ben Montgomery and added to the Davis estate." Neither the *Tribune* nor the *Clarion,* nor apparently the *New Orleans Times,* which also picked up the story, added any comment. However, a black newspaper in New Orleans, *The Louisianian,* found the account offensively racist. It asked if the white editor who published the story thought that "every rich negro should wait on the poor white men who may happen to be his guests?" The black editor labeled Ben's "obsequious behaviour" as "snobism," and added, "If Ben Montgomery has been so degraded by the influences of his former oppression that he does the work of his servants in the presence of his inferiors in position, this fact is one of the heaviest condemnations of the accursed system of slavery." It was easy and maybe even necessary for the black editor to criticize Ben, but the latter knew how much his dream depended upon the goodwill of the executors. Despite the rosy prediction of the Dun agent in November 1870 that the Montgomerys "will soon pay [the mortgage] and obtain title," Ben knew that they would have difficulty even meeting the high interest payments. He also realized that these defeated Southerners were sensitive to any black gestures of equality; it must have been galling enough for the younger Davis to find his former mansion occupied by freedmen. Hence, Ben went out of his way to appease the white men. He may not have found this brief return to service degrading at all; he had spent a lifetime outwitting whites, and no doubt he could point to material achievements far beyond those of the black editor. In the 1830s, when he was prevented from escaping shortly after his arrival at Hurricane, he had made up his mind to work within the system in a white racist society. With consummate skill and a little luck, he had succeeded beyond his wildest dreams. A bit of obsequiousness at this late date was probably a small matter to him since victors generally find a pose of humility easier to adopt than those who have not yet won their battles. However, this attitude may not have been shared by his children, who had had the way smoothed for them and who were expecting more from a life of freedom. Underneath her reticence, Virginia may well have been bitterly resentful of these white intruders, even though she found them "polished in their manners."[47]

Despite the numerous similarities between the Montgomerys' life and the lives of their white predecessors, there were some striking differences. In many ways Ben and his family were prototypes of the New Southerner, displaying a "time is money" industriousness, no prejudice against work, no habits of extravagance, and great pride in their ability to overcome obstacles. Life in the mansion at Brierfield moved at a much faster pace than it had twenty years earlier. The Montgomerys expected more of themselves and their servants than had the Davises. Neither Joseph nor Jefferson could have been termed lazy—in fact, both were very productive men—yet their life-styles followed a more leisurely tempo than the Montgomerys allowed themselves. Even during a traditional Sunday morning prebreakfast gathering on the gallery, for example, Ben brought out an essay titled "Science and Religion" for the family to discuss. And duties of the plantation or store always took precedence over social affairs; Isaiah and Thornton occasionally and Ben frequently missed Sunday dinners for business reasons. When the elder Montgomery was present, he often conducted a sort of seminar on politics and current events, efficiently providing his family education along with their recreation.

As the acknowledged head of one of the largest planter-merchant operations in Mississippi, Ben found his time infringed upon by all sorts of people who wanted to sell him land, buy his cotton or cotton seed, or win his influential backing for political office. Active supervision of his multiple enterprises, coupled with the development of new devices and techniques, left him little enough time for the self-improvement that had become a lifelong habit. In addition, many people in the community consulted him before they made personal decisions; from time to time his own children and nephews were ushered into his study to discuss their problems. When little Willie suddenly became seriously ill, Ben was hastily summoned because of his widely respected practical knowledge of medicine. His position as responsible patriarch was so time-consuming that at age fifty-three in 1872, Ben still felt driven to follow a rigid schedule that seldom included relaxation.[48]

At age fifty, Mary Montgomery was equally busy, combining the duties of a planter with those of a housewife. She hired and supervised hands who raised a quantity of cotton, corn, and sweet potatoes on 130 acres of the former Home Farm; at harvesttime, she kept five wagons employed just hauling her cotton. She remained in the field to see that the work was properly completed even when Scharff and his son were at Brierfield for dinner. She used her hired workers and young wards to cultivate the large vegetable garden and orchard, as well as to help with the flower garden. This capable woman joined eagerly in the agricultural competition, protecting her earliest cotton blooms in the hope of having the first cotton boll in the area. When her fields were harvested early, she and her crew picked cotton for other lessees on the Bend for a handsome fee. In addition, she fulfilled the usual duties of a housewife, overseeing and assisting in the routine cleaning, cooking, and sewing for her large household. Mary also found time for practical nursing when needed; she remained at Hurricane for several weeks assisting Martha during and after Willie's birth, and made several visits a day to her aged parents when they were sick. In spite of her heavy schedule, however, Mary managed to add warmly loving touches that would have done credit to her less-harried antebellum counterparts. She not only saw that her young wards were adequately dressed and cared for, and that they attended school regularly, she also provided frolics on holidays or during a rare snowfall and saw that they got treats on their birthdays and rewards such as "cake and drinks" for especially good work. She, like all of the Montgomerys, earned her own money and was generous about buying presents for others with it—a dress for one of the girls, some flower seeds for a friend or relative in the community, or a high chair for her beloved grandson. Aesthetically sensitive, one day she brought Virginia the season's first rose, and a bit later her daughter noted she "sat on the gallery with Ma in the moonlight and talked until bedtime." After the new grandchild's birth, Virginia wailed, "This house is apparently tenantless without Ma. She has been gone a week now." Three lonely days later, Virginia reported Ma's return but added, "Martha's will is not consulted." With so many demands on her time, Mary could not afford a leisurely pace.[49].

Mary herself was the product of as warm and secure a life as a slave family could enjoy. Her father, William Lewis, Sr., was a respected wheelwright, now eighty-two years old and still living in the cottage where she and her siblings were born. There her mother, Rachel, at seventy-two still enjoyed entertaining their large brood of children, grandchildren, and now little Willie, their great-grandchild. When she was eighteen, Mary Lewis had married the brilliant but mercurial Ben Montgomery only a few years after his arrival at and attempted flight from Hurricane. One can only speculate about how much her warm support and intelligent advice contributed to Montgomery's antebellum mercantile venture and postwar planter-merchant triumph.[50] There is no doubt that this busy woman was a full partner in the Montgomery enterprises, while capably fulfilling her maternal role.

The Montgomery daughters were as industrious as their parents. Virginia, as previously noted, besides fulfilling her clerical responsibilities drove herself to study early and late. She resembled her father not only in her love of books and learning but also in her mercurial disposition. For example, one day she awoke full of animation and sang as she played the piano before breakfast. As luck would have it, that day her horse ran away with her, throwing her to the ground unconscious. She was not seriously hurt but after being taken home in a carriage insisted, "I only cried because I had to give up today." The next day she remained at home nursing her bruises and studying one of the Wells' self-improvement books, but, still shaken from her accident, she brought out and dressed her dolls, rather childish behavior for a woman in her twenties. However, she took her office responsibilities very seriously and was deeply disturbed when she made a mistake. When the year-end closing of the ledgers revealed several of her errors, she was so depressed that she could neither practice nor study that night. And when her "boss," Isaiah, gave her "a severe chastigation" for some mistakes, she admitted, "I did not feel very well under the penalty." At other times she was euphoric and "full of glee"; after the birth of her nephew she was rhapsodic, and often she reported having great fun at work when "our friend Mirth has been in the office all day." She kept up with political developments and took part in the lively discussions about them. She enjoyed meeting new people and claimed to have learned a great deal from a long conversation she had with a Mr. Lane, who came to the Bend soliciting subscriptions to his new Vicksburg newspaper. Admittedly ambitious, she reported one day, "I was appointed general supervisor . . . in the transplanting business & settling with the hands. I make mention of it because I of course feel proud of having a cognizable judgment—all ambitious people do." Despite rather frequent ill health, Virginia drove herself to ever greater efforts, insisting that hard work was the best medicine. She relished holidays and the occasional days off that she allowed herself, but she always compensated for them by redoubled efforts at self-improvement. Her life bore little resemblance to that of the stereotypical languid, pleasure-seeking planter's daughter.[51]

Rebecca, too, was an industrious part of the Montgomery work force. At age twenty she displayed interests and abilities very similar to her mother's. Virginia declared that Beck was "a wheel horse at sewing"; she made clothes for the children, little Willie, her sister, and herself, as well as some shirts for sale in the store. She also excelled at cooking and enjoyed taking over the Brierfield kitchen when Aunt Martha was absent. From July through October she spent most of her time canning homegrown fruits and vegetables; she took a cart full of her preserves to Hurricane for sale. Beck spent many nights at Isaiah's house helping Martha with the baby, and she seemed to delight in all sorts of domestic chores. Less interested in intellectual activity than her sister, she nevertheless took grammar lessons from the schoolteacher. She preferred her piano lessons, though, and willingly played at parties or for the children at home. Although she was the youngest Montgomery child, in many ways Beck seemed more mature and more stable than her older sister.[52]

Thornton, at almost thirty years of age, seemed to be least overworked of all the Montgomerys. He planted cotton at Ursino, but had to borrow "plow boys" from Brierfield in March; three months later Virginia noted, "Bro. T. had to employ a great many day hands to clean his cotton crop which he is not satisfied with because tis behind in growth." His horses and mules always seemed to be sick or dying, and he was chronically short of water for plantation operations. Part of his difficulties might have been the result of taking over a neglected estate, but he seemed slow to improve it. As previously noted, although he was the postmaster, he resided almost five miles from the post office and rarely went there. He made frequent trips up- or downriver, sometimes being gone as long as a week. He was especially interested in county politics and looked after any office seeker who stopped by. The family respected his opinion, which was decisive in such matters as the naming of Isaiah's baby. However, his father assigned the heaviest task of store and office management and planting at Hurricane to his younger brother. Perhaps the gregarious and easygoing Thornton lacked some of Isaiah's drive and business acumen.[53]

As noted earlier, Isaiah was extremely busy with office and shipping duties. In addition, as planter in charge of the largest of the three places, he surveyed the fields and made contracts with lessees and hands at the first of the year, and made settlements with them after the harvest. He took an active part in the crops' cultivation, boasting in May that his corn was "the finest in the Bend" and spending so much time in the fields that Virginia remarked, "I am sure he will not fail from lack of personal attention." He engaged in a contest with a neighbor to see who could produce the greatest yield of corn; when he lost by six bushels, his sister hastened to explain, "The stock destroyed a part of Zie's." Sometimes he became weary and discouraged, but he usually seemed enthusiastic about the challenges he faced. As a new husband and father, he still found time for domestic tasks such as directing the planting of shade trees in front of the house and hanging curtains in the new kitchen. His authority was respected by those who waited to see him at the office each day; although only twenty-five years old, Isaiah was an important leader of the community.[54]

Besides the brisker pace of their lives, the Montgomerys differed from their antebellum predecessors in still another important way—their view of the proper role of women. It would have been inconceivable for Varina or Eliza Davis to oversee a work gang in the cotton fields every day, even if many of the workers were children; nor would any Davis daughter have kept the plantation books. They certainly would not have clerked in a store, because neither Joseph nor Jefferson would have demeaned himself by operating such a business. But the Montgomery women went beyond these activities: both girls, with the cooperation of their parents, actually went into the fields at harvesttime and picked cotton. Mary agreed to let Rebecca keep the proceeds from any she picked, and on August 12 the latter started accumulating what she was confident would amount to a bale of her own. Virginia remained aloof at first, but late in the month went with Ma and Beck to pick a few rows before work. The jolly spirit among the youngsters as they competed for the heaviest sack must have been appealing, for in early September Virginia again joined Beck in the fields very early, when she found "the morning cool & dewy; cotton picking was easy." After many delays because of other responsibilities, the young women, with some assistance, finally finished the bale.

On October 8, before daylight, they followed their cotton to Hurricane and saw it safely through the gin and press. Virginia reported, "It weighed 448, sample fair." They had had the satisfaction of participating in the true climax of the year for that agricultural community; no one wanted to miss being a part of the harvest. Even Isaiah's wife, Martha, left the baby with his nurse and picked for a while each afternoon.[55] Far from being frowned upon, these women were merely joining in an activity that involved the very lifeblood of the colony. If they ever gave it a thought, they probably felt sorry for the white females who had missed all the fun in the old days.

The Montgomery women were full participants in the challenging new life opening for them as free members of an expanding society. They were not hampered by the restraints that kept most nineteenth-century white women from assuming major responsibilities outside the home. Mary and Virginia and Rebecca were the heirs of generations of women who had carried their full share of the burdens and enjoyed all the benefits of equality with their men in the slave communities of the Western hemisphere. Although their family's new wealth would have made it possible for them to live frivolous lives, none of these women wanted to leave all the work and excitement to the men. A graphic demonstration of their feminine liberation came late in 1872 when both daughters left the Bend to enter Oberlin College in Ohio. Virginia had decided by summer that she wanted to do something more intellectually stimulating than planting a new flower garden each year. Perhaps she had heard about Oberlin during the two years that they lived in the black community in Cincinnati; as the first interracial and coeducational institution of higher learning in the United States, the Ohio college must have been well known among informed Negroes and women throughout its thirty-five-year existence. Or Virginia may have learned about it from Virginia Green, who gave her a letter of introduction to Miss Wyett, the art instructor there. Perhaps the exchange of letters in the *New National Era* the previous November and December had aroused Virginia's interest, although they pointed out some flaws in the alleged equal treatment of all at Oberlin. Letters from students past and present questioned the absence of a black among the student teaching assistants in the preparatory department. James H. Fairchild, president of the college, felt compelled to write in reply, claiming that race had nothing to do with the selection. Another student charged certain faculty members with discrimination in seating black students in the dining hall. This exchange might have discouraged a less-determined scholar than Virginia Montgomery. Perhaps she hoped to be the unusual black student whose performance would qualify her for one of the coveted teaching assignments.[56]

In early September, after receiving encouraging replies to her written inquiries, Virginia nervously told her parents of her plans and was overjoyed to win their wholehearted approval. When she received application forms, her father "made arrangements to procure all necessary recommendations." With many qualms about leaving friends and family for the unknown outside world, the two young women said their final farewells on November 21. Both brothers had given them advice about the journey and their new venture, and each had offered privately to assist financially if, as soon happened, the girls found their own funds inadequate. A six-day journey by boat and train took them to Oberlin, where they began a chilly round of intellectual and religious training. Since the student body that year was almost 50 percent female and about 8 percent black, they were not unique, but the strange surroundings and the cold, snowy weather left them very homesick at first. However, before Christmas Virginia passed the entrance examination with high marks and was engrossed in a curriculum that provided more intellectual stimulation than she had dreamed possible. Rebecca was less enthusiastic, getting sick the night before her first public speech and finding solace, finally, in renting a piano and immersing herself in the conservatory of music. The Montgomerys remained at Oberlin for two years, gaining more formal education than anyone they were likely to encounter in Mississippi, white or black. Even though it required contributions from each member to keep them in college, the family did not question their right to pursue their own interests.

In an era when few men and a miniscule percentage of women entered college, the Montgomery daughters were encouraged to attend. Perhaps this liberal view of the women's role, more than anything else, set the family apart from their white counterparts, both before and after the war.[57]

There were other, more superficial ways in which the Montgomerys differed from their predecessors. The women did more of the housework themselves, sweeping, dusting, ironing, and washing windows, working alongside their servants. This may well have resulted from the general postwar shortage of labor, however, and probably was common to all planters' families at that time. In fact, the wives of less-successful white planters may well have had fewer domestic servants than the Montgomerys and, therefore, performed more of the household work themselves. The Montgomerys also operated without the large stable of fine riding horses of which Joseph Davis had been so proud. Although experts agreed that a planter should have one horse or mule for every fifty acres of cleared land, the Montgomerys had only three-fourths that number in 1870. Tax records of a year later indicate they possessed only ten horses, twenty-three mules, and a mere nine wheeled vehicles, most of which must have been the essential farm wagons. Virginia frequently noted the problems they encountered because of a shortage of transportation for the family and their visitors. There were only three buggies—one old and rickety and another quite small—to accommodate the residents of all three plantations. Sometimes Virginia was late getting to the office at Hurricane because she had to wait for a vehicle to be returned by another family member or his servant, and every Sunday it took several hours for the carriages to fetch guests who had no other way to reach the dinner party. When a number of out-of-town visitors arrived, the family was completely immobilized while all vehicles were sent to the landing.

The Montgomerys found it difficult to procure satisfactory new riding horses; frequently, when a dealer sent some down on approval, they proved unsuitable. In the postwar period both animals and vehicles were scarce and expensive, so most families were forced to manage with fewer of them. Joseph Davis traveled around Vicksburg in a mule-drawn cart until the Montgomerys' success permitted him to buy a horse and carriage in 1869. For most planters, the antebellum luxuries were a thing of the past. It must have been far easier for the Montgomerys to adjust to the new conditions than it was for their neighbors; even these difficulties represented an improvement over their lives in slavery.[58]

But what of the ordinary members of the colony? How did their lives compare with their prewar existence? Unfortunately, specific evidence is very scarce. Undoubtedly they considered themselves better off as freedmen than they were before, even as welltreated slaves. Most of the associates were neither as wealthy as the Montgomerys nor as poor as their servants. Henderson Williams was a typical resident, renting twenty-five acres of productive land on which, in 1870, he raised eleven bales of cotton, forty bushels of corn, and forty bushels of sweet potatoes, for a total value of $1,180. He owned one mule worth $120 and was assisted by two hands, a young woman and a sixteen-year-old boy. The other members of his household, in addition to his wife, were the three young children of his female hand. The vast majority of farmers on the Bend held between ten and thirty acres on which they raised cotton, corn, and garden crops. Most owned a mule or a horse or both, but very few had a cow. There were only a total of twenty-nine milk cows listed on the Bend, of which the Montgomerys owned four. The total value of farm production on a typical unit was around $1,000, with only a few reaching as high as $2,000. Most residents either found or built a small house on their land, leaving the commodious former slave quarters primarily for the hands, servants, and artisans hired by the Montgomerys. Many black householders possessed $100 to $1,000 worth of personal property, although most claimed less than $500 worth.[59]

Many alarmed whites commented on "the almost entire disappearance of the colored women from the cotton-fields," or asserted that "few of the women now work at all." Although these statements were somewhat exaggerated, most of the wives of family heads at Davis Bend gave their occupation as "Keeping House" or "At Home." No doubt these women helped in the fields when the need was acute, such as during cotton-picking season, just as the Montgomery women did, but they devoted most of their efforts to their own domestic chores; this was an important improvement over prewar conditions for them and their families. Of course, there were still many female farm hands at Davis Bend; unmarried women and the wives of laborers usually could not afford the luxury of remaining at home. With the acute labor shortage, it is probable that many lessees' wives gave considerable time to field work, although they reported to the census enumerator that they were only housekeepers.[60]

In some cases, the more prosperous farmers were able to withdraw their children from the work force and send them to school. The Freedmen's Bureau had assigned at least one missionary teacher to the Bend through 1867, and there were schoolhouses at Hurricane, Ursino, and Bank plantations. In 1868 Ben Montgomery unsuccessfully petitioned the bureau for aid to their schools, but county support soon filled the breach. In the winter of 1872 nearly fifty children attended the Hurricane public school taught by Mrs. Amelia Shadd. In March she invited Virginia Montgomery to witness the school examination, and the latter maintained that the pupils "exhibited a progression that exceeded my every expectation." They were particularly well versed in American history, although they had some difficulty with geology because "twas new." In May the county closed the school for lack of funds, promising to resume instruction in October. Virginia regretted the decision, insisting that "many a poor child will fall back from this." Mrs. Shadd immediately opened a private school for those who could afford the tuition. In August the county board of education decided to postpone reopening of the public school until the next January, claiming they could support it for only five months per year, and Mrs. Shadd moved her family to Vicksburg, where her husband was active in Republican politics. After Rebecca and Virginia returned from Oberlin, they were employed as teachers on the Bend for a few months each year. The youngsters were forced to get most of their education on their own, just as the Montgomerys had.

In 1871 I. D. Shadd explained to a black editor that the 1,200 people on the Montgomery plantations were "advancing rapidly in letters," although he found them woefully ignorant about conditions beyond their neighborhood. They seemed especially uninformed about national black leaders, "ninety-nine per cent" of them having "no knowledge of the Douglasses, Remonds, Garnets, Purvises, and a host of others, who for years have filled the front ranks, battling for their liberties and rights." Shadd carefully exempted the Montgomerys from his indictment. He was probably correct in thinking that most Davis Bend freedmen were parochial and largely engrossed in their attempt to build prosperous lives. Shadd wanted to arouse their race consciousness in order to advance his own political fortunes, but found the associates unresponsive. He discovered that somehow civil and political rights were of less immediate concern to the majority than the level of the river or the progress of the army worms.[61]

Nevertheless, the Davis Bend community was not as apolitical as Shadd told the black militants regretfully, or as Ben Montgomery told the whites reassuringly. In his original prospectus for the colony, Montgomery had asserted that all political discussion would be discouraged; and in late 1869 he had reassured Davis, "You need entertain no fears of much time being lost in political affairs for it seems to be the aim of the different squads of this community to make as loud speeches as possible in the shape of cotton bales." This statement was only partly true. The people were, indeed, preoccupied with their economic enterprises, but that did not preclude an active exercise of their new political rights. Nor did the Montgomerys discourage them from such participation. As Isaiah noted later, "The Davis Bend precinct . . . was one of the most populous in the county and was of considerable importance in deciding contests." Of the 1,628 people listed as residents of the Bend in 1870, only 30 were white; this large black population provided a fertile field for Republican campaigners. Although the Montgomerys did not seek public office themselves, Isaiah claimed that they "maintained a controlling interest," using their influence to deliver an important bloc of votes.[62]

Unlike many white landlords and furnishing merchants who resorted to threats and intimidation to discourage black voters, the Montgomerys sought to convince their tenants of the value of Republican affiliation. Isaiah later claimed that he "kept membership rolls and minutes for the Union League when colored voters received their earliest instruction in balloting." His father and his uncle, William Lewis, Jr., were appointed to the board of registration in 1869; subsequently, as president of the board, Ben prepared and carried to Vicksburg a list of the names and registration numbers of some 118 black and 2 white voters who had failed to cast ballots. His disapproving tone in the letter of transmittal indicated that Ben probably rebuked those nonvoters next time he saw them. The Montgomerys maintained their civil authority, too; in 1870 and again in 1871, Ben's appointment as justice of the peace was renewed.[63] The family was well situated to wield considerable political influence.

Nevertheless, the Montgomerys continued to keep their political activities as quiet as possible when dealing with the larger white community. They realized that, although such wealth and position as theirs might have brought statewide political leverage to a white planter, they were wise to limit their operations to the Bend. In the heat of the 1871 campaign the rabidly prowhite, Democratic *Weekly Clarion* printed an eloquent letter from Montgomery & Sons that did not even mention politics but merely enumerated the steps they were taking to eradicate the army worms at Hurricane; the editor made no comment about the authors. Ben reserved his political opinions for letters to the *New York Times,* the *Cincinnati Times,* or the *Chicago Tribune.* He must have been more than a little disturbed in the spring of 1871 when the *Clarion* reprinted an item from the *Vicksburg Times* reporting the removal for malfeasance in office of the chairman of the Warren County Board of Supervisors, adding, "It is rumored that Benjamin Montgomery of Davis' Bend is to be his successor." The *Clarion* noted disapprovingly that Montgomery was "a negro." Although there was absolutely no truth to the rumor, it was the sort of publicity the Montgomerys sought to avoid.[64]

Within the confines of the Bend, however, the Montgomerys joined the other freedmen in displaying a lively interest in political campaigns. In 1872 the first federal election since Mississippi's return to national politics aroused considerable enthusiasm. There was a heated contest within the Republican party for the Fifth District congressional nomination. In June George C. McKee, an able and honest former Union general turned Republican politician, came to Brierfield for dinner with two other white Vicksburg residents; they had spoken at a large meeting at the Hurricane church the previous night. The Montgomerys liked

McKee even though he was not especially sympathetic to freedmen, regarding their presence in the party as a necessary evil. A few weeks later the Bend received another contender, Judge Brown, a conservative Whig who had deserted his fellow Mississippians to join the Republican party. His speech at Hurricane enthralled the large audience, and Virginia remarked, "I am sorry that such wavering exists among the people because they have given McKee their support." It promised to be a tight contest between these two white men, and the Montgomerys decided to use their influence for McKee.

As the day approached for the local meeting that would choose seven pledged delegates to the county convention, tension mounted and "groups of men were seen everywhere discussing politics." Captain Bourne, an eloquent champion of McKee, spoke at Hurricane four days before the meeting, but the Montgomerys still feared that "the wind is in favor of Judge Brown." On the fateful day, with "politics raging high," the store closed at noon and the entire family joined most of the men of the association in the church building. Virginia asserted:

> The house was full. Committees were organized and the delegation appointed. Bro. W. T. & Uncle Wm. were appointed with several others. A few light speeches were made in favor of McKee. 'Twas very near night when the voting took place. The house was divided and McKee rec'd all but two votes. After taking up a collection the meeting adjourned.

The delegates, pledged to McKee, succeeded in winning his nomination in Vicksburg. William Lewis was sent on to the state meeting, which he found unpleasantly chaotic; upon his return he reported "hot times at Jackson" and declared he would "*never* go to another convention."[65]

Excitement remained high through August, with the Montgomerys eagerly scanning every newspaper for political information. When the *New York Times* published a special political supplement, the family took turns reading it aloud, and the next day Ben fired off another letter to the editor. Although a Republican sweep of the Bend seemed assured, black politicians continued to stop by for rousing meetings. In September T. W. Cardozo and Henry Hunt were warmly received both at Hurricane and Ursino.

A month later Peter Crosby made an address upon the "political issues of the time," but Virginia considered him "intellectually unable to do justice to the subject of his speech." Her standards were probably more rigorous than those of the average listener, however. Three days before the election three speakers, including the white carpetbagger Charles E. Furlong, arrived at Hurricane about three o'clock in the afternoon, and the Montgomerys immediately closed both store and office so all could attend the rally. November 5 dawned bright and sunny for the new voters, who crowded the polling place at the Hurricane store. At first, "all Hands were very earnest and looked distressed" because there were no ballots. Isaiah and Joshua Montgomery and B. L. Hickman were hastily improvising some when Ben arrived with the authentic "Tickets" which had been sent down at the last minute by special messenger. There was a rush for the polls that kept all the Montgomery men busy; the final tally revealed 442 votes for Grant and only 1 for Horace Greeley. Isaiah left at four o'clock the next morning in the buggy to take the ballots to Vicksburg. Upon his return the next day the entire community rejoiced to learn of "glowing Republican victories." Virginia reported: "All in high spirits." Unsophisticated as they may have been, the freedmen recognized that the Republicans would be most likely to serve black interests, and they were proud to have contributed to their victory.[66]

Politics was not the only reason for calling meetings at Davis Bend. The farmers held ad hoc assemblies whenever a problem—such as levee building or battling the army worm—required group action. Once Virginia reported a gathering of the "Friends of Progress" that lasted well past midnight. However, that organization probably had limited appeal to the average inhabitant; she admitted that it was "not largely attended," although she and a few others "addressed the meeting extemporaneously."

Less intellectual but probably more satisfying to the majority of the people was the series of meetings during a religious revival that swept the Bend in the summer of 1872. Normally the Montgomerys did not attend church services except for a baptism now and then; however, the "Protractio" meetings even attracted most of them before they were over. The revival began on Friday, July 19, and was scheduled to end the next Sunday; however, meetings continued every night for two and a half weeks, closing with a huge gathering on Sunday, August 4.

At first Virginia reported that people were coming from neighboring plantations to attend the emotional meetings, but soon she noted the snowballing local interest. As she returned to Brierfield from the office each evening, she saw more and more freedmen traveling in the opposite direction, toward the Hurricane church. There were "children of all sizes" joining the church each night, including several from the Home Farm. One evening at the end of the first week Rebecca Montgomery and Mrs. Shadd went to the church to see what was going on; the next night, Virginia joined them there. By Sunday morning, July 28, "Everyone [of the family] except Pa. left the yard and was at Hurricane before nine o'clock to witness the baptizing" of some 130 converts, including Cousin Betsey Henry and her son, Charles, as well as 4 children from the Brierfield household. Excitement mounted during the next week, as more residents experienced conversion.

These black revival meetings were very similar to those held by the Baptists and Methodists on the American frontier a generation earlier. A white agent of the American Missionary Association described the freedmen's services as

> of the most emotional and demonstrative kind. Women go into a frenzy of excitement and roll on the floor for two or three hours together, screaming and crying, "Lord, take me," "Jesus save me," till, utterly exhausted, they fall asleep, or experience something which they call "coming through," when they jump up in ecstasy of joy, and shouting "Glory, glory, hallelujah," at the top of their voices till they are hoarse, run all over the house, hugging indiscriminately every man, woman, and child, white or black, that they may come to, and telling them with the most extravagant gesticulations that "Jesus died for me," "Jesus is the precious Saviour!" Men walk all around the house on their knees, shouting with the full compass of their voices. . . . And then they sing . . . all joining at the top of their voices, swaying their bodies to the time of the music, and clapping their hands in the most frantic manner.[67]

Undoubtedly the revival provided an emotional outlet and broke the monotony of life for the freedmen. Virginia thought it also had a positive effect on the community, noting that the growth of "the band of Christians [was] improving the place very much."

However, the experience took its toll. At the end of two weeks, "the hands [were] all broken down having to attend church every night."

It all came to a grand climax on the final Sunday, when "persons from every place covered the grounds" in the grove of trees in front of Isaiah's house at Hurricane. There, after lengthy preaching, praying, and singing, 114 more persons were baptized in the river, including Ben Green, two Brierfield children, and several of their hands. The total number of conversions during the revival amounted to some 12 percent of the residents of the three plantations, or a rather significant proportion of the population. Benjamin Montgomery apparently took no part in the movement, even avoiding the two huge Sunday jubilees. The rest of the Montgomerys attended some of the meetings, with the young women displaying the greatest interest. However, none became so involved that she was converted. Virginia seemed a bit embarrassed to note that, at the baptizings, "there was some shouting on the bank." Though she and her family may have considered themselves intellectually and culturally above such emotional demonstrations, all but Ben found them too fascinating to miss.[68]

Holidays provided other breaks in the routine for the Davis Bend colony. On May Day the church congregation gave a gala May party for the youngsters. The Fourth of July called for a more general celebration, with the Montgomerys scheduling a gathering of all four generations of the extended family. Their sumptuous dinner had to be served late, however, because Ben and Thornton each first gave great feasts for their hands. At Brierfield the Montgomerys arranged rows of tables in the dining room, where the workers were served in elegant fashion. Virginia reported that "they were highly pleased and several of them made short speeches." The community also held a patriotic demonstration complete with a "cannon's roar" and "the Stars and Stripes" floating on the breeze. To complete the celebration, that night the young people held a ball.[69] The Christmas holidays probably brought the most elaborate and extensive celebrations to the Bend; unfortunately, Virginia was at Oberlin in December 1872 and so left no record of the holiday at home.

There were other special occasions enjoyed by the colonists. A wedding often gave rise to a party that lasted well into the night.

Virginia attended the marriage of two of their hands one evening, and noted, "They looked very nice and many persons witnessed the ceremony." Afterward the couple "had a little ball in the cotton house," but, sounding as insensitive as her white predecessors, Virginia said she did not bother to attend because she felt "too tired, drowsy & cold."

Residents also enjoyed individual recreation. From time to time both men and women would take a day off to go fishing, combining pleasure with replenishing the larder. Early in June Virginia and Beck spent a delightful day on the small lake behind Brierfield, fishing from a skiff. They caught three fish, enjoyed rowing "up & down & across the Lake," and then picnicked on the bank in the shade during a long, drowsy noontime. Virginia commented, "On the whole we have had a pleasant time, not an alligator or Lake Monster appeared to marr [sic] our proceedings. We came home late & as happy as when we left." At private parties the guests enjoyed playing cards and other games.[70] Although life on the Bend was geared to the agricultural seasons and required a great deal of routine labor, there were enough holidays and celebrations to provide breaks in the monotony. Perhaps just the knowledge that no master but economic necessity kept them in the fields made most freedmen regard their lives as happy.

How well did the association work under the pressures of prosperity? Was the ideal "community of cooperation" envisioned by Robert Owen and Joseph Davis achieved under Benjamin Montgomery? Despite relative economic success, utopia remained beyond reach. Petty crimes continued to plague the colony and its leaders. Young Matthew Johnson and two associates robbed the general store across the river at Ashwood, Louisiana, one night. The next day the irate owner visited Ben Montgomery and, obtaining a search warrant, located the stolen merchandise in Matt's house. Although the guilty man had fled, Ben jailed one of his accomplices, but the prisoner escaped the next day. Believing that young Johnson could have been reformed, Montgomery suggested that he would have made restitution to the white storekeeper and let the community deal with the culprit had he not disappeared. The loss of one of their young men, perhaps to a life of crime, distressed the elder Montgomery.[71]

The branch stores at Brierfield and Ursino sometimes suffered from minor robberies if the clerks did not lock them properly when they left. Even the crops in the fields were not safe from thievery; one June day Virginia noted that "some kind neighbors have robbed Zie's fine corn field & where it was so productive is now nothing." There were also occasional brawls at the Hurricane store, and one night someone attempted to set fire to it and the adjacent schoolhouse. The Montgomerys much preferred to keep these problems within the colony. Whenever possible the guilty party was brought before the community court, which took appropriate action.[72]

All of these petty incidents involved only the inevitable unscrupulous minority of the colonists. It was the honest malcontents, who perpetually threatened to lead an exodus from the community, who posed a far greater threat. As previously noted, Ben Ousley and the three Green brothers had expressed dissatisfaction with Montgomery's rental terms in 1867 and had muttered about leaving but took no action. Every January thereafter they and others had considered the advantages offered in neighboring areas; some landowners, desperate for workers, promised impressive benefits, which they seldom delivered at the end of the year. Early in 1870, after a secret campaign of recruitment, Ben Ousley led about twenty-five residents of the Montgomery places to a plantation near Glencoe where they expected to get better financial terms. Among the defectors were Jordan Green and Matilda McKinney, who had been implicated in the attempted gin robbery two years before. Another member of a prominent slave family, Otis Joice, with his wife and children joined the dissident group, as did Sam Clark, Matilda Oakley, Adeline Plato, and Enoch Burton. Ben believed that all of them had been made restless by their new prosperity; he asserted, "Should they be so fortunate as to succeed as well elsewhere as they have here, I think they will have no cause to complain." He did not expect to have any trouble filling the vacancies; the success of the Davis Bend community was well known among freedmen in the Mississippi Valley. However, Montgomery found it wrenching to lose established members of his colony. Clearly they had not considered life there ideal.[73]

One factor that may have speeded some of the malcontents on

their way was Ben's condescendingly paternalistic attitude toward the freedmen of Davis Bend. For example, he lectured them
on health and sanitation practices, pointing out the importance of
diet and cleanliness in avoiding diseases such as cholera. He admonished them to become more self-sufficient by raising
chickens and planting larger vegetable gardens. He was especially critical of slothfulness and could not abide weed-grown
fields, frequently complaining about the people's lack of industry
and frugality, "the want of which has been a source of considerable trouble to me." On one occasion he asserted, "So soon as the
people learn the use of economy it will not be difficult to accomplish many things that at present seem unlikely." He was
delighted when he could report that "several persons who have
been slothful and shiftless heretofore are now making creditable
efforts to do something." At the same time, he claimed that "the
general industry of our community deserves praise." Like a firm,
benevolent father, Montgomery exhorted the associates to behave
properly and criticized them when they failed to live up to his
high standards. He expected a great deal of his people, almost as
much as he required of his family and himself.[74]

Unquestionably there was some social distance between the
Montgomerys and their tenants and hired hands. Virginia spoke
condescendingly of "the people in the Quarters"; one diary entry
noted coldly that "some poor woman in the Quarters lost her baby
today." And Ben seemed pleased when he could assure Davis of
the "quietude" of the people. In many ways the new owners had
assumed not only the life-style but also the attitudes and methods
of their predecessors. However, those who remained to work land
on the three Montgomery places probably expected, and some
even liked, the dominance of the family in the big house. They
must have been proud to have landlords who won cotton prizes,
read important books and newspapers, and entertained leading
white businessmen and politicians. That these leaders were
blacks and former slaves like themselves may have made a similar achievement seem possible for the laborers or their children.
On the other hand, there were likely some who resented the
Montgomerys' success and found it particularly galling to be
given instructions or reprimands by another black. Perhaps the
demonstration of the heights that could be attained by one of

their race merely made some feel more inadequate because of their own relative lack of accomplishment. Whatever their conscious or unconscious reactions to the Montgomerys, most of the members of the association recognized how much more fortunate they were than they had been in the old days. In these prosperous years, they were able to work land on their own and feed their families with minimum field labor by their wives and children; most of them even had some credit at the end of the year, which they could spend as they chose at the Hurricane store or even in Vicksburg or elsewhere. It was undoubtedly true, as Ben reported in June 1870, that for the most part the people were working cheerfully.[75] The all-black colony may not have been ideal—it may have been more authoritarian than democratic—but it provided these freedmen with the best situation they had ever known, and most enjoyed their freedom from white interference.

6

The Decline of the Colony

A SENSIBLE DARKEY—Ben. Montgomery, (colored,) of Warren County pays an annual tax of 2,447.09. Ben . . . [who owns the two Davis plantations] . . . is a good citizen, is highly respected by both black and white, attends to his own business, does not dabble in politics, and does not corrupt himself hunting offices that he is incompetent to fill.[1]

Thus did the editor of the *Hinds County Gazette* characterize the leader of the Davis Bend colony in early 1874, as native white forces in Mississippi began to organize for the overthrow of the Reconstruction governments. The "redemption" of Vicksburg and Warren County that year, and of the state government in 1875, produced racial hostility which threatened to penetrate the protective isolation of Davis Bend. In spite of Editor George W. Harper's favorable assessment of Montgomery, the changes in political climate in 1874 exacerbated local economic and agricultural difficulties so greatly as to initiate a downward trend for the colony that proved to be irreversible.

At Republican state and county conventions in the summer of 1873, black delegates had demanded a larger share of the political offices. As a result, almost half of the members of the lower house and nine of the thirty-seven senators in the new state legislature were freedmen, as were the lieutenant governor, the secretary of state, and the superintendent of education. Although freedmen did not control state government, the white Republicans suddenly saw that black domination of the party was likely in the near future, and most were unwilling to accept this prospect. By 1874 Warren County, with its large majority of black voters, had an even greater percentage of black officers than did the state; the sheriff, clerks of the chancery and circuit courts, and four of the five county supervisors were Negroes. Although there is no evidence that these black officials were any more corrupt or inefficient than their white colleagues, the white citizens of both parties were alarmed at their growing assertiveness. The Vicksburg ring that controlled both city and county government, like its antebellum counterpart, was blatantly corrupt, providing ample justification for a citizens' reform movement appealing to taxpayers of both races. While soliciting support from enlightened freedmen in the municipal election of August 1874, the victorious Democrats made clear that control would remain in white hands. The militant Taxpayers' League next turned its attention to county government with the avowed purpose of redeeming it for the native whites.[2]

Ben Montgomery carefully followed these political developments while maintaining his public image as "a sensible darkey." In August 1873 J.H.D. Bowmar reported to Jefferson Davis that Montgomery had been "spoken of as a candidate for Gov[ernor] of Miss[issippi]" but would probably not be nominated. Ben had said that he would refuse the nomination, although Bowmar believed white voters would prefer him to any white Republican nominees. The next June, Ben declined an appointment to a state commission to prepare for the national centennial in 1876. Although he pleaded the pressures of his planting and mercantile obligations, Ben actually wanted to minimize his official contacts with whites at a time when racial tensions were rising.[3]

Not all blacks from the Bend accepted Montgomery's nonparticipation policy. Thomas M. Broadwater, who had competed with the Montgomerys for leadership of the colony, moved to Vicksburg during Republican ascendancy and in 1872 was rewarded with the post of wharf and harbor master of the city. Albert Johnson, a member of one of the old Davis slave families and a signatory of the petitions for the gin concession in 1865, worked his way up in the Republican party, was named to the Warren

County Board of Supervisors by Governor Alcorn, and, while serving in that capacity, was elected to the state legislature. He seemed to be doing a creditable job in the latter post but, according to one historian, "probably became an early victim of the Vicksburg ring." Less capable but more amenable to party control was I. D. Shadd, husband of the former Davis Bend schoolteacher, who became speaker of the house in 1874.[4] However, each of these men gave up his position in the Davis Bend colony to pursue a political career, and therefore did not bring unwanted attention to that black sanctuary.

Throughout the fall of 1874 conservative whites in Vicksburg, led by prominent citizens such as J.H.D. Bowmar, agitated at public meetings and through the press for the removal of the Republican county officials. Stories of real improprieties were embellished in the retelling until white taxpayers were thoroughly aroused against the black and carpetbag regime. Finally, in early December a taxpayers' convention was called and about a hundred irate citizens forced the resignation of the entire board of supervisors, the clerk of the chancery court, and the hated black sheriff-tax collector, Peter Crosby—the black politician whom Virginia Montgomery had found an inadequate thinker and speaker in 1872. Crosby's bond was evidently improperly executed, but later examination of his books revealed no irregularities in the sheriff's discharge of his duties. When the aroused whites forced him to resign, Crosby fled to Jackson, where he received assurances of support from Governor Adelbert Ames. However, the governor was totally impotent, since he distrusted the white militia and feared race war if he mobilized black soldiers. His pleas to President Grant for federal troops to enforce the law went unheeded in that depression year when scandal threatened the national administration. Sheriff Crosby returned to Vicksburg and issued a handbill appealing to all Republicans in the county to aid him in regaining his lawful office. This notice was read in the colored churches of the county, including the one at Hurricane, on Sunday, December 6. Groups of freedmen immediately armed and made plans to march to Vicksburg, while white citizens there exchanged exaggerated rumors. As one turn-of-the-century historian commented, "The dread of negro insurrection, which has at one time or another darkened every hearthstone in the South, took possession of the people, and they saw visions of slaughter, rape, arson, and robbery."[5]

About noon the next day a large group of blacks appeared just outside the tense city, where they were met by about a hundred white militiamen. The leaders of the two forces conferred, and the blacks agreed to withdraw, but, as they started to do so, some whites shot into their ranks, killing at least seven freedmen. Several other skirmishes occurred later on other roads with much the same results. When the blacks withdrew, the final toll stood at thirty-six blacks and two whites dead.[6] Crosby was not able to reclaim his office until several months later, after belatedly dispatched federal troops dislodged a replacement elected by the white citizens of Vicksburg. By this time race relations were at a very low ebb, and it was apparent that the white Democrats were determined to regain control of local governments at all costs.

Ben Montgomery, fearing a disastrous outcome from any foray by armed blacks, had used all his persuasive powers to prevent the Davis Bend colonists from joining the black posse to Vicksburg after the inflammatory church service on December 6. According to a Jackson newspaper, "about 700 negroes . . . from Hurricane armed with guns . . . started out, but old Ben confronted them and bade them return to their homes. He spoke so eloquently they turned back: thus was much bloodshed spared." Montgomery received warm praise from several local papers, with one concluding, "If such men as Old Ben were more plentiful, what a land of peace and harmony we should have!" Nevertheless, he must have been disturbed at the direction of the political movement and wondered how long he could protect his small colony from white intrusion. As it happened, the politicians who disfranchised Mississippi freedmen by economic and physical coercion in the next two years generally left Davis Bend alone; in the presidential election of 1876, the precinct remained staunchly Republican, returning more than 400 votes for Hayes and only 7 for Tilden. However, the Montgomerys cooperated with the dominant whites in local contests, supporting what came to be called the "fusion principle," which allotted some minor offices to Negroes in exchange for black community backing for white Democrats who controlled the government.[7]

It was in this inauspicious racial climate that the Montgomerys, with uncharacteristically poor judgment, chose to expand their business to Vicksburg. Five years of successful operation as planters and merchants probably led them to expect continued profits from established enterprises and unlimited increases for those with the courage to expand. Thornton may have grown impatient with the limitation of their mercantile operations to the small population on the Bend. Perhaps, in his frequent visits to the city, he saw profitable stores that seemed to be operated much less efficiently than their own at Hurricane. As the business began to accumulate a bit of surplus capital despite the burden of payments for the Davis estates and Ursino, Thornton may have craved larger fields to conquer. The Dun credit-rating agency gave them consistently glowing reports, quoting Montgomerys' own statement of February 24, 1874, that their net capital totaled $75,000 to $100,000. It is possible that the Montgomery men disagreed about the wisdom of expanding their operations beyond the Bend, and therefore Ben and Isaiah took no active part in the new enterprise. At any rate, in late summer 1874 Thornton opened a store in downtown Vicksburg at the corner of Grove and Washington streets where the Freedmen's Savings Bank had recently closed its doors. Organized with $10,000 capital as W. T. Montgomery & Co., the business was backed by Montgomery & Sons of Davis Bend, according to the Dun reporter. Thornton also had two silent partners, B. L. Hickman and W. Lewis. Since both of these men performed vital functions in the parent corporation at Hurricane, it seems doubtful that they spent much time at the Vicksburg branch, although they probably invested some of their money in the venture. Within a few months the new firm was placing advertisements in newspapers as far away as Jackson, calling themselves "Commission Merchants, Wholesale & Retail Dealers in Groceries, Provisions and Plantation Supplies, Etc."[8]

No doubt Thornton expected to serve the dynamic black community in Vicksburg, which had grown by almost 500 percent from 1,433 in 1860 to 6,805 in 1870. Although there had been some erosion of the economic base of the community as a result of the financial panic of 1873, this recession had relatively little impact on local small businesses. A greater threat to the freedmen's prosperity was posed by the increasingly effective discrimination against black artisans and day laborers as a result of heightened political tensions. Vicksburg merchants began to hire white porters; railroad shops and a foundry barred Negro laborers; and the Vicksburg & Meridian Railroad replaced its colored mail agents with whites. Still, most black men and women continued to be employed as domestics, draymen, porters, or laborers because few whites were willing to fill these low-paid jobs. These black workers were a natural market for the black-owned W. T. Montgomery & Co. Furthermore, the store also catered to agricultural workers from the surrounding area, many of whom preferred the excitement of shopping in Vicksburg; for them, the advertisement promised "Liberal advances made on cotton."

For a time the store appeared to do well. It received good credit recommendations based largely on Ben's reputation as a man "of good character with white people & much influence with his own race." Eighteen months after the new firm opened, a Dun observer concluded that the Montgomerys were "a family of remarkable Negroes, who seem[ed] to be flourishing." All through 1876 the store continued to prosper, and the proprietors were "considered good for what they buy." As late as January 1877 a Dun report stated "Character &c. good. Capital $5,000 or $10,000, prospects good. Pay their paper promptly, & are generally considered good customers." However, just two months later, the agent announced cryptically, "Out of business here & gone to Hurricane." A July entry in the credit ledger for Montgomery & Sons commented, "W. T. Montgomery & Co. Vicksburg had to quit business."[9] Thornton's attempt to transfer the family's business success to the city had ended in failure. Perhaps the unfamiliar, transient clientele made Ben's way of extending credit too risky. Or, as political developments led to increased incidents of racial violence, fewer farmers may have chosen to patronize city merchants, preferring the security of plantation stores. Furthermore, the competitive market in Vicksburg may have proven too different from the more monopolistic setting at Hurricane; perhaps Thornton had made some unwise inventory and credit decisions in order to meet his competition. Whatever the reasons for its failure, the Vicksburg venture cost the Montgomerys dearly both in lost capital and in lowered standing with their creditors.

This first blemish on Ben's pristine credit rating came at a time when the family's enterprises were in greatest need of assistance.

Considering the times, perhaps the real question is not why the Vicksburg store failed but how it managed to operate for more than two years. The year 1874 was as disastrous for planters of the river counties as had been the early postwar years. The spring brought two waves of floods on the Mississippi following heavy rains upstream in March and again late in April. That summer the late plantings of cotton were seared by two months of drought; in July, Ben reported to Joseph Davis's granddaughter, "We have experienced extra difficulties in our cropping operations this season." The cotton yield along the river was reduced substantially, but the shortage was too localized to affect the world market. Prices continued to fall, averaging about 30 percent below those of the bumper year of 1870. Like all furnishing merchants, the Montgomerys suffered heavy losses when their customers were unable to produce enough cotton to cover their debts. Since their own crop was equally poor, the family was not able to recoup these losses in order to meet their own obligations to suppliers and mortgage holders. The Vicksburg store may have escaped the brunt of this disaster because, opening in midsummer, it probably sold primarily for cash until the beginning of the next crop year.[10]

Although 1875 did not bring such severe agricultural difficulties, the Montgomerys realized that they were overextended. Land prices had continued to fall with the decline of cotton, and the high interest payments on Hurricane and Brierfield were becoming more and more of a burden. In 1871 the plantations for which the Montgomerys had paid $300,000 five years earlier were assessed for $60,000 for tax purposes, and the next year a special act of the state legislature reduced the assessment of the mortgage to $75,000. The freedmen applied to the executors for a reduction in the mortgage itself, but were granted only a $3,000 decrease in the annual interest payments. As times worsened, even $15,000 proved more than the Montgomerys could pay.[11]

The disastrous summer of 1874 brought still another event that affected the Montgomerys and the association at Davis Bend: desperate for funds to support his family, Jefferson Davis brought suit against the other executors and heirs of Joseph Davis's estate, claiming that Brierfield was legally his. Acknowledging that his brother had never given him written title, Jefferson asserted that Joseph's verbal gift and his own occupation and development of the plantation since 1835 gave him a legal right to it. No one denied that Joseph had given his younger brother the land to use as his own; however, Joseph's will failed to make the gift explicit. As a skilled lawyer, Joseph must have been aware of the omission; perhaps he still feared federal confiscation of Jefferson's property, or he merely may have followed his lifelong habit of retaining control of his gifts to the family. At any rate, of the $300,000 combined estate, Joseph left bequests to his two grandchildren totaling $150,000 and to Jefferson's four children a total of $80,000. The remaining $70,000 was unassigned; Jefferson contended that it represented the value of Brierfield, which Joseph recognized was not his to bequeath. The younger Davis chose this time to press his claim because his four-year venture as president of a life-insurance company had ended with the failure of the firm, and he was in dire financial straits. His lawyers, noting that the statute of limitations would bar legal action after 1875, advised that, by acting promptly Jefferson might successfully contest the will.[12]

Joseph Davis's grandchildren, Joseph D. Mitchell and Lise Mitchell Hamer, countered with the contention that by 1869, when the will was written, their grandfather had realized that the decline in land values made his plantations worth no more than $230,000. He had made specific bequests for that amount, with the grandchildren receiving residuary rights to the additional $70,000 if the Montgomerys were ever able to pay it. Mitchell and Hamer cited the provisions of the will directing the executors to deal liberally with the Montgomerys as proof that Davis had not expected the latter to fulfill the entire sale contract.[13]

The Montgomerys, named as codefendants in the suit, were thus caught in the middle of a family quarrel that became increasingly acrimonious. Their first response was to renew their request to the executors to be released from their purchase agreement. In a formal reply to the suit they stated that they would be unable to make the stipulated payments on the two plantations because of agricultural disasters and the vast depreciation in land values; therefore, they were willing, "with the consent of all parties in interest, to cancel the purchase as to the whole, or as to Brierfield plantation, provided that their obligations to pay be cancelled."[14] The executors made no reply.

Ben was eager to maintain good relations with both sides in the controversy. He complied with Jefferson's request for a written statement that Joseph had sold the plantations with the understanding that, if his younger brother wanted possession of Brierfield upon his release from prison, the Montgomerys would rescind that part of their purchase. Later, Ben repeated the same information in a letter to Lise Hamer. In his testimony, Ben was carefully noncommittal, claiming that he knew nothing about the legal title to Brierfield; however, he had assumed it belonged to Jefferson since he lived there, paid taxes on it, and received the returns from its crops. He also stated that Joseph Davis remitted a part of the Montgomerys' interest payments to Jefferson, but denied knowledge of the amount of the payment or the proportion of the estates contained in Brierfield.[15] Whatever the outcome, the Montgomerys feared the factionalism that divided the Davis family.

The year 1874 dealt one final blow to the black family, which proved to be the most damaging of all. On the last day of the year Ben Montgomery was helping a crew raze one of the old houses in the quarters at Hurricane when a wall collapsed on him. According to Thornton, "one rib was broken and his hips and spine so injured that he could not walk." Two months later Dr. C. J. Mitchell stated that Ben had suffered a serious injury to the spinal cord that would be very slow to heal. In March Virginia reported that, although her father was now able to sit up, he was still unable to walk. Even after he recovered mobility Ben continued to be wracked by pain; although he seldom complained, he told his family that "something was very wrong inside." His forced confinement for almost six months and the aftermath of continuing pain effectively removed Ben from active management of the colony at Davis Bend. Having once relinquished his predominant role, the elder Montgomery seemed reluctant to resume it; he encouraged Thornton and Isaiah to continue in command. With the best will in the world, the sons could not exercise the same authority that Ben had built up over the years; they had neither his experience nor his business acumen. As outside forces brought increasing problems, the family sorely missed Ben's sure hand at the helm.[16]

Throughout the year 1875, Davis family members kept busy lining up favorable witnesses, thus forcing relatives and friends to take sides. The search extended to the Bend, where Jefferson secured testimony from former slaves Hagar Allen and Sam Charlton, among the first group he had bought in 1835. He sought to prove that his own bondsmen had cleared and developed Brierfield. The Hamer-Mitchell faction countered by persuading old Frank McKinney to testify that many of Joseph's slaves had also participated in that effort. This encouraged division within the black community and exacerbated discontent already prevalent in those difficult years. Ailing Ben Montgomery only hoped for an early decision of the court.[17]

On January 8, 1876, the chancellor dismissed the suit, ruling that Jefferson Davis was estopped from such action because he had accepted the terms of Joseph's will by administering it as an executor for four years prior to making his claim. The Hamers, Mitchell, and the Montgomerys immediately went to Vicksburg prepared to make some compromise with Jefferson, but the latter declared himself "weary of their trickery and vacillation" and refused to meet with them. Instead he directed his attorneys to prepare an appeal, which he filed in the Mississippi Supreme Court three months later, when two of the three Republican justices had been replaced by friendly ex-Confederates.[18]

These developments did nothing to solve the Montgomerys' worsening financial problem. Poor crops, the declining price of cotton, severe credit losses among their tenants, and the large interest payments on Hurricane and Brierfield combined to push them to the edge of bankruptcy. Their operations had always been conducted on a dangerously small capital reserve; now that narrow margin had disappeared, and they found themselves unable to obtain the necessary operating funds. Desperate for relief, Ben had hoped that Jefferson Davis would win his suit so that they might get out from under the Brierfield debt without penalty. When this failed, he proposed to Joseph's grandchildren that they take back Hurricane. Since the Montgomerys were unable to pay the interest on it, the Hamers and Joseph Mitchell agreed to occupy and cultivate the place rent-free, but they refused to release the freedmen from their contractual obligations. The Montgomerys were compelled to accept this arrangement, providing mules and supplies in lieu of the most recent overdue interest. By March 1876 the blacks' financial condition was so unsatisfactory that their New Orleans commission merchant would no longer honor their drafts, and Thornton hurried from New Orleans to Vicksburg, trying to find someone to accept their paper, payable in September.[19]

The Montgomery holdings were shrinking. With Lise and her husband and brother established at Hurricane, Isaiah moved his family into the Brierfield house with his parents and sisters. Gradually he transferred their greatly diminished store operations from Hurricane to Ursino. By October the Dun agent reported that their small stock of merchandise on the Bend was supplied weekly from the Vicksburg store. The year 1876 proved to be another poor cotton year along the river, so the Montgomerys were not able to recover any of their credit losses or, in turn, diminish their own debts.[20]

The rapid crumbling of the family's fortunes took its toll on an enfeebled Ben Montgomery. It was a wrenching experience to lose Hurricane, which had been either his home or his property for nearly forty years. The dissension within the Davis family was distressing, especially since the Montgomerys were dependent upon their goodwill. The freedmen had been unable to pay anything on the principal, all $300,000 of which was due January 1, 1876. Furthermore, the impeccable credit record Ben had maintained since 1841, which had carried him through the difficult postwar years, seemed irrevocably damaged as a result of the unfortunate Vicksburg store failure. All of these troubles aged the elder Montgomery very rapidly. As early as 1874, even before his injury, a Vicksburg newspaper had referred to him as "old Ben." In 1875, as the family's problems mounted, the elder Montgomery's slow recovery prompted Jefferson Davis to write suggesting a change in medical treatment. Nevertheless, Ben failed to regain normal health. The slender, intense black man had never been robust, and yet his strong will had driven his wiry frame through many hardships. However, on May 12, 1877, with no warning, his body finally gave up the struggle, and, at age fifty-eight, Benjamin Montgomery died.[21]

Strangely, considering his familiarity with legal procedures, Ben died intestate; the amount and complexity of his possessions only a few years earlier would seem to have mandated the preparation of a will. However, by the time of his death its lack posed no serious problem. In November Thornton petitioned the chancery court to be named administrator of the estate, and the next month his request was granted. As cosigner of his bond, Thornton secured J.W.N. Harris, one of the most prominent white lawyers in Vicksburg, who probably had handled all of the Montgomerys' legal affairs. The small size of the administrator's bond, in this case $500, shows how low Ben's fortunes had fallen by the time of his death; normally the bond was set at double the estimated worth of the estate. In subsequent years Thornton failed to file the required inventory or annual accounts of his administration of the estate, but, although the court cited him in 1880, there is no record that any action was taken.[22] The meager assets of the estate had simply melted away.

Ben's death was greeted with dismay in many quarters. Joseph Davis's executors noted that this further complicated their task, already made difficult by Jefferson's pending appeal. Commission merchants in New Orleans, St. Louis, and Vicksburg, although recently accustomed to dealing with Thornton, had based their original opinion of the Montgomerys' credit worthiness upon Ben's proven reliability; they felt uneasy without his steadying influence on the business. The Dun agent, noting that the freedmen had gotten behind in their payments, worried that "Montgomery Sr is dead" and the firm was now, in fact, "Montgomery's Sons." The colonists too must have felt disturbed; although Ben may not have assumed as large a paternal role as Joseph Davis, he had been for more than a decade the authority figure at Hurricane, Brierfield, and Ursino, and had been a person of considerable importance on the Bend for many years before that. His decisions had carried not only economic but also legal and moral weight in the community. Perhaps most important of all, his dream of an ideal "community of cooperation" had inspired them with the hope of creating a truly satisfying life on the old Davis plantations. Although there had always been some resentment, and the results of their efforts had become increasingly disappointing, many members of the association must have felt both grief and insecurity with the passing of Benjamin Montgomery.[23]

Ben's death, undoubtedly hastened by the decline in the Montgomery fortunes, seemed to accelerate that decline still further. Yet another tragedy struck the family that year: Martha, now living at Brierfield with Isaiah, five-year-old Willie, and his two-year-old sister Addie, gave birth to another son, who was named Benjamin, in honor of the deceased patriarch. However, the child, sickly from birth, survived only a few months.

In April 1878 the state supreme court reversed the lower court decision, and, with the two ex-Confederate justices overruling the lone remaining Republican, awarded Brierfield to Jefferson Davis. The legal aspects of the case are complex, and there is no doubt that Joseph had once given Brierfield to his younger brother; however, the court's decision seems clearly to have been based on political loyalties. It was nonetheless binding, and the Davis executors soon filed suit in chancery court to foreclose the Montgomery mortgage, which was by then two years in default. Thornton and Isaiah appealed the foreclosure decree to the state supreme court, delaying its enforcement in an effort to gain more favorable terms.[24]

The year 1879 brought the final demise of Montgomery & Sons as a mercantile firm. In January a Dun reporter noted that they owed $35,000 to Myer Weis & Co. of New Orleans, "and have judgements against them to the amount of $3,000 that can't be made." The situation had not improved by July, when the agents concluded, "We don't think it possible that they can work out." In December Dun canceled further reports on Montgomery & Sons, stating cryptically, "Owned by Myer Weis & Co." By this time all Montgomery operations had been gathered at the Ursino store, which continued to function as a small plantation commissary. Except for a brief period in 1880, Thornton still served as postmaster, having the title of the post office officially changed from Hurricane to Ursino in 1881.[25]

As their fortunes declined, Thornton became more interested in politics. Even after native white Mississippians had regained control of the local and state governments, Democratic politicans still came to the Bend seeking black votes. In the 1879 elections the plantations were visited by six of these men, "all Bourbon Democrats of old Southern lineage, except [one], and he was an

Ex-Confederate soldier." After listening to their speeches at the Hurricane schoolhouse, Thornton took them to Brierfield for the night. The next morning the Montgomery women served their guests an elaborate breakfast, but, unlike their father, Thornton and Isaiah shared the meal at the table with the white gentlemen. Even though he was less subservient than Ben, Thornton managed to win the approval of these and other powerful whites, who found him well read and "an agreeable talker." One Chicago reporter who interviewed him asserted, "His manners are better than those of nineteen-twentieths of the white men at the North; but he has to ride in the texas [lower, stern deck of a steamboat] here, and take a backseat in all public places. The gentlemen who know him, however, have a thorough respect for him." Through the operation of the fusion principle, Thornton was invited to serve as treasurer of Warren County for the year 1879. Affairs at Davis Bend no longer required the diligent effort that had marked the prosperous years of Montgomery ownership. Without his father to warn against it, Thornton probably welcomed both the salary and the duties of the office, which kept him in Vicksburg most of the year.[26]

Not only were the Montgomerys out of the retail business, their planting operations also were greatly curtailed. During the 1879 season they tilled only 1,000 acres instead of the 3,700 they had cultivated ten years earlier. Their landholdings at Ursino, valued at $50,000, were encumbered for at least $30,000. They listed the total value of their farm production at $50,000, compared with $192,000 in 1869. The entire focus of their farming had changed; by 1879 they raised only 800 bales of cotton, compared with 1,900 bales a decade earlier, but the value of their livestock was almost the same. They had more horses, mules, and cows at the later date and, in addition, listed 140 sheep and lambs, and 50 swine, none of which were included in the earlier inventory. As a result of this shift in emphasis toward livestock, the Montgomerys produced 6,000 bushels of corn instead of the 2,000 produced in 1869; they also raised 1,000 bushels of sweet potatoes, ten times their earlier yield, 300 bushels of oats, and 250 bushels of Irish potatoes. Thornton and Isaiah were attempting to diversify farm products and reduce their dependency upon cotton as the price continued its trend downward. Also, the poorer quality of the cotton lands at Ursino may have suggested the shift in products; their neighbor, W. S. Lovell, produced more than twice as many bales of cotton on half again as many acres. At the same time, he raised less than half as many sheep and hogs as the Montgomerys.[27]

By 1879 the planters on the Bend had changed their method of providing the necessary labor. At the beginning of the decade the Montgomerys had paid no wages, instead leasing the land to farmers to be worked on shares. However, in 1879 they reported paying $12,000 in wages for farm workers. Lovell and the Hamers also hired labor, paying $0.50 per day without board or $9 or $10 per month when board was included. Lovell maintained that the drop in the price of cotton to about ten cents per pound made these low wages necessary; he claimed that in order to attract and keep an adequate labor supply, he had reduced credit prices in his store to levels below that for cash the previous year.[28]

Nevertheless, many workers on the Bend and throughout the South were discontented. The economic downturn, combined with new political restraints and worsening race relations, culminated in a movement among the freedmen to emigrate to Kansas. In 1879, spurred on by a few messianic leaders, colorful advertisements of transportation companies, and their own disappointment with conditions in the South, several thousand freedmen sought a better life in the West. Most of those who joined the migration from Davis Bend came from the Montgomery lands; twenty-five families including some seventy people left in the month of March alone. In some cases their dissatisfaction was the result of personal antagonism; in 1875 Jefferson Davis told his wife that his favorites, Hagar Allen and Sam Charlton, had told him that they hated Ben Montgomery, adding, without citing evidence, "I fear that he has been unjust to those in whose special interest the places were sold to him." These few who blamed the Montgomerys for their misfortunes were joined by those who felt trapped in hopeless peonage to creditors who were themselves failing year by year. The *Chicago Tribune* reporter who visited the Bend in early May noted, "Many of [the Montgomerys'] laborers are heavily in debt to them for supplies, and these ran away."[29]

As a result of poor planning, the emigrants suffered great hardship on the journey westward. On the boat from St. Louis many contracted dysentery from drinking impure Missouri River water or pneumonia from exposure as deck passengers. Poor accommodations in Wyandotte, Kansas, only worsened their condition, and many sank into despair. William M. Nervis, who had been keeping those remaining at the Bend informed of the migrants' progress, now telegraphed the Montgomerys for help in bringing the people home. Isaiah immediately went to their assistance, finding "many sick and them all in bad condition generally. . . . Some eight or ten had died. . . ." Since the Montgomerys desperately needed their labor, Isaiah wired his brother that he was sending back fifty-nine of them by the first available steamer.[30]

However, this was not the sole reason why the younger Montgomery son had gone to Kansas. Perhaps more than Thornton, Isaiah had adopted the goal and belief of his father and his former master that the dream of an ideal black community could be realized under proper conditions. As the family's financial situation worsened, he sought reasons for the failure of the Davis Bend experiment. The *Tribune* reporter concluded, "their misfortunes are largely due to their liberality in dealing with their laborers." Isaiah became convinced that the fundamental problem lay elsewhere. In his view, success was impossible without the wholehearted cooperation of all the workers; there was too much discontent at Davis Bend, where "every little accident would make them get up and leave." As Isaiah later recounted, he "began to see that if a permanent colony was to be formed, the colored people must own the land themselves." This had proved to be impossible at Davis Bend, so he decided to investigate land in Kansas "for the purpose of establishing an agricultural colony where the negro might flourish under his own vine and fig tree."[31]

According to a reporter from the *Boston Herald*, Isaiah, "after journeying through the State, was so well pleased with the soil and prospects for moneymaking, that he decided to buy a section (640 acres) in Waubansee County." The newly formed Kansas Freedmen's Relief Association, a charitable group of Topeka citizens and officials concerned about the plight of the migrants, bought four sections of land adjacent to Isaiah's, which they proposed to divide into forty-acre plots to be sold to freedmen on easy terms. In addition to the sixty-four families occupying Relief Association land, Isaiah, who was to lead the colony, would provide plots for several more families on his section. John M. Brown, "a prosperous colored Mississippian," would superintend the construction of temporary barracks for the early settlers until they could build "shanties" for themselves. The cautiously optimistic Boston journalist asserted, "Should it do well, the frequently heard statement that the negro cannot thrive in Kansas will be disproved."[32]

In fact, the colony was successfully established, but, despite his high hopes for the project, Isaiah Montgomery never moved there as its leader; instead he returned to Davis Bend with most of the members of his delegation. Certainly he had no illusions about racial conditions in Mississippi. He asked the governor of Kansas to send communications to him without a return address to avoid attracting attention; he added, "Nothing is too hard to suspicion of this country, where it has been the custom for a century or more to ransack the Mails to prevent the circulation of documents breathing the spirit of freedom." Nonetheless, Isaiah rejected the move to Kansas. Perhaps he was uneasy about the climate and crops; or it might have been that their financial resources were too limited to risk a new start just then. It is also possible that the confusion attendant upon the mass migration of thousands of freedmen to Kansas discouraged Montgomery from choosing that location for his new experiment. In any case, although he decided not to join the emigrants who came to be known as the "Exodusters," he did not abandon the idea of establishing another ideal community.

Meanwhile, back in Mississippi, the foreclosure proceedings worked their way through the courts, and in February 1881 Thornton and Isaiah were notified that, unless they immediately remitted $392,000, Hurricane and Brierfield would be sold at public auction. There was no possibility of averting the sale; they had been able to pay only $6,000 interest for 1879 and nothing since then. Accordingly, on September 12, 1881, the plantations were auctioned to the Jefferson Davis family and Joseph Davis's grandchildren for a total of $75,288. Although a forced sale seldom brings the full value of the property, this sum probably was not far below the market price of the land. Isaiah later claimed that, even though they paid nothing on the principal, he and his family paid between $130,000 and $140,000 in interest during the years they held the plantations. This meant that during each of the ten years in which they fully cultivated both places, the Montgomerys paid an average of less than $3.50 per acre for the use of the land. Although a small portion of the acreage consisted of unimproved woodland and swamps, prime cotton lands constituted the bulk of the two estates. In 1868 Ben charged his tenants $4 to $6 per acre, which easily covered the landlords' average expenses; however, in later years rents undoubtedly declined with the value of the land. All things considered, including the fact that they posted no collateral, the Montgomerys' land costs seem to have been quite reasonable. By the same token, the Davis family had not suffered any loss. Their property had been saved from federal confiscation, and Joseph and his executors were convinced that the Montgomerys' management provided as great a return as they could have expected from any alternative. In fact, incomplete as the Montgomery interest payments were, they proved to average more than the heirs were able to realize in subsequent years. Extensive levee building upriver caused annual floods, which, combined with falling prices and the difficulty of retaining an adequate labor supply, prevented the Davis plantations from ever regaining their prewar prosperity.[33]

The final loss of Brierfield as well as Hurricane effectively ended Montgomery dominance of the Bend. After their fourth child was born at Brierfield in 1879, Isaiah and Martha moved their family to Ursino, where they had another son in 1880 and a daughter in 1882. By 1884 Thornton had moved on to other interests beyond Mississippi, although he remained the official postmaster at Ursino until February 1886. Family ties with the Bend were further weakened when Mary Montgomery died there in 1885. About this time Isaiah suffered a long illness and was unable to keep up the mortgage payments on Ursino, so that plantation too was lost. By 1886 all the living Montgomerys had left Davis Bend, and the experiment was at an end.[34]

What effect did this failure have on the ordinary members of the community? Unfortunately, it is impossible to know the extent to which they had adopted the Davis-Montgomery dream. It seems likely that Ben was able to build considerable enthusiasm for the experiment when he drafted and published his original appeal for members in 1866. He probably gave inspiring descriptions of his proposed utopia to the early recruits. Two difficult years discouraged some, but most were still hopeful in 1869, at the beginning of the prosperous years. However, after 1874 the combination of circumstances that led to the Montgomerys' failure also brought distress and discouragement to many colonists. Their hopes of achieving prosperity and independence gradually dimmed as their newfound political and civil rights were withdrawn. After reaching a level of affluence that was almost unprecedented for their race in the South, the Montgomerys lost everything in a few short years; observing this process, their associates must have lost faith in their own prospects.

Many of the early settlers had drifted away before the final foreclosure of Brierfield and Hurricane; no more than 10 percent of the families resident on the Montgomery plantations in 1870 were still there in 1880. Hurricane had the most long-term residents, including some former Davis slaves such as Willis Payne, who labored there with his wife and five children. Of the three Green brothers, only fifty-year-old Henry was still a resident; he, his wife, and their three sons were all laborers, with only their two young daughters exempt from field work. At Ursino the remnants of the Montgomery family were joined by three of Mary's brothers. William Lewis, Jr., still listed on the census roll as a planter, was able to support his wife, Susanna, and their three children at home; his household also included his wife's sister and three farmhands. Tony Lewis's wife too remained at home as a housekeeper; their son Isaac was employed as a schoolteacher, but their twenty-four-year-old daughter worked as a field hand. Moses Lewis and his wife, listed as farmer and housewife in 1870, were now both employed as laborers at Ursino. This downgrading, common to most Davis Bend households in the 1880 census, may have been a mere semantic change, since we noted earlier that most women spent some time each year in the fields. However, it seems likely that the new classification represented a real decline of status of both the women and their husbands. It now required the full-time effort of all the members to provide bare subsistence for most families.[35]

Among the oldtimers still resident on the Bend was Frank McKinney, born in Georgia shortly after 1800, sold South to Natchez when he was about twenty-five, and brought to Hurricane by Joseph Davis before 1830, in time to help develop both plantations. Under Davis's generous policies, Frank not only profited from legitimate petty trade, but, until discovered, also dealt in contraband whiskey with a poor white on a nearby island. After Yankee gunboat men destroyed the mansion, he tried to flee from Hurricane but was captured by Confederate raiders and spent the rest of the war in a labor gang. He returned to the Bend to join the Montgomery association, and by 1870 he and his old wife, Sally, had managed to accumulate $800 worth of personal property. However, in 1880 Frank was still listed as a laborer, although he was eighty years old. Sally had died and Frank had married a thirty-year-old woman with three young children; their household also included three male and one female field hands.[36]

Although old Frank seemed to feel at home only at Davis Bend, his attachment was not shared by many of his contemporaries. In addition to the former Davis slaves who left with Ben Ousley in 1870—settling near Newton, Mississippi—some of those who went to Kansas in the exodus of 1879 never returned to the Bend. Still others scattered after all of the Montgomerys moved away. Granderson Bray and his wife, Amanda, remained at Hurricane through 1880, but subsequently migrated to Arkansas. There, in 1895, at the age of seventy-eight, Granderson died of a heart attack in the field where he and Amanda were picking cotton. Their neighbors at Corner Stone, near Pine Bluff, included former Davis hands George Steward, William Kannigan, and "old lady Hagar Allen," who had told Jefferson Davis twenty years earlier that she hated Ben Montgomery.[37]

By the mid-1880s there were few traces left of the cooperative experiment that Ben Montgomery had launched with such high hopes in 1866. It had fallen victim to the inexorable forces of the world cotton market, the domestic economy, floods, insect pests, and the changing political climate. But it was also a casualty of the Montgomerys' mismanagement, based at least in part on their commitment to an impossible dream. With a dangerously inadequate capital reserve, Ben had insisted upon premature expansion to Ursino, when the profits of prosperity should have been plowed back into a more limited enterprise. Without Ursino, they might not have been able to save their firm, but perhaps they could have remained afloat somewhat longer. On the other hand, if the Davis executors had been willing to release the Montgomerys from their contract for Hurricane and Brierfield in 1870, the model colony might have had a chance for success at Ursino. However, Ben's goal was a black cooperative community embracing most, if not all of the island, and he could not resist an early opportunity to broaden its scope. In his view, the more land he had to lease, the more able members of the association he could attract. His hopes were built upon a conviction that honest, industrious people working in independence and harmony would create an ideal society, free from the ruinous competition and needless friction that marred most societies. He insisted that Montgomery & Sons continue to extend credit to all members whom he deemed men of goodwill. When many of them fled, leaving the firm with huge, unrecoverable debts, Ben must have questioned his own judgment of individuals but probably did not doubt the capacity of mankind to create a utopia. There were so many outside forces that made for credible scapegoats that Montgomery may well have died with his convictions intact.

However, the dream was not interred with Ben Montgomery. His second son had imbibed the concept as a boy while listening to discussions between his master and his father. Just as Ben saw crippling flaws in the Davis system, so Isaiah thought he knew what had gone wrong with his father's experiment. Ben had believed that the essential element lacking in the antebellum community was the personal freedom of its members; he saw the basic contradiction in the concept of a "community of cooperation" among slaves. Given the opportunity to come together voluntarily and operate as independent agents, free from white control, Ben thought they could achieve true harmony. When dissension and dishonesty arose among the associates, the elder Montgomery blamed individual character weakness, but Isaiah believed they lacked sufficient motivation. The younger man recognized the great hunger for landownership, which had sparked the development of much of early America. In the agrarian society of the South, the possession of land was still the true measure of success, as it had been when Joseph Davis acquired Davis Bend in the 1820s. The first goal of most freedmen after the war was to buy a plot of their own, but Ben Montgomery had made no provision for this in his model colony. Isaiah himself knew the thrill of working his own fields and sympathized with the desires of his fellow freedmen. Only by owning their own land could they be expected to become stable, responsible members of the association.[38] Although Isaiah had rejected Kansas as a suitable site for a new venture, he still cherished the hope of someday establishing a successful agricultural community owned by the blacks themselves. When he left the Bend permanently, Isaiah took with him his own version of the Davis-Montgomery dream.

IV

Isaiah Montgomery Revives the Dream

7

Mound Bayou

It was with the same notion of carrying out, under new conditions, the plan which his father and his former master had formed years before, that, in 1887, Mr. Montgomery—as he says in a brief autobiography—"sought to begin anew, at the age of forty, the dream of life's young manhood."[1]

Isaiah Montgomery tried to create a satisfactory life for himself and his family in Vicksburg's black community. In 1885 he set up a small mercantile firm on the outskirts of town near the national cemetery. Perhaps by avoiding the central business district he hoped to minimize opportunities for racial harassment. He also became active in black civic affairs, joining James Hill and J. J. Spelman in organizing the first Colored Fair held at Jackson that year. The leaders succeeded in getting generous subscriptions from white merchants for prizes to be awarded to blacks who exhibited the best livestock, agricultural products, baked goods, and needlework. Isaiah was invited to join the governor, two white senators, and ex-Senator Blanche K. Bruce in addressing the crowd during the four-day fair. In 1886 Montgomery solicited a premium from the Jefferson Davises to be awarded in their name at the Second Annual Colored Fair. However, despite his prominence in black society, Isaiah was not satisfied with his life or that of his fellow freedmen in Vicksburg.[2]

Thornton Montgomery had chosen to begin a new venture far from the scene of their previous failure. After serving a term as county treasurer, he had become disillusioned with the prospects for Negroes in Mississippi and decided to try his luck in the northern Great Plains. There, land was cheap and it was said that a man was judged by his skill and industriousness rather than by the color of his skin. By 1884 Thornton had settled south of Fargo in the Dakota Territory on a section of land bisected by the new Chicago, Milwaukee, St. Paul, and Pacific Railroad. There, surrounded by Scandinavian homesteaders, the elder Montgomery prospered, enlarging his holdings from the original 640 acres to 1,020 acres and building a grain elevator, which became the center of a small community called Lithia, a stop on the all-important railroad. Thornton was respected by his neighbors and by leading citizens of Fargo. In September 1884 the *Fargo Daily Argus* reported that Montgomery, "a most worthy man," had been asked to represent Dakota in the World's Exposition at New Orleans. By 1889 a black newspaper in Minneapolis–St. Paul labeled him "the largest colored farmer in the Northwest."[3]

Thornton was well satisfied not only with his financial success but with race relations in the new region. He hired the Joseph Hollands, white migrants from Wisconsin, to keep house for him and manage the farm. They remained close friends even after the Hollands left his employ to take up a place of their own in the neighborhood. Montgomery hired a series of white managers, housekeepers, and farmhands over the years in that labor-short area and never felt that his color was a handicap. However, there were other disadvantages that made the Dakota venture seem undesirable to the Mississippians whom Thornton tried to persuade to join him. First, the cultivation of wheat in a semiarid climate required entirely different methods than those employed in cotton culture in the lower Mississippi Valley; Thornton's family and friends were unfamiliar with these techniques. Furthermore, the severity of the winters was frightening to people who seldom saw snow or felt temperatures more than a few degrees below freezing. Stories of blinding blizzards and paralyzing sub-zero temperatures discouraged prospective migrants among the Vicksburg freedmen. Thornton himself found the Dakota winters intolerable. After spending the first one in a Fargo hotel, he decided to leave the management of his farm to his employees and subsequently wintered in Vicksburg. Although he remained active in the Republican party, he missed the involvement in race politics that had intrigued him in Mississippi. Avid reading of current newspapers and an extensive correspondence with such leaders as the venerable Frederick Douglass failed to compensate for his isolation.[4] Thornton tried unsuccessfully to induce his brother to lead a group of former Davis blacks to take up land in his neighborhood. Although Isaiah was restless in Vicksburg, he was convinced that his dream could never be realized on the vast plains of Dakota Territory.

However, Isaiah learned from his brother's experience that a railroad could be just as effective a highway of commerce as the Mississippi River, and it had the advantage of never flooding the fields. Therefore, he was immediately interested when James Hill told him that the Louisville, New Orleans, and Texas Railroad was offering bargains in rich, alluvial land along their new line from Memphis to Vicksburg, through the Yazoo Delta. As a result of encouraging correspondence with Major George W. McGinnis, manager of their land office, Isaiah made several trips through the bayous that bordered the railroad right-of-way. Exploration was difficult because hardwood trees and dense undergrowth of cane and briers formed an almost impenetrable wall on either side of the railway embankment through which he had to hack his way; however, he noted that the lush growth promised rich soil for the settler. Finally, in the spring of 1887 he chose a site almost midway between Memphis and Vicksburg, fifteen miles east of the Mississippi and four miles west of the Sunflower River. He called it Mound Bayou for the large Indian mound at its center where two bayous converged.

Isaiah returned home and, after consulting Martha, decided to sell their Vicksburg interests and invest everything in a new colony in the virgin delta. He persuaded his cousin, Ben Green, to give up his small store in Newton and join them in buying 840 acres at the new site. The Montgomerys and Green began to advertise their venture among blacks in and around Vicksburg. They especially sought out remnants of the Davis Bend community who had shared in the prosperous years of that experiment. As a friend later noted, "It was not easy . . . to find settlers in that early day. The task of taming this wild country seemed hopeless to men with so few resources and so little experience." However, by midsummer they had recruited a little band made up primarily of former Davis slaves seeking "social and economic as well as physical . . . freedom." Despairing of achieving their goal in an integrated society, the migrants later claimed that they "set out to develop their institutions unencumbered by the handicaps imposed upon them by the dying traditions of the past."[5]

Legend has it that, after the small group of pioneers got off the train and it chugged away, Isaiah, "the black Moses who had led them through the wilderness to this place," gave a powerful speech that inspired them to undertake the tremendous task of carving out a colony. Montgomery himself later reported, "I told them . . . that they might as well buy land and own it and do for themselves what they had been doing for other folks for two hundred and fifty years." This philosophy of self-help and independence from white interference must have seemed familiar to the veterans of the Davis Bend colony. However, this time they were to start out as owners of their own plots of forty or more acres which the railroad sold them for seven dollars per acre, one dollar down and the balance in five equal payments. By the end of the year more than 700 acres had been purchased on these terms, and Isaiah's theory that landownership would make steady, responsible colonists was about to be tested.[6]

Life was difficult for the first permanent settlers who arrived at Mound Bayou in early 1888. The men built crude cabins from the first timber they cleared on their own land, then some of them who had exhausted their savings hired out to Montgomery and Green to clear some five acres for the town. One of the pioneers sent his wife and children to do that work while he cut staves in the woods. Others maintained themselves by cutting railroad ties, for which there was a ready market. Martha Montgomery and Ben Green set up a sawmill, which they operated in conjunction with the small mercantile firm they had established on some of the first cleared land in the village. Timber agents eagerly bought all the cypress, oak, and ash lumber they could supply. By this means the colonists harvested a cash crop while clearing their fields for cultivation. Even so, many of them suffered real hardship. During cotton chopping or picking season, the women and children worked for white planters on the nearest plantations, some nine or ten miles away, and the men sometimes tried to cut timber in the daytime and roll logs at night. In spite of all this effort, one man reported that he and his family often existed on bread and water, with meat a rare luxury. They considered it a stroke of luck when he managed to kill two bear cubs one day, especially since bears and raccoons had been ravaging the patches of corn the settlers had planted between the stumps. The forests were also full of deer, panthers, and wolves, all fair game for black hunters.[7]

The colonists managed to survive the rigorous first three years, having earned a total of $8,780 from timber sales, and, in addition, having produced 379 bales of cotton and 3,045 bushels of corn on the 655 acres they had cleared. Within three months after his arrival, Isaiah had persuaded the Post Office Department to allow him to open a branch in Mound Bayou; according to the town historian, "The first post office consisted of a wooden soap box partitioned to form 'pigeon holes' " located in the hall of the Montgomery home. Mary Virginia, who, with Rebecca, had accompanied Isaiah's family on the venture, had soon set up a school in one room of the Montgomery house, where she taught the children whose parents could spare them from field work. As one observer reported, "The wilderness had become the frontier. The colonists came in faster now. The ragged outline of the forest steadily receded in all directions." Mound Bayou was well on its way to becoming an independent Negro community.[8]

By 1907, twenty years after its founding, the village had become the center of a thriving agricultural colony of some 800 families, with a total population of about 4,000 blacks. Of the 30,000 acres owned by the colonists, between 5,000 and 6,000 were under cultivation, producing about 3,000 bales of cotton annually and more than half the corn and fodder consumed by the community. The town site now included some 96 acres for its population of about 500. Business enterprises had grown along with the number of colonists; there were 13 stores and a number of small shops doing a combined annual business of about $600,000. The train station in the center of town was a hub of activity, handling $40,000 in freight and $6,000 in passenger traffic each year. The sawmill, still turning out valuable lumber from the local hardwood, had been joined by three cotton gins, all of which were busy during harvest season. Communication with the outside world was facilitated by a telephone exchange; the company engineer who installed it, the only white man ever resident in the town, remained only long enough to train local operators. A weekly newspaper, *The Demonstrator,* carried church and social news and racially oriented editorials, along with advertisements for local and regional products.[9]

According to one minister, the six churches in town and four more within the colony were "by far too many," certainly more than the people could adequately support. One of the two private schools in the settlement, the Mound Bayou Normal and Industrial Institute, had been established with American Missionary Association assistance when the colony was only three years old. Twenty years later it was headed by the Reverend B. F. Ousley, a descendant of Ben Ousley, the former Davis slave who led the group migration from Davis Bend in 1870. This school and one sponsored by the Colored Baptist Church of Bolivar County each accommodated more than a hundred pupils, mostly from the country, who paid one dollar per month for the vocational and religious education they could not get in the brief term at the public schools.

The heart of the business community was the Bank of Mound Bayou, organized in 1904 with a capital stock of $10,000 by Charles Banks, formerly a businessman in Clarksdale, Mississippi. The president of the bank, John Francis, had come to the village from New Orleans as a clerk in Montgomery & Green's store; after Ben Green's murder in 1896, he married his widow and managed her large estate. The bank's board of directors included the most prominent men in the colony: R. M. McCarthy, who owned one of the gins as well as considerable real estate; T. C. Jordan, proprietor of a bakery and meat market; H. A. Godbold, who ran a general store; C. R. Stringer, town treasurer; and J. H. Barker, town marshal. Thornton Montgomery was also a director of the bank; before the turn of the century the inhospitable climate and difficulty of securing capable managers had induced him to sell his Dakota lands at a sizable profit and join his brother in the Mound Bayou venture. A contemporary observed:

> The bank and its directors, because they represent and are so completely identified with the interests of the town, have come to have

the position of a sort of chamber of commerce, guarding the credit of the various enterprises and directing and inspiring the economic and business development of the colony.[10]

Thornton Montgomery and Charles Banks also established the Mound Bayou Loan and Investment Company as a means of preventing the intrusion of white ownership in the colony. The Louisville, New Orleans, and Texas Railroad held mortgages on much of the land sold to freedmen since the colony's founding. A few years after the Illinois Central bought the railroad and renamed it the Yazoo and Mississippi, there were rumors that the new owners planned a wholesale foreclosure of Mound Bayou mortgages. Banks and his associates in the bank managed to get the loans renewed, but the threat prompted these town leaders to seek an alternative credit source for the colonists. The new loan company, capitalized at $50,000, planned to sell stock to farmers at $50 per share, payable in monthly installments of $1. Thus local capital would be accumulated to cover defaulted mortgages while more successful farmers built up their savings. Banks and the Montgomerys hoped by this means eventually to be able to finance new settlers, keeping more business control within the community rather than in potentially hostile white hands.[11]

The government of the colony also was kept under black control. The village of Mound Bayou, incorporated in 1898, had the usual officials—a mayor, three aldermen, a constable, and a town marshal—all local people, elected by the adult males of the village. In practice, however, all questions of importance were decided by an informal town meeting much like the ones held at Davis Bend, in which the women took as active a part as the men. For example, in January 1906, after a particularly poor crop year, the citizens assembled to discuss their situation. Speakers pointed out that not only the weather but also bad planning must be blamed for their straitened circumstances. It was suggested that the colonists should strive to drain more land, plant earlier, and produce more than one annual crop of vegetables on each garden plot. Speakers generally agreed that everyone must work harder and learn to live within his means, foregoing luxuries bought on credit. Sharecroppers and day laborers were admonished to increase their working hours and improve "the character of their services." Furthermore, all idlers who congregated in the town, "contributing to the enticement and demoralization of the community," were warned that they would no longer be tolerated. The consensus of the meeting was printed in a leaflet and circulated by a committee headed by Isaiah Montgomery.[12]

A town meeting was called to deal with the problem of illicit liquor sellers who ran what were called "blind tigers," where farmers in town on Saturday bought drinks and then frequently started fights. The citizens delegated the mayor, the treasurer, and the town marshal to gather evidence and prosecute the guilty; as a result, six persons were fined and forced to cease operations. Montgomery subsequently reported that four of these had been reformed simply by returning to their farms and engaging in useful work; a fifth, a woman, left town; and the sixth was still under suspicion. Another meeting of the citizens was held when white liquor interests attempted to influence some local voters in order to repeal the county prohibition law. Montgomery explained to the assembly how damaging it would be to their people to have saloons readily available, even if the local ones were run by blacks. He noted later, "We voted the law down and there has been no serious attempt to open the county to liquor traffic since."[13]

The townspeople were determined to create a proper moral environment within their model community. One year, each church delegated a member to serve on a committee that made a house-to-house canvass "to determine to what extent loose family relations existed." Subsequently, a town meeting decided that the forty unmarried couples found living together must either marry or leave the colony; most chose the former course. Less choice was given to the prostitutes who frequented the town on payday. The colonists agreed that no one should provide lodgings for them; instead, the women would be ordered to leave on the next train. Within a few weeks word of this ruling spread through the Delta, and from then on Mound Bayou was free of this problem.[14]

The settlement was remarkably free of serious crime; in its first twenty years, there were only two homicides. As a friendly observer reported, "Both of these were committed by strangers—men who drifted into the community in the early days before the local self-government and the traditions of the town had been established." Ben Green's assailant, who murdered him in a quarrel over a box of tacks, was identified as a fugitive wanted for a serious crime in Alabama. Most of the cases in the mayor's court involved petty crimes such as gambling, selling liquor, or failing to pay the street tax of three dollars or its equivalent in work each year. When Isaiah was asked how he explained their lack of law-enforcement problems, he replied:

> I attribute it to the force of public opinion. The regulations that we enforce have public sentiment behind them. The people recognize that the laws . . . represent the sentiment of the community and are imposed for their own good. It is not so easy for them to realize that where the government is entirely in the hands of white men.[15]

Like colonial New England towns or tribal villages in West Africa, Mound Bayou relied on public opinion in a close-knit, homogeneous society, rather than on the sanction of law, to prevent undesirable behavior.

Isaiah Montgomery was convinced that the colony's achievements could have been accomplished only in a segregated environment. He was disturbed by the tendency of young residents to move to larger towns or cities where they were forced to live in the poorest sections and exposed to the worst influences. Still adhering closely to the Jeffersonian belief in the virtue of the yeoman farmer, which Joseph Davis had advocated so persuasively, Isaiah was inclined to prescribe a back-to-the-farm movement as the cure for all social ills. He was sure that this formula would reform anyone, whether he was guilty of gambling, selling or drinking liquor, living in sin, or planning to move to the city. However, he did not want to see the new generation adopt the outmoded farming methods of their parents. He was troubled by the fact that so much of the farming at Mound Bayou was still done "in the sticks," that is, among the tree stumps, because of the difficulty of clearing the fields completely. Like his father and his former master, Isaiah was an advocate of scientific cultivation and insisted that "the people must be induced to take up intensified and diversified farming." In 1907 his immediate goal was the establishment of an agricultural school in the village using the curriculum and personnel from Tuskegee, where his friend, Booker T. Washington, was at the height of his power.[16]

By the turn of the century the position of the Negro in the South had worsened dramatically. In 1901 Isaiah commented on "the political circumstances which render the lives and property of colored people insecure all over the South." Although organized Ku Klux Klan activities had declined after the reestablishment of southern white control of local and state governments, terrorist tactics were regularly employed by white mobs to keep blacks in subservient positions. Evidence of financial success of members of the recently enslaved race was often sufficient provocation for violence. For example, Montgomery received an appeal for assistance from a black man who ran a printing shop and published a Baptist newspaper at West Point in Clay County. He had "a decent home and a Piano" and kept a horse and buggy to take his daughter to and from the shop, where she served as his cashier and bookkeeper. One day while he was in Jackson on business, a white mob chased his daughter home, terrorized the family, and ordered them to leave town within three days. When he wrote Isaiah, the printer was negotiating with the county sheriff and the local banker in an effort to sell his property, though he was forbidden to enter the town. Another Montgomery correspondent, a small grocer, was forced to flee from town, leaving his business because he was considered too prosperous. A successful merchant was forced to sell his carriage and walk, while a black man who ran two hacks from the depot was ordered to sell one of them. All of these men thought themselves fortunate to escape the beatings or lynchings that were all too common. Such stories enraged black citizens of the state, but there seemed little they could do about it. Normal political avenues of redress were increasingly closed to them; black voters were kept from the polls by physical threat or fear of economic reprisal. In this atmosphere, Mound Bayou stood out as an oasis of freedom and autonomy for oppressed Negroes.[17]

As a resident of Bolivar County, Montgomery took a more active part in politics than his father had deemed wise at Davis Bend. Isaiah was well acquainted with the black Republican politicians in Vicksburg and Jackson, working closely with them after he left the Bend. In 1884 he served as a delegate to both the Warren County and the district party conventions and campaigned actively for James G. Blaine throughout the congressional district. Early in 1888, soon after he arrived at Mound Bayou, Isaiah was contacted by the leading black Republican there, Circuit Clerk Joseph E. Ousley, another ex-slave from Hurricane and named for his former master. Ousley immediately placed Montgomery on the Bolivar County Republican Committee. Two years later, the Republicans in that heavily black county decided to oppose the Democratic slate for the impending state constitutional convention on the grounds that the dominant whites had totally ignored the fusion principle in recent elections, refusing to give even minor offices to freedmen. Isaiah was persuaded to stand for election, although he declined to campaign actively, making only an initial address of announcement. He claimed to have told his Republican supporters that he had little hope of positive accomplishment at the convention, although he evidently did not inform them of his attitude toward the goal of the white delegates, which was to legalize the disfranchisement of black voters. At any rate, he was elected and seated as the only Negro and the only avowed Republican at what the Democrats had billed as an all-white constitutional convention.[18]

By supporting the faction that favored reducing representation in the black counties and, in effect, barring black but not white illiterates from the polls, Isaiah was given a seat on the crucial franchise committee. He later reported, "Such a prolonged and fiery discussion took place over this live subject, that I was induced to give it close study." He decided to support the committee report and gave a long, eloquent speech to the convention, advocating the virtual disfranchisement of blacks in Mississippi. He claimed that his mission was "to bridge a chasm that has been widening and deepening for a generation . . . that threatens destruction to you and yours, while it promises no enduring prosperity to me and mine." He reminded his listeners that slaves had developed the state's plantations where "every acre represents a grave and every furrow a tear." He traced the history of black performance during the recent "fratricidal war," and subsequently, when Northerners gained the freedmen's confidence but not their affection. Montgomery conceded that the ex-slaves lacked political experience but told the whites, "You have suffered your prejudice to set bounds and limits to our progress." As a result, he asserted, "we . . . lack confidence in your professions of good will," and confidence must be restored before the racial conflict could be ended. He claimed that the dispute had weakened both the treasury and the moral fiber of the state, and he supported the committee's goal of eliminating the "blood-shed, bribery, ballot-box stuffing, corruption, and perjury" that had characterized recent elections. Montgomery admitted that the new law would disfranchise more than 123,000 black voters and only 11,000 whites, giving the latter a safe majority of 40,000 voters. However, he was willing to sacrifice black voting rights for a scheme that would, he believed, end "the grave dangers" of a race conflict and "inaugurate an era of progress" for the entire state.[19]

Isaiah's accommodating speech not only spurred the convention to prompt passage of the measure, but also elicited considerable reaction around the nation. Not surprisingly, assessments divided along racial lines. Democratic newspapers in the state gave the speech high praise; the *New York World* printed it in full and dispatched a correspondent to Jackson to get a photograph and biography of "this hitherto obscure Orator." Even former President Grover Cleveland hailed the enlightened stand of this remarkable freedman. Almost fifty years later a Mississippi senator still recalled with admiration the courage of "this quiet unassuming man . . . who boldly advocated restriction of the right of suffrage in the interest of future development of the race . . . although the negroes were at the time in the majority in the state in the ratio of about two to one."[20]

Leading black spokesmen saw Montgomery's speech in a different light. In New York Henry F. Downing, president of the United States African News Company, sent a copy of the full text to a number of black leaders, inviting expressions of opinion for publication. Downing said, "[Montgomery's] surrender of the rights of 123,000 Negroes upon the altar of expediency is an act unprecedented either for its heroism or for its audacity. Which?" Not one of the replies published in T. Thomas Fortune's *New York Age* supported Isaiah's stand. The venerable Frederick Douglass, while cautioning that "we may denounce his policy, but must spare the man," went on to label his address "a positive disaster to the race." Claiming that Isaiah had been taken in by the lying whites, Douglass concluded, "No thoughtless, flippant fool could have inflicted such a wound upon our cause as Mr. Montgomery has done in this address." In more moderate language T. McCants Stewart suggested that Montgomery, on the scene, might be better able to judge what must be done, but pointed out that the scheme he advocated would allow election judges to enfranchise illiterate whites while barring all colored people. The Mississippi politician, John R. Lynch, by this time an auditor in the U.S. Treasury Department, restrained his rage with difficulty:

> The entire scheme is a fraud, a sham and a swindle, the sole purpose of which is to perpetuate the ascendency of the Democrtatic party in the State. That Mr. Montgomery should have made the mistake of advocating the adoption of such a scheme is a great disappointment to his friends, although no one who knows the man will impute to him any other than honest motives and sincere purposes.[21]

Historians since that time have found Isaiah's behavior at the 1890 convention difficult to explain. Lynch, in his *Autobiography,* suggested that Montgomery might have been merely placating the whites in order to retain his seat, but admitted he found that an inadequate explanation. He concluded that the reasons for such action by a man of more than average intelligence with "the reputation of being honest and honorable" would always remain "an inexplicable mystery." This judgment was echoed by Vernon Wharton in 1947 and Louis Harlan in 1974. However, J. Saunders Redding found a credible explanation in Montgomery's desire to prevent "the white man's intrusion upon his private domain."[22] There is little reason to doubt that Isaiah was concerned about the security of his infant colony, which was only three years old; the lynching and "white cap" terrorism of the era was enough to frighten any black leader. Ben Montgomery had taught his son that the best security came from the patronage of powerful members of the white elite, so Isaiah naturally sought to win the favor of the convention leaders. However, there is little reason to believe that he saw the new law as a wrenching sacrifice of black rights. In his view, blacks had little useful political power to sacrifice; their legal voting rights could be exercised only at great physical or economic risk. The dominant whites were determined to maintain white supremacy, and there was no effective way the freedmen could oppose them until they had gained more education, experience, and above all, wealth. Montgomery believed that this process of "race elevation" could occur only in segregated communities such as Mound Bayou; until it happened, voting rights were of minor importance. This did not mean that he considered blacks incapable of political participation—he confidently instituted self-government in Mound Bayou. He merely believed that the time was not ripe for their entry into white politics at the state and national levels. Modern critics may say that his advocacy of disfranchisement delayed this entry in the twentieth century, but Montgomery could not see that possibility in 1890. He thought he was acting in the best interests of his colony, and their example would benefit all Mississippi blacks. Given local conditions at the time, his judgment was not implausible.

At any rate, Isaiah's fame as a result of his speech brought some tangible benefits to Mound Bayou. That same year he joined a black delegation to Washington seeking appropriations to build effective levees along the Mississippi-Yazoo delta. When this lobbying effort succeeded, he represented his section before the commission charged with allocating the appropriated funds. Montgomery also became more influential in state Republican politics, working to ensure federal appointments for men sympathetic to black interests. However, the most significant and enduring result of his 1890 speech was his friendship with Booker T. Washington, soon to become the most important Negro in America. In 1895 Isaiah served as one of the black commissioners at the Atlanta Exposition where Washington gained national attention for his famous speech disavowing any desire for immediate social or political equality and advocating economic progress through hard work as the means of black advancement. Washington's philosophy of self-help and racial solidarity sounded both sensible and familiar to Montgomery, who had heard his father advocate the same course of action during his childhood at Hurricane. Isaiah shared Ben's faith in hard work and economic achievement as a means of winning acceptance in the white world. Washington's establishment of a vocational agriculture program at Tuskegee Institute in Alabama institutionalized the very goals toward which Ben Montgomery had always worked: development of the best methods of scientific farming, and their dissemination among black farmers in the South. Isaiah's model colony at Mound Bayou was the perfect testing ground for those ideas that he and Washington shared. As Washington's influence grew, Montgomery and his community became the beneficiaries of his favor. In 1911 the founder of Tuskegee labeled Mound Bayou a "place where a Negro may get inspiration by seeing what other members of his race have accomplished . . . [and] where he has an opportunity to learn some of the fundamental duties and responsibilities of social and civic life."[23] The colony had gained a powerful ally.

In 1900 Montgomery joined Washington in organizing the National Negro Business League in Boston. At this and subsequent conventions, Isaiah gave enthusiastic speeches describing Mound Bayou and its prospects; as a result, he won some vigorous new settlers for the town. Charles Banks, a vice-president of the league who owned a thriving general store in Clarksdale, Mississippi, was so inspired by Isaiah's presentation at the Chicago meeting in 1901 that he arranged to sell his firm and by 1904 had organized and opened the Bank of Mound Bayou. In 1911 Booker T. Washington called Banks "the most influential Negro business man in the United States" and "the leading Negro banker in Mississippi."[24] Another member of the Business League who deserted Clarksdale to join Mound Bayou's business community was Eugene P. Booze, who married one of Isaiah's daughters and, in 1909, assisted Banks and Montgomery in establishing the Farmer's Cooperative Mercantile Company, which became one of the town's major enterprises.

After 1890 Montgomery never again stood for elective office, but he accepted an appointive government position, which proved to be an even greater mistake; the compensating benefits to Mound Bayou that followed his controversial speech at the constitutional convention were totally absent from his venture as a federal official.

President Theodore Roosevelt was eager to place capable Negroes in federal posts in the South. With the approval of Booker T. Washington, Roosevelt's major advisor on race matters, he directed Edgar S. Wilson, who headed the U.S. Land Office in

Mississippi, to offer Montgomery an appointment as collector of government monies. The busy mayor of Mound Bayou, echoing his father a generation earlier, asserted, "I am loath to turn aside for political preferment." However, Wilson and other state Republicans urged him to accept; hence, in the spring of 1902 Montgomery took up his new duties at the state capital. He had never administered anything larger than Montgomery & Sons of Davis Bend or the village government of Mound Bayou, and seemed a bit bewildered by the complicated bureaucracy of the Interior Department. At the end of the year his job was further complicated by budget cuts that forced a reduction in his experienced clerical staff; early the next year, his able assistant was promoted out of the land office. With his many responsibilities in Mound Bayou taking much of his time and attention, Montgomery really had not mastered his federal duties when, one Sunday morning in May 1903, a special agent from Washington conducted a surprise inspection of his operations. Thornton later claimed that the audit was instigated by a Republican faction in the state that wanted to oust all black officeholders; certainly there was considerable rivalry within the party at that time. Whatever his purpose in making the unusual visit, the agent treated Montgomery rudely after he discovered that almost $5,000 of government funds had been deposited in Isaiah's personal account. Although the money was immediately returned, the agent recommended that the black official be asked to resign and, if he failed to comply, "be summarily removed from office." The inspector feared that the story might leak out and "result in an attack on the administration for shielding and whitewashing a nigger."[25]

As Booker T. Washington's secretary, Emmett Jay Scott, reported to his boss, Isaiah was "terribly broken up & disconcerted" when they met in New Orleans to discuss the wisest course of action. Scott insisted that Montgomery resign at once instead of waiting until fall "to save his face." Although, as his brother asserted, Isaiah was "not a combative man," he remained obdurate on this score and retained his government position until the following November, even though President Roosevelt told Wilson of his resignation in June. In the interim Montgomery appealed to Captain A. A. Sharp, president of the Roundaway Manufacturing Company, which operated a very profitable 10,000-acre cotton plantation in the Delta. Sharp wrote to Stuyvesant Fish, president of the Illinois Central Railroad—which owned both the local rail line and Roundaway—asking him to plead Isaiah's cause with Secretary of the Interior E. A. Hitchcock. Sharp insisted that Montgomery, a man of the highest integrity, had been guilty of no more than a technical error, and deserved a fair hearing. The black man had "always been a conservative good citizen," guiding the people of his race "in the right way," and Sharp wished his section had "more men of his kind." However, if Fish did intervene in Montgomery's behalf, it was to no avail.[26]

Booker T. Washington's response was less cordial. As he well knew, even a hint of malfeasance in office by one of Roosevelt's black appointees threatened the success of his race program. When Montgomery appealed to him, Washington, summering in Massachusetts, directed Scott to "tell him that I have no power to change the decision of the Administration: I merely acted as a go-between." Washington suggested that Isaiah appeal directly to Roosevelt if he had any information that might reverse the president's decision. Washington remained cool toward Montgomery for some months after the latter returned to Mound Bayou and immersed himself in the colony that had been his first concern. Isaiah never again addressed the president of Tuskegee as "Dear Sir and Friend," but he soon resumed correspondence with "Doctor Washington" about mutual plans for the improvement of Mound Bayou.[27]

President Roosevelt too eventually forgave Montgomery his mishandling of the federal appointment. In 1907, at Isaiah's request, Roosevelt halted his train at Mound Bayou and, much to the citizens' delight, spoke to them for ten minutes from the rear platform. Booker T. Washington was pleased to note that the president's address praising the independent black colony was telegraphed throughout the nation. In 1909, on the centennial of Lincoln's birth, the Lincoln Farm Association dedicated a permanent memorial at his birthplace near Hodgenville, Kentucky. On that occasion, President Roosevelt gave the major address, representatives of the Union and Confederate armies made brief remarks, and Isaiah Montgomery, representing former slaves, deposited a copy of the Emancipation Proclamation in the cornerstone. Montgomery was honored by the assignment and spent hours preparing his brief speech, which he then asked B. T. Washington to edit. The resulting flowery praise of the Great Emancipator and plea for national unity only briefly mentioned "the presence of grave and unsolved difficulties" in the nation, and ended on an optimistic note.[28]

Although Montgomery and Booker T. Washington might have been called "sensible darkies," who behaved toward whites in an accommodating manner, both were very much concerned about practical ways to improve conditions for their fellow blacks. Isaiah was always ready to listen to the schemes or test the inventions of aspiring black businessmen, and he frequently recommended their projects to Washington or other influential friends. He grew especially indignant when white terrorists in Mississippi harassed small black entrepreneurs because of their economic success. Often when a victim wrote him for advice, Montgomery sent him money and suggested that he relocate in or near Mound Bayou. In at least one instance he wrote Captain Sharp at Roundaway plantation recommending for settlement there "a number of moneyed land-owning people" who were fleeing from "the white cap districts" of the state. On another occasion, Isaiah sent Booker T. Washington a list of cases of outrages against black businessmen and asked if they should not be presented to the governor with a petition for redress; they might be given to the press, "but it seems impossible to get that body out of the Machine groove."[29]

Montgomery watched closely the trend of white behavior toward his race, and sometimes privately expressed doubt about its future, warning against complacency because alleged reforms in the "white cap counties" were usually illusory. However, these moments of doubt were shared only with his family or associates such as Washington; he never failed to reply optimistically when ordinary black folk wrote him of their concerns. When James K. Vardaman, a man whom Thornton called "the Traducer and Maligner of a race, and a [w]recker of its hopes and ambitions," won the nomination for governor of Mississippi, Isaiah wrote such a reassuring letter to a worried black farmer that the *Memphis Commercial Appeal* published it in full. He advised against taking seriously the campaign rhetoric in this contest between two white factions, where the race problem had been "seized upon as the most available political quandary." Although Montgomery admitted that "the good people of Mississippi faltered," he was convinced that "it must be only a temporary halt," and counseled the farmer to continue to work hard and trust his white friends.[30]

Isaiah was well aware of the importance of maintaining his good reputation among local whites, realizing, as he told a reporter, that the very safety of the colony depended upon their goodwill to prevent terrorist raids. When Booker T. Washington asked him to respond to a request from a Massachusetts editor for particulars about outrages against successful members of the race, Montgomery refused, saying "For reasons which you well understand, I cannot afford any special notoriety in connection with these matters." On his way home from the Republican national convention in 1904, Montgomery told a reporter from the *St. Louis Globe Democrat* that Mississippi Democrats would be "very much disappointed with the result" if they raised the race question in the upcoming campaign. The *Vicksburg Herald* seized upon Montgomery's statement, asserting that it sounded like a threat and warning him of the dire consequences of acquiring "the reputation of a race agitator." The editor suggested that this man, who had voted so sensibly in the 1890 constitutional convention, must have "been carried away by the Roosevelt race political cult, which turned the heads of Booker Washington and so many other of the non-political leaders." Thornton was so disturbed by the unfavorable publicity that he sought Washington's advice even before Isaiah returned home.[31] In that tense racial climate, the Montgomerys feared to jeopardize their successful experiment.

From the time the colony was founded one of Isaiah's major concerns had been to provide the best possible educational facilities. In 1892 he and Ben Green donated a tract of land in the village for the establishment of the Mound Bayou Normal and Industrial Institute. Soon Montgomery secured partial sponsorship from the American Missionary Association, which supplied northern teachers for some years and contributed funds for a number of years after that. As the colony grew, Isaiah became increasingly indignant about the inequitable distribution of county education funds, which were drawn primarily from the poll tax. In

1909, for example, $7,000 for Bolivar County schools came from Negro poll taxes and only $1,300 from whites, but the funds were always divided equally between the races. That meant that 1,300 white children received the same education allotment as 12,000 colored pupils; as a result, black schools could pay teachers only $15 to $35 per month for four-month terms, while white teachers received $55 or more per month for a six-month session. In an effort to compensate for this inequity, Montgomery not only sought to publicize the facts through Booker T. Washington but in later years successfully solicited additional funds from the Rosenwald and Jeanes philanthropic foundations. As a further aid to education, Andrew Carnegie donated $4,000 for the erection of a library in Mound Bayou, but the town had some difficulty maintaining its services in later years.[32]

The largest infusion of philanthropic funds came to aid a project that originated as an exclusively black self-help venture. Charles Banks, who had organized the Mississippi Negro Business League as a chapter of B. T. Washington's national organization, suggested that the state group sponsor a manufacturing plant "that would broaden the racial activities, and afford legitimate channels for the encouragement of the mechanical and business development of the negro people." They chose a cotton-seed-oil mill, first, because "our people are cotton-growers; whatever money they make is from handling cotton." Second, there was a great demand for cottonseed oil and meal, as well as husks; oil mills were earning from 15 to 40 percent on their investments. With a logic Ben Montgomery would have approved, these black men reasoned that since they ginned and marketed their own cotton, why not reap the additional value of manufacturing the by-products? They decided to offer stock in the new mill at only one dollar a share "in order that every negro in Mississippi might have the chance of investing his savings in the venture." Mound Bayou seemed the proper location for the plant because it had become the "racial capital" of the state. In 1908 Montgomery and Banks began selling shares of stock in the Mound Bayou Oil Mill & Manufacturing Co., and by 1910 construction had begun.[33]

From the beginning the organizers of the project seemed less interested in financial returns than in the psychological benefits in terms of race pride. From time to time they held mammoth stockholders' meetings at Mound Bayou that attracted blacks from a wide area. There, in a camp-meeting atmosphere, the people shared basket lunches while listening to inspiring speeches from prominent and successful members of their race. On one such occasion a black bishop summed up the underlying purpose of the venture: "The organization of this oil mill will show the youth of our people the things of which we are capable, and will be inspiration to them to become fit for better things."[34]

However beneficial this may have been to race pride, such efforts did not raise sufficient money to launch the business. By 1912, with the plant valued at $100,000 and completed except for the final equipment, Montgomery and Banks, with Washington's aid, began an aggressive fund-raising drive among white philanthropists in the North. Isaiah made several trips to New York and Chicago armed with a six-page pamphlet entitled "Introduction to Mound Bayou," which described the colony in glowing terms. Montgomery hoped not only to sell $40,000 worth of mill bonds but also to establish a half-million-dollar fund from which to make low-interest loans to black farmers who were being charged exorbitant rates by white bankers. He secured expressions of interest from officers of the American Bankers Association and the Illinois Central Railroad. The latter sent an inspection team, which published a very favorable assessment of the prospects of the Mound Bayou colony; Montgomery used it in his continuing campaign. Julius Rosenwald, president of Sears Roebuck and Company, promised to subscribe a substantial sum to the loan fund if his stringent conditions were met.[35]

On November 25, 1912, an elaborate ceremony was held to dedicate the heavily indebted oil mill. The editor of the *Memphis Commercial Appeal* made a few remarks to the assembled black stockholders, and then Booker T. Washington congratulated "the founder of this town and his coworkers, because from the very beginning of this settlement they have had the good sense and farsightedness to keep in close and sympathetic touch with the best white people in the state of Mississippi." He admonished the black citizens to work harder and improve their farming methods in order to increase their productivity. He predicted improving race relations throughout the South, concluding, "As we go on year by year demonstrating our ability to make good and law-abiding citizens and our ability to create something the white man wants and respects, in the same degree will our relations be further cemented in the direction of peace and prosperity."[36] There could be no clearer statement of the Washington-Montgomery philosophy.

However, despite this impressive dedication, the oil mill was unable to start operations; creditors' demands had absorbed all available funds, and there was nothing left for operating expenses. In response to an urgent plea from Banks and Washington, Julius Rosenwald agreed to buy $25,000 worth of the remaining $40,000 in unsold bonds, providing the money was used to put the mill into operation. B. B. Harvey, a Memphis mill owner, bought the remaining bonds and leased the mill for five years. Thus billed as a great Negro enterprise in spite of the white lessee, the Mound Bayou Oil Mill began operations on October 9, 1913, nearly eleven months after its dedication. There were problems with Harvey from the first. He was supposed to pay the outstanding debts but, at the end of the first year, refused to make a financial statement, and Banks and Montgomery were forced to meet the obligations for interest, taxes, and insurance. The recession of 1914 brought the failure of Harvey's Memphis mill, and there is some evidence that he misappropriated funds from the Mound Bayou venture for his own needs. Another employee, the mill's financial agent, had sold some bonds under false pretenses and pocketed the money. Distressed by hints of these problems, Banks turned to Rosenwald for assistance to force Harvey out and operate the mill entirely under black direction. Even in these critical circumstances, the Mound Bayou leaders rejected a bid by a subsidiary of Proctor and Gamble to take over operations, fearing it would mean "the loss of our identity as a race with the Oil Mill." Harvey put the unprofitable plant on a half-time schedule for a few months and, in January 1915, suspended operations entirely. Although Rosenwald and others gave some additional aid, the mill operated only sporadically from then on. By the fiftieth anniversary of the colony in 1937 the oil mill building was labeled "a tragic reminder of a more prosperous past. . . [and] a loss to stockholders and promoters of $100,000."[37]

The Bank of Mound Bayou also encountered difficulties. As

early as September 1913 Washington urged Banks to get his bank "in a strong and active condition" during the years of prosperity. He also warned Banks to carry out fully every promise he had made to Rosenwald, because "if [he] be disappointed in this investment he will lose faith in our entire race." However, in spite of a $5,000 loan from the president of Sears Roebuck, the Bank of Mound Bayou failed in August 1914. These difficulties apparently caused some temporary strain between Montgomery and Banks, but both men joined the effort which resulted in the establishment of a new bank in the town a year later.

Nevertheless, the days of prosperity and expansion for Mound Bayou were over. The World War I boom encouraged some colonists to seek work in northern cities such as Chicago. In 1920 the price of cotton fell from a dollar to fifteen or twenty cents a pound, and as a result, the price of prime land around Mound Bayou plummeted from $300 to $175 an acre. The year 1922 brought the failure of the Farmer's Cooperative Mercantile Company, which E. P. Booze had managed for the Montgomerys. As one historian noted, "A financial blight settled on the town. Women who formerly had kept their own homes and worked their land were forced to seek domestic employment in white homes [in nearby towns]. Men became sharecroppers on the big plantations to the south. Homes were broken."[38]

In 1912 Isaiah Montgomery wrote Andrew Carnegie that he hoped to devote his old age to putting the Mound Bayou community on a sound financial footing, but "circumstances beyond my control. . . render my efforts in this behalf hazardous and uncertain." As time proved his fears to be justified and the colony's condition weakened, the aging Isaiah increasingly turned his attention to his family. Thornton had died in 1909, leaving few material possessions; his investments in grain futures and in Canadian prairie land had proved failures. By comparison, Isaiah's ventures in Mound Bayou real estate and commerce had prospered. In 1920 the younger Montgomery built an elaborate twenty-one-room mansion of red brick at a cost of $30,000; he claimed to need the space for his two divorced daughters and their children as well as his extensive library and the family's "collection of handmade furniture of the antebellum type." On May 11, 1921, Isaiah and Martha celebrated their golden wedding anniversary. They had been full partners in the colonial experiment; Martha's business ability had maintained their mercantile interests along with the sawmill and cotton gin, while Isaiah had concentrated on building the colony. In late summer 1923 "Miss Mat," as she was known to the townspeople, died, and Isaiah survived her by only about seven months. His death on March 7, 1924—two weeks before his seventy-seventh birthday—left Mound Bayou without a founder and patriarch. Although the Montgomerys had had twelve children, no son survived them; within a few months two of their four daughters had moved away, leaving only Lillian Belle, who was severely handicapped, and Mary Booze, who became a Republican national committeewoman while managing the Montgomery estate.[39]

What was the significance of the Mound Bayou experiment? Although it never became a perfect "community of cooperation," for a time it approached that goal. Mound Bayou governed itself, and major decisions were reached by a consensus of the citizens, although its leaders exercised a great deal of influence. Citizens were encouraged to work together to solve mutual problems, but there was no attempt to collectivize the economy; that had never been an aim of Robert Owen or Joseph Davis or any of the Montgomerys. The goal had always been to provide opportunities within the free enterprise system for individual advancement through hard work in an atmosphere of cooperation with one's fellows. Within these limits, Mound Bayou in its prime might well have appeared a success to Owen and Davis and Ben Montgomery.

For contemporaries, the true importance of the colony lay in its position as a symbol of black achievement. For at least twenty-five years, when black esteem was being severely buffeted by the fiercest forms of white bigotry, Mound Bayou was a thriving, well-publicized example of a successful Negro colony. It stirred race pride in blacks across the nation when such prominent figures as Booker T. Washington and Theodore Roosevelt cited Mound Bayou as a shining example of black success. In Mississippi it seemed a beacon of hope and a place of refuge to beleaguered blacks in a senselessly hostile white world; there was always the knowledge that, if life became too intolerable, there was some place to which they might flee. In later years there was no color stigma attached to Mound Bayou's decline, because it paralleled that of every small town in the region.

Mound Bayou was also critically important to the handful of children who were privileged to grow up there in an environment free from discrimination. Many years later Benjamin A. Green, son of founder Ben T. Green and a graduate of Fisk University and Harvard Law School, asserted in regard to his Mound Bayou childhood, "Everything here was Negro, from the symbols of law and authority and the man who ran the bank down to the fellow who drove the road scraper. That gave us kids a sense of security and power and pride that colored kids don't get anywhere else."[40] This one of Isaiah Montgomery's goals was completely, if temporarily, achieved. He was less successful in persuading these young people to remain in the colony on their own land, away from the urban vices; national demographic tides moved in the opposite direction.

The colony was not free from internal friction. The removal of an ever-present white menace merely allowed the citizens time for jealousy and infighting. The Montgomery family itself did not escape this problem; Ben Green's wife resented Isaiah's preemption of the top leadership role in the young colony, and feelings had grown so hard that some said Isaiah did not regret Ben's murder. The tradition of violence lingered within the first family. Isaiah's son-in-law, a divisive force in town himself, was shot from ambush outside his store in 1939, shortly after one of the Montgomery daughters died a violent death.

By 1940 a visitor described Mound Bayou as a dilapidated, depopulated town with little left to excite race pride. The Davis-Montgomery dream enjoyed a brief half-life in the mind of the middle-aged mayor, Ben A. Green. He had returned from World War I with a Harvard law degree and the determination to implement at least some of old Isaiah Montgomery's idealistic goals. However, by then the town was already dying and he had little chance for success. Twenty years later the disillusioned mayor admitted that "pride and power and a sense of security no longer apply to the situation here." The dream of creating an ideal "community of cooperation" was finally dead.[41]

For one hundred years that dream had inspired four valiant, if only partially successful efforts. From the stagecoach conversation of Robert Owen and Joseph Davis in 1825 had grown a plan that bore abortive fruit in the model slave plantation at Davis Bend. There, for thirty-five years, Davis strove to build a cooperative community and succeeded only in creating an innovative system of slave management; the realities of bondage precluded any greater achievement. However, Davis's attempt allowed some very able slaves to obtain education and experience that permitted them to launch a more successful postwar effort. Although Davis never voluntarily abandoned slavery, he honestly believed in the importance of the dream and persuasively propounded it to the Montgomerys even as he stressed the importance of material wealth.

The Civil War ended the restraints of slavery at Davis Bend, and replaced the master with well-meaning but inept Yankees. The officers of the navy, the army, and the Freedmen's Bureau each in turn tried to set up a demonstration colony for the freedmen, but their tenure was too brief, their authority too limited, and their problems too great to permit more than modest success. However, the Yankees did manage to preserve the dream and encourage a further effort to implement it.

Ben Montgomery and his sons seized the opportunity that the aged Joseph Davis offered and launched an ambitious enterprise at Davis Bend that made them, for a time, the third largest planters in the state. It also provided an all-black community, largely self-governed, where the freedmen could pursue an agrarian life for the most part free from outside interference. For a decade this successful venture provided a haven for some and an example of black achievement for many more. The former Davis slaves knew that, if they chose to, they could continue to live and work on the old home place. However, even as free men and women, the colonists often found cooperation difficult, and many left the experiment before economic and political circumstances brought its collapse. Ben Montgomery's mixture of sternly authoritarian and benevolently paternal rule did not create the utopia he had envisioned.

Isaiah Montgomery's revival of the dream at Mound Bayou created a colony that prospered for twenty-five years and provided a refuge and an example of black success when the fortunes of the race were at a low ebb. The small landowners in the community could escape much of the crushing burden of oppression that hampered most Mississippi blacks at the turn of the century. Here, as at Davis Bend, total separation was not possible in a complex, interdependent world, and eventually forces beyond the colony's control brought about its decline. However, as Mayor Ben Green insisted in 1940, Mound Bayou's failure "proves nothing about the Negro. It proves plenty about humanity."[42] The same observation holds true for each of the experiments. None was ever completely free from discord and dissension, even during periods of success and prosperity. Robert Owen, Joseph Davis, the Union officers, and Benjamin and Isaiah Montgomery all underestimated the strict limits to human capacity for selfless cooperation. Within these bounds both postwar Davis Bend and Mound Bayou enjoyed considerable success as model "communities of cooperation." And all four of the experiments, extending over a full century, attest to the persistence of a dream.

Notes

Abbreviations used in Notes:

BRFAL	Bureau of Refugees, Freedmen, and Abandoned Lands
LC	Library of Congress
LR	Letters Received
LS	Letters Sent
MDAH	Mississippi Department of Archives and History
MSE	Mississippi Superintendent of Education
NA	National Archives (Washington, D.C.)
NYPL	New York Public Library
OAG/CTD	Office of Adjutant General, Colored Troops Division
RG	Record Group
WNRC	Washington National Records Center (Suitland, Md.)

Chapter 1

1. Robert Owen, *A New View of Society* (London, 1813), p. 33; reprinted in *The Life of Robert Owen Written by Himself* (London, 1857), 1: 285.
2. Margaret Cole, *Robert Owen of New Lanark* (New York, 1953), pp. 148–149; A. E. Bestor, *Backwoods Utopias* (Philadelphia, 1950), pp. 104–114.
3. Varina Howell Davis, *Jefferson Davis, Ex-President of the Confederate States of America: a Memoir* (New York, 1890), 1: 49–50, 171–172; Donald MacDonald, *Diaries. 1824–1826* (Indianapolis, 1942), pp. 299–301; Hudson Strode, *Jefferson Davis, American Patriot, 1808–1861* (New York, 1955), pp. 39, 111; James Daniel Lynch, *The Bench and Bar of Mississippi* (New York, 1881), pp. 73–74; Dunbar Rowland, ed., *Mississippi* (Atlanta, 1907), 1: 630–631.

4. V. Davis, *Memoir*, 1: 50; Cole, *Owen*, p. 58; Bestor, *Utopias*, p. 80. Owen's ideas on education are summarized from Owen, *A New View*, "Second Essay," pp. 20–34, and Cole, *Owen*, pp. 75–87.

5. Lynch, *Bench and Bar*, p. 73; Rowland, *Mississippi*, p. 630; Davis v. Bowmar et al., manuscript court record, Mississippi Department of Archives and History (hereafter abbreviated MDAH) pp. 174–175, 212, 219. For a description of Mississippi in the early years, *see* Joseph G. Baldwin, *The Flush Times of Alabama and Mississippi: A Series of Sketches* (New York, 1854).

6. Joseph E. Davis to President A. Johnson, Sept. 22, 1865, in Davis v. Bowmar, MDAH, p. 441; Frank E. Everett, Jr., *Brierfield: Plantation Home of Jefferson Davis* (Hattiesburg, Miss., 1971), pp. 7–9; V. Davis, *Memoirs*, pp. 47–48.

7. [Joseph Holt Ingraham], *The Southwest. By a Yankee* (New York, 1835), 2: 84–86, quoted in Charles S. Sydnor, *Slavery in Mississippi* (Baton Rouge, 1933), pp. 186–187.

8. Lynch, *Bench and Bar*, p. 76; Rowland, *Mississippi*, p. 631; Joseph E. Davis to Jefferson Davis, July 9, 1832, Monroe, Haskell M., Jr., and McIntosh, James T., eds., *The Papers of Jefferson Davis* (Baton Rouge, 1971), 1: 246; 2: 15, 21, 256–259, 296 (Baton Rouge, 1974); Henry Stuart Foote, *The Bench and Bar of the South and Southwest* (St. Louis, 1876), p. 226.

9. *See* transcript of an interview with V. Blaine Russell, July 31, 1972, Old Court House Museum, Vicksburg, Mississippi. There is some confusion about the number of children Joseph fathered, one descendant reporting four while a brief biography published early in this century lists nine; however, all agree that he had no children by his legal wife, Eliza Van Benthuysen Davis. T. C. DeLeon, *Belles, Beaux and Brains of the '60's* (New York, 1909), p. 76. Varina Howell Davis, Joseph's sister-in-law, who wrote the most detailed account of the family (*Memoirs*, 2 vols.), mentioned no earlier marriage. *Vicksburg Weekly Herald*, September 24, 1870.

10. Cole, *Owen*, pp. 144–160.

11. Bestor, *Utopias*, pp. 218–226.

12. Mahala Eggleston Roach to her son, Aug. 22, 1897, miscellaneous manuscripts, MDAH; V. Davis, *Memoir*, I, 192; Eron Rowland, *Varina Howell: Wife of Jefferson Davis* (New York, 1927), 1: 65–66.

13. V. Davis, *Memoir*, 1: 193; Roach to son, August 22, 1897, MDAH; Mary Mitchell White, "Interludes," typescript, in possession of Betty White Wells, Tulsa, Oklahoma, p. 167.

14. Roach to son, Aug. 22, 1897, MDAH; White, "Interludes," p. 168. In 1853 Frederick Law Olmstead noted the fashion for the newly rich cotton planters in the Mississippi Valley to import European gardeners to add to their prestige. Frederick Law Olmstead, *A Journey in the Back Country* (New York and London, 1907), p. 26.

15. V. Davis, *Memoir*, 1: 194–205; "Autobiographical Sketch" in Monroe, *The Papers of Jefferson Davis*, 1: lxviii; *A Journey*, p. 31. Olmstead found young men in the Natchez area "all 'talking horse.'"

16. Letter fragment from Joseph E. Davis, October 9, 1865, Jos. Davis Papers, MDAH; Sydnor, *Slavery*, p. 185; J. E. Davis to Jefferson Davis, February 13, 1847, Confederate Museum, Richmond, Virginia.

17. U.S. Census, 1840, Slave Schedules, Warren County, Miss.; Warren County Tax Rolls, MDAH; Sydnor, *Slavery,* p. 193.

18. White, "Interludes," p. 169; M. E. Hamer to W. L. Fleming, Jan. 30, 1908, Walter Lynwood Fleming Collection, New York Public Library (hereafter abbreviated NYPL); Roach to son, Aug. 22, 1897; U.S. Census, 1860, Slave Schedules, Warren County, Miss., MDAH; Sydnor, *Slavery,* p. 43. Davis's neighbors, Turner and Quitman, as well as his brother Jefferson, averaged slightly less than four slaves per cabin. However, R. Y. Wood, another neighbor, had almost seven in each of his slave huts. For a discussion of the ideal slave dwelling, *see, De Bow's Review,* 10: 623, and 17: 422–423; *Farmer's Register,* 5: 32–33; *Commercial Review,* 3: 419. For a discussion of the usual slave housing, *see* Sydnor, *Slavery,* pp. 39–41; Kenneth M. Stampp, *The Peculiar Institution* (New York, 1956), pp. 292–295.

19. Hamer to Fleming, Jan. 30, 1908, Fleming Papers, NYPL; U.S. Census, 1850, Agriculture Schedules, Warren County, Miss., MDAH.

20. *Farmer's Register,* 5: 32; V. Davis, *Memoir,* 1: 174.

21. Lynch, *Bench and Bar,* p. 76; V. Davis, *Memoir,* 1: 174; Roach to son, Aug. 22, 1897, MDAH; Hamer to Fleming, n.d., Fleming Papers, NYPL.

22. *New Orleans Times Democrat,* February 18, 1902.

23. V. Davis, *Memoir,* 1: 176–177; Hudson Strode, *Jefferson Davis, Private Letters, 1823–1889* (New York, 1966), p. 101.

24. Sydnor, *Slavery,* p. 76.

25. V. Davis, *Memoir,* 1: 174; Hamer to Fleming, Jan. 30, 1908, Fleming Papers, NYPL. For a general discussion of slave incentives, *see* Stampp, *Peculiar Institution,* pp. 164–168.

26. Joe D. Howell to W. B. Howell, Sept. 5, 1845, William Burr Howell Papers, MDAH; Hamer to Fleming, Jan. 30, 1908, Fleming Papers, NYPL.

27. V. Davis, *Memoir,* 1: 179, 193.

28. Ibid., p. 47; Monroe, *Papers of Jefferson Davis,* 1: 408; Zachary Taylor to Jefferson Davis, April 18, 1848, and July 10, 1848, Zachary Taylor Papers, Library of Congress (hereafter abbreviated LC).

29. *Commercial Review,* 3: 420; Strode, *Private Letters,* p. 94; Strode, *Patriot,* pp. 327–328, 333–335; Ben Montgomery to Jefferson Davis, August 1, 1859, in Dunbar Rowland, ed., *Jefferson Davis, Constitutionalist: His Letters, Papers, and Speeches* (Jackson, Miss., 1923), 4: 92; W. L. Fleming, "Jefferson Davis, the Negroes and the Negro Problem," *Sewanee Review,* 16: 412. Stampp, *Peculiar Institution,* p. 305; Stampp asserts that most slaves suffered from tooth decay and "few received dental care."

30. U.S. Census, 1860, Slave Schedules, Warren County, Miss., MDAH.

31. V. Davis, *Memoir,* 1: 179; Davis v. Bowmar, MDAH pp. 415, 425.

32. Strode, *Patriot,* p. 118; Walter L. Fleming, "The Religious Life of Jefferson Davis," *Louisiana State University Bulletin,* vol. I, no. 5 (n.d.), pp. 330–331; Ben Montgomery to Joseph Davis, Feb. 3, 1870, Jos. Davis Papers, MDAH.

33. *New Orleans Times Democrat,* February 18, 1902. Ben's age is derived from U.S. Census, 1870, Population Schedules, Warren County, Miss., MDAH.

34. Sydnor, *Slavery,* pp. 149, 165–166; *New York World,* September 28, 1890.

35. *New York World,* September 28, 1890; Booker T. Washington, *The Story of the Negro* (New York, 1909), 1: 154.

36. *New York World,* September 28, 1890; Washington, *Story of the Negro,* 1: 154–155; Davis v. Bowmar, MDAH, p. 393; Joseph Davis letter fragment, October 9, 1865, Jos. Davis Papers, MDAH; *Cincinnati Daily Gazette,* December 25, 1863; William C. Weneta, Center for Polar and Scientific Archives, National Archives and Records Service, Washington, D.C., to Janet S. Hermann, May 23, 1978; Eleanor S. Brockenbrough, The Confederate Museum, Richmond, Virginia, to Janet S. Hermann, Aug. 2, 1978; Henry E. Baker, "The Negro in the Field of Invention," *Journal of Negro History,* 2: 24; Tuskegee Institute, *Negro Year Book, 1921–22* (Alabama, 1922), pp. 317–318.

37. Roach to son, Aug. 22, 1897, MDAH; Hamer to Fleming, Jan. 30, 1908, Fleming Papers, NYPL; V. Davis, *Memoir,* 1: 174–175; Ben Montgomery to Joseph Davis, June 27, 1866, Jos. Davis Papers, MDAH.

38. Isaiah T. Montgomery Pension Record, Civil War, XC2997096 Washington National Records Center (Suitland, Md.); Roach to son, Aug. 22, 1897, MDAH.

39. Isaiah T. Montgomery to Booker T. Washington, Nov. 9, 1905, Booker T. Washington Papers, LC.

40. *New Orleans Times Democrat,* February 18, 1903.

41. T[homas] P. Leathers to Hon. J[ames] Campbell, Jan. 10, 1856, John A. Quitman Papers, MDAH.

42. Roach to son, Aug. 22, 1897, MDAH.

43. Admiral David D. Porter to General Lorenzo Thomas, Oct. 21, 1863, Letters Received, Office of the Adjutant General, Colored Troops Division, Record Group 94, National Archives (hereafter abbreviated LR, OAG/CTD, RG, NA).

44. Isaiah T. Montgomery to Booker T. Washington, July 28, 1904, Booker T. Washington Papers, LC. For a discussion of free blacks in the South, *see* Charles S. Sydnor, "The Free Negro in Mississippi," *American Historical Review,* 30: 785; Ira Berlin, *Slaves Without Masters* (New York, 1974). For a clear picture of the plight of free Negroes in the North, *see* Leon Litwack, *North of Slavery* (Chicago, 1961).

45. *Vicksburg Daily Times,* September 26, 1870.

46. The 1860 census figures must be regarded with some skepticism when they list only twelve bales of cotton and no corn produced on the Joseph Davis plantation the previous year.

47. Gignel and Jameson to Joseph Davis, Nov. 23, 1866, Jos. Davis Papers, MDAH.

48. Zachary Taylor to Jefferson Davis, April 18, July 10, 1848, Zachary Taylor Papers, LC; *Vicksburg Daily Times,* September 20, 1870; *Weekly Clarion* (Jackson), September 29, 1870; Lynch, *Bench and Bar,* p. 75; Hamer to Fleming, January 30, 1908, Fleming Papers, NYPL.

49. *Weekly Clarion,* September 29, 1870; *Vicksburg Daily Times,* September 20, 1870; Lynch, *Bench and Bar,* pp. 75–76; Roach to son, Aug. 22, 1897; Bettie Bradford to her sister, Nannie, Dec. 21, 1853, Lise Mitchell Papers, Tulane University; White, "Interludes," p. 168.

50. *Vicksburg Sentinel and Expositor,* September 6, 13, 1842; *South-Western Farmer* (Raymond, Miss.), September 9, 1842; *Yazoo Whig and Political Reg-*

ister, September 12, 1842; *Woodville Republican,* September 24, 1842; Joseph E. Davis to Jefferson Davis, Feb. 13, 1847, Confederate Museum; Davis v. Bowmar, MDAH, pp. 588–596; Henry Stuart Foote, *Casket of Reminiscences* (Washington, 1874), p. 186; V. Davis, *Memoir,* 1: 171; *The Papers,* 1: 274; 2: 8, 14, 15.

51. *New Orleans Times Democrat,* February 18, 1902; V. Davis, *Memoir,* 1: 478–479.

52. *New Orleans Times Democrat,* February 18, 1902; WPA Slave Narratives, Warren County, Miss., Record Group 60, Old Court House Museum, Vicksburg, Miss.; George P. Rawick, ed., *The American Slave: A Composite Autobiography* (Westport, Conn., 1972), 7: 93–94. Supplementary Series I, vol. 8, pp. 996–1006, 1158–1160, 1338–1339.

53. Newspaper clipping, *Commercial Appeal,* n.d., enclosed in letter from the editor of *The Century Magazine* to Mrs. Jefferson Davis, June 13, 1902, Jefferson Davis Papers, University of Alabama.

54. V. Davis, *Memoir,* 1: 479; 2: 18; Stampp, *Peculiar Institution,* pp. 103–104.

55. *New Orleans Times Democrat,* February 18, 1902; Whitelaw Reid, *After the War* (New York, 1866; Harper Torchbooks edition, 1965), p. 283.

56. Isaiah Montgomery to Booker T. Washington, July 28, 1904, Booker T. Washington Papers, LC. The claim of Union Colonel John Eaton that Jefferson Davis had a slave mistress who was Joseph Davis's daughter was merely Yankee propaganda with no basis in fact. *Report of the General Superintendent of Freedmen, Department of the Tennessee and State of Arkansas for 1864* (Memphis, 1865), p. 93. For a different but undocumented assumption, see Phyllis M. Sanders, "Jefferson Davis: Reactionary Rebel, 1808–1861," unpublished Ph.D. thesis, UCLA, 1976.

57. Hamer to Fleming, Jan. 30, 1908, Fleming Papers, NYPL.

58. Stampp, *Peculiar Institution,* p. 329; Rowland, *Mississippi,* p. 631; V. Davis, *Memoir,* 1: 176–177; Fleming, "Jefferson Davis, the Negroes and the Negro Problem," *Sewanee Review,* 16: 407–427.

59. Isaiah Montgomery to Booker T. Washington, Jan. 29, 1909, B. T. Washington Papers, LC; Jos. Davis to Senator Henry Wilson, Dec. 24, 1865, Records of the Bureau of Refugees, Freedmen and Abandoned Lands (hereafter abbreviated BRFAL), National Archives Microfilm Publication M826, reel 16.

60. I. Montgomery to B. T. Washington, Jan. 29, 1909, B. T. Washington Papers, LC; Strode, *Patriot,* p. 114.

61. V. Davis, *Memoir,* 1: 311.

62. [Frederick Douglass], *Life and Times of Frederick Douglass* (New York, 1962; reprinted from 1892 edition), p. 150.

Chapter 2

1. V. Davis, *Memoir,* 2: 10, 18; Lise Mitchell Journal, Tulane University, pp. 22–36.

2. Jeff. Davis to Jos. Davis, Feb. 22, 1862, in *New York Times,* May 15, 1864; Jos. Davis to Jeff. Davis, April 17, 20, 21, 22, 1862, Jefferson Davis Papers, Transylvania University.

3. Jos. Davis to Jeff. Davis, May 2, 22, 1862, Transylvania University; Jos. Davis to Jeff. Davis, June 13, 1862, Jefferson Hayes-Davis collection in possession of Mrs. Adele Hayes-Davis Sinton, Colorado Springs, Colorado.
4. Jos. Davis to Jeff. Davis, May 22, 1862, Transylvania University; Hudson Strode, *Jefferson Davis, Confederate President* (New York, 1959), pp. 262–263.
5. *Vicksburg Whig,* June 6, 13, 1862; *Hinds County Gazette* (Raymond, Miss.), June 18, 25, 1862; Jos. Davis to Jeff. Davis, June 6, 18, 1862, Transylvania University; Deposition of Nicholas E. Barnes, Davis v. Bowmar [1874], pp. 277–300, MDAH.
6. Lise Mitchell Journal, Tulane University; Strode, *President,* p. 287; M. L. Smith to Jeff. Davis, telegram, June 26, 1862, Jefferson Davis Papers, Duke University.
7. Jos. Davis to Jeff. Davis, June 18, 20, 21, 22, Aug. 31, Sept. 1, 22, Octo. 7, 29, Nov. 1, 15, 21, 27, Dec. 8, 1862. Transylvania University; Jos. Davis to Jeff. Davis, Aug. 23, 1862, Jeff. Davis Papers, University of Alabama; Dr. Banks Acct., June-August, 1862, Jos. Davis Papers, MDAH.
8. Ben Montgomery to Jeff. Davis, Jan. 11, 1863, Alabama State Department of Archives and History; Isaiah Montgomery to Booker T. Washington, Nov. 9, 1905, B. T. Washington Papers, LC.
9. Admiral David D. Porter, *Incidents and Anecdotes of the Civil War* (New York, 1885), p. 133; *Natchez Daily Courier,* February 27; March 3, 6, 1863.
10. Admiral David D. Porter to General Lorenzo Thomas, Oct. 21, 1863, LR, OAG/CTD, RG 94, NA; Ben Montgomery to My Dear Son, October 14, 1863, enclosed in above letter; Isaiah T. Montgomery Pension Record, Civil War XC2997096, WNRC; Isaiah T. Montgomery to Booker T. Washington, Nov. 9, 1905, B. T. Washington Papers, LC; *New York World,* September 28, 1890; *Harpers Weekly,* February 7, 1863, p. 94; *New Orleans Tribune,* July 9, 1865.
11. D. D. Porter to L. Thomas, Oct. 21, 1863, LR, OAG/CTD, RG 94, NA; William T. Montgomery Pension Record, Civil War, Application No. 47101, Certificate No. 33531, NA; *New York World,* September 28, 1890.
12. Jos. Davis to Jeff. Davis, Sept. 16; Nov. 1, 11; Dec. 1, 1863, Transylvania University.
13. Ibid., Aug. 15, 1863.
14. Ibid., Aug. 15, 16; Nov. 1, Dec. 1, 1863; Lise Mitchell to Cousin Nannie, Aug. 20, 1863, Lise Mitchell Journal, Lise Mitchell Papers, Tulane University.
15. Report of Samuel R. Shipley, President of the Board, of his visit to the Camps of the Freedmen on the Mississippi River, in *Statistics of the Operations of the Executive Board of Friends' Association of Philadelphia for the Relief of Colored Freedmen* (Philadelphia, 1864), pp. 14–15; John Eaton, Jr., *Grant, Lincoln, and the Freedmen* (New York, 1907), pp. 3–8; Ulysses S. Grant, *Personal Memoirs* (New York, 1885), 1: 424–425.
16. Senate Executive Documents No. 53, 38th Cong., 1st Sess., June 30, 1863, p. 14.

17. Eaton, *Grant, Lincoln,* p. 32; *Report of the General Superintendent of Freedmen, Department of the Tennessee and State of Arkansas for 1864* (Memphis, 1865), p. 7.

18. Eaton, *Grant, Lincoln,* p. 33; *National Cyclopedia of American Biography* (New York, 1936), 25: 31; General Samuel Thomas obituary, *New York Times,* January 12, 1903.

19. Eaton, *Grant, Lincoln,* pp. 105, 109, 126.

20. Ibid., pp. 85–86; *Report of the General Superintendent,* p. 39; Everett, *Brierfield,* p. 7.

21. Shipley, *Report,* pp. 24–25.

22. Notes of the testimony before the Freedmen's Bureau Board of Inquiry at Vicksburg, November 1865, manuscript in Jos. Davis Papers, MDAH.

23. Thomas W. Knox Dispatches, *New York Herald,* December 28, 1863; *War of the Rebellion, Official Records,* ser. III, vol. 4, pp. 708–709; ser. I, vol. 38, pt. V, p. 318; vol. 39, pt. II, p. 334, pt. III, p. 568.

24. Porter, *Incidents,* p. 226.

25. Ibid., pp. 228–229. The price of cotton in New York averaged $155 per 500-pound bale in 1861–62, rose to $335 in 1862–63, and peaked at $505 in 1863–64. John S. McNeily, "War and Reconstruction in Mississippi, 1863–1890," *Publications of the Mississippi Historical Society, Centenary Series,* 2 (1918): 193.

26. Eaton, *Report,* pp. 14–15.

27. Eaton, *Grant, Lincoln,* p. 148. The Army-Treasury dispute is discussed there, pp. 142–166; Vernon Lane Wharton, *The Negro in Mississippi, 1865–1890* (Chapel Hill, 1947), Harper Torchbooks edition (New York, 1965), pp. 35–38. *See also* James E. Yeatman, *Report to the Western Sanitary Commission in regard to Leasing Abandoned Plantations* (St. Louis, 1864) and *Suggestions of a Plan of Organization for Freed Labor and the Leasing of Plantations* (St. Louis, 1864).

28. Mississippi Plantation Register, n.d., 330: 46, 162, and Mississippi Leased Plantations, Treasury Department, Vicksburg, 79: 26, 92, BRFAL, RG105, NA; S. Thomas to Gen. L. Thomas, June 15, 1864, LR, OAG/CTD, RG 94, NA.

29. Special Orders No. 15, March 28, 1864, Box 35, BRFAL, RG 105, NA.

30. Eaton, *Report,* pp. 39–40; Notes of testimony before Board of Inquiry, Jos. Davis Papers, MDAH.

31. Eaton, *Report,* pp. 39–40; B. T. Montgomery to the Officers of Genl. Wood's Staff, June 11, 1866, Jos. Davis Papers, MDAH. As Montgomery pointed out, "But for much exertion and some expense on the part of the Freedmen who were in possession of stock and plantation utensils, very little would have been here at that time worth seizing."

32. Eaton, *Report,* p. 41; Consolidated Report, Freedmen's Department, Vicksburg, January 4, February 1, 1864, Box 35, BRFAL, RG 105, NA; Eaton, *Grant, Lincoln,* p. 135; Henry Rountree to Cincinnati Contraband Relief Commission, March 1, 1864, Vol. 122 BRFAL (Miss.), NA; Notes of the Testimony, Jos. Davis Papers, MDAH.

33. H. Rountree to Cincinnati Contraband Relief Commission, April 13, 1864, Vol. 122, BRFAL (Miss.), RG 105, NA.
34. Ibid., April 14, 1864.
35. For complaints of the Davis freedmen *see* Notes of the Testimony, Jos. Davis Papers, MDAH, and Report of Investigating Board, November 24, 1865, Letters Received, Office of Assistant Commissioner, State of Mississippi, BRFAL, RG 105, Microfilm 826, Reel 10, NA.
36. People Record, Home Colony, Davis Bend, Miss., 1864, Vol. 123, BRFAL, RG 105, NA (this is the source of all information about the residents of the Home Farm); Eaton, *Grant, Lincoln*, p. 133; John T. Trowbridge, *The South* (Hartford, 1867), p. 383.
37. Jos. Davis to Jeff. Davis, April 23, 1864, Transylvania University.
38. Morning Report for Freedmen's Hospitals, March 19, 1864, Vol. 299, Special Orders No. 49, Medical Director of Freedmen, March 5, 1864, Vol. 296, BRFAL (Miss.), RG 105, NA; Notes of the Testimony, Jos. Davis Papers, MDAH.
39. H. Rountree to Cincinnati Contraband Relief Commission, April 13, 1864, Vol. 122, BRFAL (Miss.), RG 105, NA; Morning Reports for Freedmen's Hospitals, April 2, May 14, June 11, July 9, August 6, September 17, October 29, November 26, December 24, 1864; January 16, February 25, 1865, Vol. 299 BRFAL (Miss.), RG 105, NA.
40. J. H. Carter & Co., Answers to Questions for Planters, n.d. [probably November 1864], Box 36, BRFAL (Miss.), RG 105, NA.
41. H. Rountree to Cincinnati Contraband Relief Commission, April 14, 1864, Vol. 122; Reports of Missionaries and Teachers, October 28, November 28, December 28, 1864; Reports of Freedmen and Employees, March, April, May 1865, Box 36; Joseph Warren to Lt. Stuart Eldridge, Report for November 1865, Letters Sent, Mississippi Superintendent of Education (hereafter abbreviated LS/MSE) vol. 49, BRFAL (Miss.), RG 105, NA.
42. J. Warren to Miss Maggie Littell, Nov. 16, 1865, Vol. 49; J. Warren to Rev. James I. Frazer, Nov. 7, Dec. 4, 1865, Vol. 49, LS/MSE, BRFAL (Miss.), RG 105, NA.
43. Diary of Samuel D. Barnes, September 19, 1864, Samuel D. Barnes Papers, Manuscript Divison, LC.
44. J. Warren to S. Eldridge, Sept. 30, Nov. 15, 1865, LS/MSE, vol. 49, BRFAL (Miss.), RG 105, NA.
45. Barnes Diary, May 18, 1865, LC; *Vicksburg Daily Herald,* July 6, 1864.
46. *Vicksburg Daily Herald,* July 6, 1864.
47. Reid, *After the War* (New York, 1866); Harper Torchbooks edition (New York, 1965), p. 284.
48. H. Rountree to Cincinnati Contraband Relief Commission, April 14, 1864, Vol. 122, BRFAL (Miss.), RG 105, NA.
49. H. Rountree to Samuel Adams, April 29, 1864; H. Rountree to A. M. Taylor, Feb. 23, 1864; notes of H. Rountree to Wm. R. Woolman, April 25, 1864, Vol. 122, BRFAL (Miss.), RG 105, NA.
50. J. H. Carter & Co., Answers, n.d., Box 36, BRFAL (Miss.), RG 105, NA; *Vicksburg Daily Herald,* November 11, 1864.

51. J. H. Carter to Col. S. Thomas, Feb. 17, 1866, LR, West District, Box 53, BRFAL (Miss.), RG 105, NA.

52. Quoted in McNeily, "War and Reconstruction," 2: 189; S. Thomas to Gen. L. Thomas, July 29, 1864, LR, OAG/CTD, RG 94, NA.

53. Eaton, *Report,* p. 40; *Grant, Lincoln,* p. 165.

54. *Official Records,* ser. I, vol. XLI, pt. IV, p. 437; *Vicksburg Daily Herald,* November 10, 1864.

55. Eaton, *Report,* p. 41.

Chapter 3

1. Rules and Regulations . . . for the Government of Freedmen at Davis Bend, Miss., Record of Capt. Norton's Business, 122: 23–24, BRFAL (Miss.), RG 105, NA: *Senate Executive Documents* No. 27, 39th Cong., 1st Sess., p. 38.

2. Norton to Superintendents of Colonies, April 7, 1865, 122: 28–29; Monthly Citizen Employees, July 1865, Vicksburg West District Rosters, Box 54, BRFAL (Miss.), RG 105, NA; J. P. Williston to O. O. Howard, June 14, 1865, M826-12; S. Thomas to Howard, Sept. 19, 1863, M826-1.

3. Norton to Superintendents of Colonies, April 7, 1865, 122: 28–29, BRFAL (Miss.), RG 105, NA.

4. Record, Court of Freedmen, Davis Bend, Miss., BRFAL (Miss.), NA.

5. Ibid.; Norton to Capt. J. H. Weber, Sept. 25, 1865, Box 53, BRFAL (Miss.), NA.

6. Record, Court of Freedmen; Isaac Green and Henry Green to Capt. Donaldson, Aug. 5, 1865, Box 39, BRFAL (Miss.), NA.

7. Joseph Warren to Lt. Stuart Eldridge, Sept. 30, 1865, vol. 49; Norton to Weber, Sept. 25, 1865, Box 53, BRFAL (Miss.), NA; Thomas to Howard, Oct. 12, 1865, M826-1.

8. Diary of Samuel D. Barnes, April 16, 23, 1865, Samuel D. Barnes Papers, Manuscript Division, LC.

9. Eaton, *Grant, Lincoln,* p. 165; George R. Bentley, *A History of the Freedmen's Bureau* (New York, 1974), p. 60; Clifton L. Ganus, Jr., "The Freedmen's Bureau in Mississippi" (Ph.D. diss., Tulane University, 1953), p. 31.

10. Thomas to Eaton, July 16, 1865, John Eaton Papers, University of Tennessee; Eldridge to Weber, July 15, 1865; Thomas to Howard, Sept. 21, 1865, M826-1; Circular No. 7, July 29, 1865; Circular No. 9, Aug. 4, 1865, Asst. Comr., BRFAL (Miss.), NA; *House Executive Documents* No. 70, 39th Cong., 1st Sess., pp. 157–160.

11. Thomas to Eaton, July 16, 1865, John Eaton Papers, University of Tennessee.

12. *Daily Clarion* (Meridian, Miss.), August 8, 1865, reprinted from *Vicksburg Journal,* n.d.

13. Thomas to Howard, Sept. 19, 1865, M826-1.

14. *Daily Gazette* (Cincinnati), December 25, 1863; Charles B. Boynton, comp., *History of the Great Western Sanitary Fair* (Cincinnati, 1864); William T. Montgomery, Pension Record, Civil War, Certificate No. 33531, NA.

15. *New York World,* September 28, 1890; Isaiah T. Montgomery to Booker T. Washington, Nov. 9, 1905, B. T. Washington Papers, LC; Record of Rations issued at Davis Bend, Feb. 10–July 8, 1865, Vol. 122, BRFAL (Miss.), NA. A letter from Ben Montgomery at Hurricane to "Mas J. E. Davis" is erroneously dated "Jany 15th, 1865"; the correct date, "Jany 15th, 1866," appears at the bottom of the page.
16. Record, Court of Freedmen; Warren to J. Fraser. Dec. 4, 1865, Vol. 49, BRFAL (Miss.), NA.
17. Capt. A. W. Preston, report to Lt. Stuart Eldridge, June 15, 1866, with affidavits of Edward Grant and Henderson Adams, M826-15.
18. Thomas to Lt. Col. R. S. Donaldson, May 19, 1865, Box 39, BRFAL (Miss.), NA.
19. July 15, 1865, Jos. Davis Papers, MDAH; also in Register of Letters Received, M826-6.
20. Montgomery to Jos. Davis, n.d., Jos. Davis Papers, MDAH.
21. Ibid., July 20, 1865; *see also* M826-6 and M826-10.
22. Ibid., July 30, 1865, Jos. Davis Papers, MDAH; also in M826-11.
23. Ibid., Aug. 4, 1865, Jos. Davis Papers, MDAH; M826-1.
24. Norton to Thomas, Aug. 3, 1865, M826-6.
25. Thomas to W. T. Montgomery, J. A. Gla, B. T. Montgomery, Thos. Bland, Thos. Broadwater & Others, Aug. 4, 1865, Jos. Davis Papers, MDAH; M826-1.
26. Com. of Five to Thomas, Sept. 3, 1865, Jos. Davis Papers, MDAH.
27. Montgomery to Davis, Oct. 14, 1865, Jos. Davis Papers, MDAH.
28. Statement of John T. Donaly in Jos. Davis to Samuel Thomas, Oct. 21, 1865, Jos. Davis Papers, MDAH; M826-9.
29. Enclosed in Davis to Thomas, Oct. 21, 1865, M826-9.
30. Manlove to Thomas, Oct. 25, 1865, M826-11.
31. Thomas to Manlove, Oct. 26, 1865, M826-1.
32. Davis to O. O. Howard, Oct. 27, 1865, M826-10.
33. Davis to Thomas, Oct. 28, 1865, M826-10.
34. Davis to Howard, Oct. 27, 30, 1865, M826-10.
35. Special Orders No. 46, Oct. 30, 1865, M826-28.
36. Davis to President Andrew Johnson, Sept. 22, 1865, M826-9; Davis v. Bowmar [1874], MDAH, pp. 440–448.
37. Davis to Johnson, Nov. 4, 1865, Jos. E. Davis file, Land Division, BRFAL, NA.
38. Montgomery to Davis, Nov. 10, 1865, Jos. Davis Papers, MDAH.
39. Complaint of J. E. Davis vs. Col. Saml Thomas, n.d., Jos. Davis Papers, MDAH.
40. n.d., Jos. Davis Papers, MDAH.
41. S. Eldridge, "for Col. Thomas," to Chaplin J. A. Hawley, Nov. 24, 1865, M826-1.
42. Davis to Burwell, Nov. 16, 1865, Jos. Davis Papers, MDAH; Card of A. Burwell, Nov. 20, 1865, with report of Investigating Board, M826-10.
43. Card of A. Burwell, Nov. 20, 1865, M826-10.

44. "Notes of the testimony taken before a board ordered by Col. Thomas," n.d., Jos. Davis Papers, MDAH.
45. Davis to the Board of Officers, n.d., Jos. Davis Papers, MDAH.
46. J. A. Hawley, S. G. Swain, L. P. Woodworth to Thomas, Nov. 24, 1865, M826-10.
47. Davis to Sen. James Guthrie, Jan. 28, 1866, Land Div., BRFAL, NA; Davis to Pres. Johnson, Feb. 28, 1866, Jos. Davis Papers, MDAH.
48. Montgomery to Davis, Nov. 18, 1865, Jos. Davis Papers, MDAH.
49. J. A. Gla, Thomas Broadwater & 112 others to Freedmen's Bureau, State of Miss., Nov. 23, 1865, M826-10. Thomas evidently knew of this effort because two days earlier he wrote Howard that, as soon as the investigation was completed, he would forward the report of the Board "together with a statement of the Freedmen themselves." Thomas to Howard, Nov. 21, 1865, M826-1.
50. Thomas to Howard, Dec. 22, 1865, M826-1.
51. Ibid.
52. Davis to Johnson, Jan 17, 1866, M826-15; Davis to Johnson, March 1, 1866, Jos. Davis Papers, MDAH; Davis to Guthrie, Jan. 28, 1866, and Burton N. Harrison to Gen. R[ichard] Taylor, March 27, 1866, Land Div., BRFAL, NA.
53. Davis to Wilson, Dec. 24, 1865, M826-16.
54. Note on Gen. T. J. Wood to Howard, March 13, 1866, M752-4.
55. For example, Thomas to Howard, Jan. 1, 1866, M826-1.
56. Senate Executive Documents No. 27, 39th Cong., 1st Sess., pp. 38–39.
57. Thomas to Howard, Jan. 1, 1866, M826-1.
58. Montgomery to Thomas, Nov. 30, 1865, M826-11.
59. Bedford to Thomas, Jan. 17, 1866, M826-11; Montgomery to Davis, Jan. 8, 1866, Jos. Davis Papers, MDAH.
60. Montgomery to Davis, Jan 22, 1866, MDAH.
61. Montgomery to Davis, Feb. 5, 1866, MDAH.
62. Thomas to Howard, Dec. 13, 1865, M826-1.
63. Senate Executive Documents No. 27, 39th Cong., 1st Sess., p. 43.
64. Thomas to Howard, March 13, 1866, M826-1.
65. Thomas to Manlove, Feb. 9, 1866, in Vicksburg Herald, February 10, 1866, reprinted in The Standard (Port Gibson), February 17, 1866; Thomas to Howard, March 8, 1866, M826-1; The Cincinnati Commercial, March 17, 1866; Thomas to Wood, March 26, 1866, M826-1.
66. House Executive Documents No. 11, 39th Cong., 1st Sess., p. 30; Thomas to Howard, Jan. 30, 1866, M826-1.
67. Special Order No. 53, April 10, 1866, BRFAL, Washington, D.C., reprinted in Vicksburg Journal, April 20, 1866; House Executive Documents No. 120, 39th Cong., 1st Sess., p. 3.
68. O. O. Howard, Autobiography of Oliver Otis Howard, Major General, United States Army (New York, 1907), 2: 283.
69. C. J. Mitchell to Davis, June 16, 1866, Lise Mitchell Papers, Tulane University; Davis v. Bowmar [1874], MDAH, pp. 206, 347, 360.
70. Thomas to Gen. Lorenzo Thomas, June 15, 1864, OAG/CTD, RG 94, NA.
71. Samuel Thomas obituary, New York Times, January 12, 1903.

72. J. H. Carter to Thomas, Feb. 17, 1866, LR, Western Dist., BRFAL (Miss.), NA.
73. Montgomery to the Officers of Genl. Wood's Staff, June 11, 1866, M826-15.
74. *New York Times,* July 7, 1866.
75. Varina Davis to Jefferson Davis, April 12, 1866, in Hudson Strode, *Private Letters of Jefferson Davis* (New York, 1966), p. 244. Joseph included this accusation in a rough draft of a letter to President Johnson, March 1, 1866, MDAH. There is no evidence that he actually made such a charge to Johnson or any other official to whom he sent appeals.
76. Special Orders No. 117, Oct. 24, 1865, M826-28; Special Orders No. 59, Dec. 18, 1865, Box 53; Western District Roster of Officers, July, 1865–Jan. 1866, Box 54; Special Orders No. 24, Feb. 27, 1866, Special Orders No. 25, Feb. 28, 1866, Box 39, BRFAL (Miss.), NA.
77. B. T. Montgomery, sworn statement, May 18, 1866; Jos. E. Davis to Pres. Johnson, Aug. 2, 1866, MDAH; *House Executive Documents* No. 1, 39th Cong., 2nd Sess., Nov. 1, 1866.
78. Ritter to Bestow, June 12, 1866, M826-16.
79. Preston to Eldridge, June 15, 1866, M826-15.
80. E. S. Bedford, affidavit, June 25, 1866; B. T. Montgomery to the Officers of Genl. Wood's Staff, June 11, 1866; A. D. W. Leavens to Capt. Preston, June 11, 1866; J. H. Leitch to Capt. Preston, June 21, 1866; Samuel Parker (col'd), affidavit, June 11, 1866; Isaac Martin (col'd), affidavit, June 1, 1866; Edward Grant (col'd), affidavit, June 12, 1866; William Canigan (col'd), affidavit, June 13, 1866; Henderson Adams, affidavit, June 10, 1866; all the above enclosed in Preston to Eldridge, June 15, 1866, M826-15; B. T. Montgomery, affidavit, May 18, 1866, Jos. Davis Papers, MDAH.
81. Eldridge to Ryan, June 4, 1866; Wood to Howard, July 13, 1866, M826-2; Montgomery & Sons per B. T. Montgomery to Maj. Genl. Wood, June 25, 1866, M826-15; Bentley, *History of Freedmen's Bureau,* p. 133; Special Orders No. 66, June 20, 1866, M826-28.
82. Montgomery to Davis, June 27, 1866, Jos. Davis Papers, MDAH; Wm. T. Montgomery, affidavit, June 26, 1866; Special Orders No. 67, June 26, 1866, M826-28.
83. *New York Times,* July 7, 11, 1866; Gen. A. C. Gillem to Gen. J. B. Steedman, Sept. 28, 1867, M826-3.
84. Montgomery to Davis, Aug. 6, Sept. 3, 1866; Hurricane Acct., white occupants of houses, Oct. 24, 1866, Jos. Davis Papers, MDAH; Preston report, June 15, 1866, M826-15.
85. Ryan to Preston, Oct. 1, 1866, M826-16; Preston to Ryan, Oct. 6, 1866, M826-2; Card of P. G. Carter, n.d., enclosed in Ryan to Preston, Oct. 1, 1866, M826-16; Carter to Wood, June 29, 1866, M826-16; Montgomery to Davis, Aug. 6, 1866, MDAH.
86. Montgomery to Davis, July 23, 1866, MDAH; Capt. Ryan's Report, Sept. 4, 1866; Ritter to Bestow, June 12, 1866, M826-16; Preston to Eldridge, June 15, 1866, M826-15.
87. Montgomery to Davis, Aug. 9, Oct. 10, 1866, MDAH; Montgomery to Wood, Sept. 28, 1866; D. L. Glascott to Ryan, Oct. 17, 1866, with endorsements by

A. W. Preston, Sept. 29, Henry M. Whittlesey, Sept. 30, A. W. Preston, Oct. 2, and Ryan, Oct. 17, M826-15; newspaper clipping, n.d., Jos. Davis Papers, MDAH.

88. W. T. Montgomery, Lewis and Boyd to Wood, May 18, 1866, M826-15; W. T. Montgomery to J. D. Nicholson, May 22, 1866; with Wood's endorsement, June 1, 1866, Jos. Davis Papers, MDAH.

89. Eldridge to Ryan, June 16, 1866, M826-2; Ryan's Report, July 9, 1866; Ritter to Bestow, June 12, 1866, M826-16; Preston to Eldridge, June 15, 1866, M826-15.

90. Green to Preston, Oct. 24, 1866, M826-14; Ryan's Report, Aug. 13, Sept. 4, 1866, M8256-16; Ganus, "Freedmen's Bureau in Miss.," pp. 311, 335.

91. Montgomery to Davis, Sept. 10, Oct. 3, Oct. 7, 1866, Jos. Davis Papers, MDAH; Montgomery to Davis, Sept. 13, 1866, Confederate Museum, Richmond, Virginia.

92. Joseph E. Davis, petition to the President, May 9, 1866, with additional names, May 29, 1866; Davis to Wood, Sept. 8, 1866, J. E. Davis file, Land Div., BRFAL, NA; Bowmar to Davis, Sept. 28, 1866, Lise Mitchell Papers, Tulane University; Jos. Davis Amnesty Papers, OAG, RG 94, NA.

93. Davis to Wood, Oct. 8, 1866, M826-13; Davis to Preston, Oct. 28, 1866, M826-13; Wood to Howard, Oct. 31, 1866, *Senate Executive Documents* No. 6, 39th Cong., 2nd Sess., p. 88; Montgomery to Davis, Dec. 31, 1866, Jos. Davis Papers, MDAH; Deed to Benjamin T. Montgomery, Deed Book VV, Land Records, Office of Chancery Clerk, Warren County, Miss.

94. Montgomery to Davis, Oct. 3, 1866, MDAH; Wood to Howard, Oct. 31, 1866, *Senate Executive Documents* No. 6, 39th Cong., 2nd Sess., p. 97; *Vicksburg Daily Times*, November 24, 1866; Jos. Davis to Jeff. Davis, March, n.d., 1867, Strode, *Private Letters,* pp. 262–263.

95. *Vicksburg Journal,* August 3, 1865, reprinted in the *Daily Clarion* (Meridian), August 8, 1865.

96. Ryan Report, Oct. 1, 1866, M826-16; Preston to Eldridge, June 15, 1866, M826-15.

Chapter 4

1. Handwritten copy, Jos. Davis Papers, MDAH [the date is erroneously given as Nov. 15]; mortgage recorded in Warren County, Miss., Land Records, Office of Chancery Clerk, Deed Book VV, 14.

2. U.S. Department of Agriculture, *Report of the Commissioner of Agriculture for the Year 1867* (Washington, 1868), pp. 105–106.

3. [Geo. C. Benham], *A Year of Wreck* (New York, 1880), p. 8; Davis v. Bowmar, MDAH, p. 351; Reid, *After the War,* pp. 291, 414.

4. Jos. Davis to Jeff. Davis, March 26, 1867, Manuscripts Collection, University of Alabama Library; Montgomery to Jos. Davis, Jan. 31, 1867, Jos. Davis Papers, MDAH; Wood to Howard, Dec. 10, 1866, M826-2; Wharton, *Negro in Mississippi,* pp. 87, 90, 93; James W. Garner, *Reconstruction in Mississippi* (New York, 1901), Louisiana Paperbacks edition (Baton Rouge, 1968), pp. 114, 116.

5. Davis v. Bowmar, MDAH, pp. 196, 134, 351, 530–533, 586–587; Booker T. Washington, "A Town Owned by Negroes," *The World's Work,* vol. 14, no. 3 (July 1907), 9131.

6. Montgomery to Davis, Oct. 7, Nov. 25, 1866, Jos. Davis Papers, MDAH. The commissioner of agriculture stressed the crucial labor shortage in *Report of the Commissioner . . . 1867,* p. 106.

7. *Vicksburg Daily Times,* November 21, 1866.

8. Wood to Howard, Nov. 21, 1866, M752-38, NA.

9. *Vicksburg Times,* November 21, 1866; *Hinds County Gazette,* November 30, 1866; A. T. Bowie of St. Joseph, La., to Wood, Dec. 13, 1866, M826-6; Wood to Howard, Dec. 14, 1866, M752-5.

10. *New York Times,* December 2, 3, 1866.

11. Jeff. Davis to Jos. Davis, Dec. 17, 1866; Davis v. Bowmar, MDAH, pp. 586–587.

12. Jos. Davis to Jeff. Davis, Mar. 26, 1867, University of Alabama; *St. Louis Globe Democrat,* October 24, 1886.

13. Montgomery to Davis, Jan. 24, 31, 1867, Jos. Davis Papers, MDAH.

14. Montgomery to Davis, Nov. 25, Dec. 3, 1866, Jan. 24, 1867, Jos. Davis Papers, MDAH; Reid, *After the War,* p. 280; Davis v. Bowmar, MDAH, pp. 308–309.

15. Montgomery to Davis, March 28, also Feb. 28 and March 21, 1867, Jos. Davis Papers, MDAH; Dabney O. Elliott, *The Improvement of the Lower Mississippi for Flood Control and Navigation* (St. Louis, 1932), p. 111.

16. Montgomery to Davis, April 15, 1867, Jos. Davis Papers, MDAH; Huntington & Pitkin to Maj. A. W. Preston, April 2, 1867, M826-19.

17. Montgomery to Davis, April 18, 22, May 6, 9, 1867, Jos. Davis Papers, MDAH; Montgomery to Davis, May 2, 30, 1867, University of Alabama.

18. Caleb G. Forshey, "Cut-Offs on the Mississippi River," in American Society of Civil Engineers, *Transactions,* 7 (1878): 248; *Natchez Weekly Courier,* June 23, 1866.

19. Montgomery to Davis, Feb. 28, March 21, May 6, Oct. 14, Dec. 30, 1867, Jos. Davis Papers, MDAH; sketch enclosed in Wm. T. Montgomery to Assistant P. Master, Post Office Dept., Washington, D.C., June 4, 1867, ser. 187, Geographical Site Location Reports, Records of the Post Office Dept., RG 28, NA.

20. Jerry N. Hess, Civil Archives Division, NA, to Janet Hermann, May 18, 1978; T. P. Leathers to Hon. J. Campbell, Postmaster General, Jan. 10, 1856, John A. Quitman Papers, MDAH; Jos. Davis to Jeff. Davis, Feb. 1, 1858, Jefferson Hayes-Davis Papers; *New York World,* September 28, 1890.

21. Montgomery to Davis, Nov. 25, 1866, Jan. 24, 1867, Jos. Davis Papers, MDAH; Garner, *Reconstruction in Mississippi,* pp. 148–150; Reid, *After the War,* p. 416.

22. Montgomery to Davis, Jan 24, 1867; petition for reestablishment of Hurricane Post Office, n.d., Jos. Davis Papers, MDAH.

23. Montgomery to Davis, Feb. 11, 16, July 8, 1867, Jos. Davis Papers, MDAH; Hess to Hermann, May 18, 1978; Wm. T. Montgomery to Asst. P. Master, June 4, 1867, Ser. 187, Geographical Site Location Reports, RG 28, NA.

24. Montgomery to Davis, Dec. 31, 1866, May 9, July 4, 1867, Jos. Davis Papers, MDAH.

25. Montgomery to Davis, June 13, July 4, 18, 1867; Thos. T. Swann, Auditor, to B. G. Humphreys, Governor, June 18, 1867, with Humphreys' endorsement; B. T. Montgomery to Genl. Ord, June 25, 1867; copy of report of Board of Police meeting, July 8, 1867, Jos. Davis Papers, MDAH; Scharff Bros. to Ord, June 19, 1867; B. T. Montgomery to Ord, July 1, 1867, enclosing petition, July 1, 1867, LR Register, Officer of Civil Affairs, 4th Mili. Dist., vol. 28, part 1, pp. 366, 538, RG 393, NA.

26. Montgomery to Davis, letter fragment, n.d. (probably late May 1867), Jefferson Davis Papers, Confederate Museum; Montgomery to Davis, June 13, Jos. Davis Papers, MDAH; Jos. Davis to Jeff. Davis, June 1, 1867, University of Alabama; Jos. Davis to Jeff. Davis, June, n.d., 1867, Strode, *Private Letters,* pp. 282–283.

27. *Vicksburg Daily Times,* October 24, 1866; Mrs. Betty Bentley Beaumont, *A Business Woman's Journal* (Philadelphia, 1888), p. 301; Reid, *After the War,* p. 285; Ryan to Preston, Aug. 23, 1866, M826-16; Ryan to Wood, Oct. 18, 1866, M826-6; Moore, "Mississippi During Reconstruction," pp. 351–353.

28. Montgomery to Davis, April 15, May 6, June 13, 1867, Jos. Davis Papers, MDAH.

29. B. T., Wm. T. and I. T. Montgomery to Gen. O. C. Ord, Aug. 12, 1867, M826-21; summary in LR Register, M826-7 and Office of Civil Affairs, 4th Reconstruction District, vol. 29, part I, p. 380, RG 393, NA.

30. Ord to Gillem, Aug. 13, 1867, M826-19; Alvan C. Gillem to O. O. Howard, Jan. 20, 1867, M826-2; Lt. J. Tyler endorsement on Montgomery to Ord, Aug. 12, 1867, M826-21.

31. Montgomery to Ord, Aug. 15, 1867, M826-27.

32. Endorsement, Aug. 30, 1867, on Montgomery to Ord, Aug. 15, 1867, M826-27; endorsements, Aug. 16, 29, 1867, on Montgomery to Ord, Aug. 12, 1867, M826-21.

33. Statement of Bryan [sic] Wood against the Mate & Deck Crew of the Str. Grey Eagle, Aug. 21, 1867; "Witnesses introduced on the 24th," Box 54A, BRFAL (Miss.), RG 105, NA.

34. C. P. Huntington to Platt, Sept. 22, 1867; B. T. Montgomery to Platt, Sept. 2, 1867, Box 54A, BRFAL (Miss.), RG 105, NA.

35. Hunt and McCaleb, Atys., to Gen. E.O.C. Ord, Sept. 17, 1867; endorsement of Alvan C. Gillem, Sept. 18, 1867; Lt. J. Tyler to Gillem, Sept. 18, 1867, with endorsement, Gillem, Sept. 18, O. D. More, Sept. 20, and Gillem, Nov. 14, 1867; Deputy Marshal I. W. Resor to Gillem, Nov. 18, 1867, Box 54A, BRFAL (Miss.), RG 105, NA.

36. Montgomery to Davis, Aug. 22; Ord endorsement, Aug. 24, 1867, M826-21.

37. Huntington to Ord, Sept. 2, 1867; Special Orders No. 117, Headquarters 4th Military District, Aug. 27, 1867, LR, Box 1, RG 393, NA.

38. S. O. 117, Aug. 27, 1867; Huntington to Ord, Sept. 2, 1867; Wm. Thornton Montgomery Oath, Aug. 31, 1867, 4th Military District, LR, Box 1, RG 393, NA.

39. Huntington to Platt, Sept. 26, 1867, Box 54A, BRFAL (Miss.), RG 105, NA.
40. *Weekly Clarion,* September 19, 1867; Montgomery to Ord, Sept. 16, 26, 1867, LR Register, 4th Reconstruction District, Vol. 29, Part I, pp. 402–409, RG 393, NA; Montgomery to Davis, Sept. 16, 30, 1867, Jos. Davis Papers, MDAH; John Hope Franklin, ed., *The Autobiography of John Roy Lynch* (Chicago, 1970), pp. 43, 57; Speech of Adelbert Ames at Natchez, November 20, 1870, quoted in Ames, Blanche Butler, comp., *Chronicles from the Nineteenth Century: Family Letters of Blanche Butler and Adelbert Ames* (Clinton, Mass., 1957), 2: 219. In 1901 James Garner claimed that Justice of the Peace Montgomery "was probably the first negro in the state to hold public office." *Reconstruction in Mississippi,* p. 164.
41. "A Mississippi Planter," *Southern States Farm Magazine,* 5 (February 1898): 559; *Autobiography . . . Lynch,* pp. 56, 59–65.
42. Montgomery to Freedmen's Bureau, Vicksburg, Dec. 18, 1867, M826-7.
43. Chas. E. Furlong, Sheriff, Warren Co. to Office of Civil Affairs, Nov. 4, 1867, LR, 4th Military District, RG 393, NA, Box 1; E. W. Raymond, B. T. Montgomery, W. T. Montgomery to Maj. O. D. Greene, Nov. 8, 1867, Records of the Secretary of State, RG 28, MDAH.
44. Montgomery to Davis, June 3, July 4, 18, Aug. 8, Sept. 9, 16, 30, 1867, Jos. Davis Papers, MDAH; Wharton, *Negro in Mississippi,* pp. 122–123; Montgomery to Jos. Davis, May 30, July 29, 1867, Jeff. Davis Papers, University of Alabama; Montgomery to Davis, Aug. 22, 1867, M826-21; John Q. Anderson, ed., *Brokenburn: The Journal of Kate Stone, 1861–1868* (Baton Rouge, 1955), p. 368; Beaumont, *Journal,* p. 311.
45. Montgomery to Davis, Jan. 31, April 15, Nov. 14, Dec. 11, 19, 1867, Jan. 6, 1868; Payne, Huntington & Co. to J. E. Davis, Dec. 7, 17, 1867, Jos. Davis Papers, MDAH; Davis v. Bowmar, pp. 69–70, 128, MDAH; Jos. Davis to Jeff. Davis, June, n.d., 1867, Strode, *Private Letters,* p. 283.
46. [George C. Benham] *A Year of Wreck;* Anderson, *Brokenburn,* p. 369; Montgomery to Davis, Nov. 14, Dec. 11, 1867, Jan. 6, 1868, Jos. Davis Papers, MDAH.
47. Montgomery to Davis, July 29, Nov. 14, Dec. 19, 1867, Jan. 6, 1868, Jos. Davis Papers, MDAH.
48. Montgomery to Davis, July 29, 1867, Jeff. Davis Papers, University of Alabama; Montgomery to Davis, Jan. 6, 1868, Jos. Davis Papers, MDAH.
49. Montgomery to Davis, April 15, Nov. 14, Dec. 30, 1867, Jan. 6, 1868, Jos. Davis Papers, MDAH.
50. Elliott, *Flood Control,* p. 111; Montgomery to Davis, Jan. 6, 23, Feb. 11, June 8, 1868, Jos. Davis Papers, MDAH.
51. Montgomery to Davis, June 8, 29, July 23, Aug. 6, Sept. 24, 1868, Jos. Davis Papers, MDAH.
52. Montgomery to Davis, March 23, May 11, 18, June 4, 1868, Jos. Davis Papers, MDAH.
53. Montgomery to Davis, Jan 23, March 23, April 13, May 11, 25, June 8, 1868, Jos. Davis Papers, MDAH.
54. Montgomery to Davis, June 29, July 23, 30, Sept. 13, 1868, Jos. Davis Papers, MDAH.

55. Montgomery to Davis, Oct. 15, 22, 26, Dec. 31, 1868, Jos. Davis Papers, MDAH.
56. Montgomery to Davis, Dec. 17, 31, 1868, Jos. Davis Papers, MDAH.
57. Jeff. Davis to Jos. Davis, Dec. 26, 1868, Davis v. Bowmar, MDAH, pp. 585–586.
58. Montgomery to Davis, Nov. 9, 1868, Jos. Davis Papers, MDAH.
59. Montgomery to Davis, Nov. 30, Dec. 7, 1868, Jos. Davis Papers, MDAH.
60. Montgomery to Davis, Dec. 31, 1868, Jos. Davis Papers, MDAH.

Chapter 5

1. *Vicksburg Daily Times,* September 20, 1870; Col. C. E. Hooker to Davis, Jan. 24, 1870; Davis to Wm. Yerger, July 11, 1870; Montgomery to Davis, Aug. 9, 1869, Sept. 9, 1869, April 7, 1870, Jos. Davis Papers, MDAH.
2. J. D. Lynch, *Bench and Bar,* p. 78; Jefferson Davis to Lize Mitchell, Nov. 20, 1867, Fleming Papers, NYPL. Joseph E. Davis obituaries also appeared in the *Vicksburg Weekly Herald,* September 24, 1870; *Weekly Clarion* (Jackson), September 22, 29, 1870; *Weekly Mississippi Pilot,* September 24, 1870; *Hinds County Gazette,* September 28, 1870.
3. Jos. Davis Papers, MDAH.
4. Warren Watt to Davis, May 19, 1867; George Green to Davis, Dec. 2, 1868; Simon Gaiter to Davis, June 11, 1868; Henderson Newton to Davis, May 19, July 1, 1867; Davis to Genl. Gillem, June 6, 1867; Montgomery to Davis, Dec. 23, 1868, Jos. Davis Papers, MDAH; J. E. Davis to Gillem, June 6, 1867 with endorsement, June 7, 1867, M826-6; Jos. Davis to Jeff. Davis, Dec. 28, 1868, University of Alabama.
5. Montgomery to Davis, June 6, 1866, Feb. 15, 18, March 4, 15, Aug. 9, Sept. 9, Nov. 2, 29, 1869, Feb. 10, May 29, 1870, Jos. Davis Papers, MDAH.
6. Will of Joseph Emory Davis, Minute Book Probate, Vol. O; Will Book B, Office of the Chancery Clerk, Warren County, Miss.; Davis v. Bowmar, pp. 32–33, MDAH.
7. Jeff. Davis to Jos. Davis, April 5, 1860, Davis v. Bowmar, MDAH; *Natchez Tri-Weekly Courier,* January 20, 1868; *Vicksburg Herald,* February 13, 1868; V. Davis, *Memoir,* 2:804; Hudson Strode, *Jefferson Davis, Tragic Hero, The Last Twenty-five Years, 1864–1889* (New York, 1964), pp. 326–327.
8. Extract from Journal of Proceedings of Executors, Davis v. Bowmar, MDAH, pp. 95–96.
9. Montgomery to Davis, Jan. 4, 1869, Jos. Davis Papers, MDAH.
10. Montgomery to Davis, Dec. 23, 1868, Jan. 25, Feb. 4, 1869, Feb. 3, 17, April 7, 1870, Jos. Davis Papers, MDAH; Montgomery to Davis, Jan. 27, 1870, University of Alabama.
11. Davis v. Bowmar, MDAH, pp. 100–101; Land Records of Warren County, Miss., Book II, p. 355.
12. Indenture of Ursino, pp. 37–44; Extract from Journal of the Proceedings of Executors, pp. 94–102, Davis v. Bowmar, MDAH. Montgomery to Jeff. Davis, Dec. 19, 1870, Confederate Museum, Richmond, Virginia.

13. J.H.D. Bowmar to Jeff. Davis, April 1, 8, 1872, May 7, 1873, Confederate Museum, Richmond, Virginia; Extract from Journal of the Proceedings of Executors, pp. 94–102, Davis v. Bowmar, MDAH.
14. F. W. Loring and C. F. Atkinson, *Cotton Culture and the South Considered with Reference to Emigration* (Boston, 1869), pp. 55–57; Diary of Mary Virginia Montgomery, Jan. 17 to Dec. 29, 1872, Benjamin Montgomery Family Papers, Manuscripts Division, LC.
15. Montgomery to Davis, July 23, 1868; for discussion of cotton seed varieties, *see* July 30, 1868, Jan. 25, Feb. 4, 1869, March 27, 1870; for early production, *see* March 22, 1869, Jos. Davis Papers, MDAH; Mary Virginia Montgomery's diary, June 5, 1872, LC; Loring and Atkinson, *Cotton Culture,* p. 63; Eugene W. Hilgard, Special Census Agent, *Report on Cotton Production of the State of Mississippi* (Washington, 1884), p. 149.
16. Interview with Jefferson Davis, *New York Tribune,* May 25, 1871, reprinted in the *Hinds County Gazette,* October 12, 19, 1870; *Vicksburg Weekly Herald,* October 15, 1870; *Weekly Clarion* (Jackson), October 22, November 3, 1870; *Weekly Pilot,* October 15, 1870.
17. *New York Times,* July 30, September 28, 1878; *Daily Picayune* (New Orleans), October 10, 1878. The award at Philadelphia may be the one referred to by Thomas S. Dabney April 14, 1884, when he recalled a successful black planter "a few miles below Vicksburg" whose cotton "at the Cincinnati Exposition, a few years ago, took *all* the prizes!" Thomas S. Dabney to William H. Dabney, quoted in Susan Dabney Smedes, *Memorial of a Southern Planter* (New York, 1965), p. 305. Perhaps this is the source of the statement "In 1873, Montgomery & Sons . . . won all the prizes for cotton at the Cincinnati Exposition," in James W. Loewen and Charles Sallis, eds., *Mississippi: Conflict and Change* (New York, 1974), p. 187. In fact, no cotton was exhibited at the Fourth Cincinnati Industrial Exposition that opened September 3, 1873, the only fair held there that year, according to the *Cincinnati Enquirer.*
18. U.S. Census, 1870, Agricultural Schedule, Warren County, Miss.; *Hinds County Gazette,* November 2, 1870; *Vicksburg Times and Republican,* October 20, 1870; *Weekly Clarion,* October 12, December 22, 1870, May 11, 1871; Robert Somers, *The Southern States Since the War, 1870–1871* (New York, 1871), p. 254.
19. Montgomery to Davis, April 5, Aug. 9, 1869, Jan. 6, 23, Feb. 11, 1868, Jos. Davis Papers, MDAH; U.S. Census, 1870, Agricultural Schedule, Warren County, Miss.; for advice to diversify crops, see *Vicksburg Times and Republican,* October 20, 1870; *Weekly Clarion,* October 8, 1874.
20. Montgomery to Davis, Sept. 10, 1866, Jos. Davis Papers, MDAH.
21. Roger L. Ransom and Richard Sutch, *One Kind of Freedom* (Cambridge, 1977), p. 116; Harold D. Woodman, *King Cotton and His Retainers* (Lexington, Ky., 1968), p. 273, 301–302; Montgomery to Davis, Dec. 17, 1868, Jos. Davis Papers, MDAH.
22. Montgomery to Davis, Feb. 21, April 7, May 29, June 5, 1870, Jos. Davis Papers, MDAH; Mary Virginia Montgomery's diary, March 28, June 21, 1872, Montgomery Papers, LC.

23. Mary Virginia Montgomery's diary, Aug. 15, 26, 27, Oct. 3, 1872, Montgomery Papers, LC. J. H. D. Bowmar to Jeff. Davis, October 22, 1873, Confederate Museum, Richmond, Virginia.

24. For Montgomery's antebellum store operation, *see* chapter 1, pp. 18–19; for the re-establishment of the store, *see* Chapter 3, pp. 66–67.

25. *See* chapter 4, pp. 133–134; R. G. Dun Credit Ledgers, Baker Library, Harvard University, Vol. 21, Warren Co., Miss., 81E, 82. These extracts from the Dun Ledgers are used with the permission of Dun and Bradstreet, Inc., New York. In the quotations from the ledgers, obvious abbreviations have been spelled out. For definitions of the ratings, *see* Ransom and Sutch, *Freedom*, pp. 137–138, 306–313.

26. *Boston Evening Transcript*, n.d., quoted in the *New Orleans Times Democrat*, February 16, 1902; Isaiah T. Montgomery to Booker T. Washington, Nov. 9, 1909, B. T. Washington Papers, LC, Box 847.

27. Mary Virginia Montgomery's diary, 1872, Montgomery Papers, LC.

28. Ibid., June 12, 13, Sept. 21, Oct. 19, 1872, Montgomery Papers, LC.

29. Ibid., for information about William Lewis, Jr., *see* March 28, April 18, 20, July 11, Aug. 25, Sept. 1, 2, 7, 28, Nov. 11; for Ben Green, *see* May 11, Sept. 20, Oct. 21, 1872, Montgomery Papers, LC.

30. Thomas D. Clark, *Pills, Petticoats and Plows: The Southern Country Store* (Indianapolis, 1944), p. 82; Mrs. Betty Bentley Beaumont, *A Business Woman's Journal* (Philadelphia, 1888), p. 294; Mary Virginia Montgomery's diary, 1872, Montgomery Papers, LC.

31. Mary Virginia Montgomery's diary, July 26, Aug. 27, Sept. 11, Oct. 4, 1872, Montgomery Papers, LC; for a discussion of patent medicines sold in general stores, *see* Clark, *Pills, Petticoats and Plows*, chap. XIII.

32. Ransom and Sutch, *Freedom*, p. 345, n. 23; Mary Virginia Montgomery's diary, Jan. 20, 22, Feb. 17, July 27, Aug. 3, 24, Sept. 7, 14, 21, 28, Oct. 12, Nov. 19, 1872, Montgomery Papers, LC; Montgomery to Davis, April 18, 22, 1867, Jos. Davis Papers, MDAH.

33. Mary Virginia Montgomery's diary, Feb. 3, 16, 17, March 2, 4, May 6, 1872, Montgomery Papers, LC.

34. Ibid., April 25, May 2, June 5, 27, July 11, Aug. 15, 22, 29, 1872, Montgomery Papers, LC.

35. Loring and Atkins, *Cotton Culture*, p. 75; Woodman, *King Cotton*, pp. 296, 332.

36. Ransom and Sutch, *Freedom*, pp. 237–242; Somers, *Southern States*, p. 241.

37. Everett, *Brierfield*, pp. 42–49.

38. U.S. Census, 1870, Population Schedule, Davis Bend Precinct, Warren County, Miss. At the bottom of the page there is a note in a hand different from the enumerator's, referring to the Benjamin Montgomery listing, stating "Color Doubtful." Evidently the authorities could not believe that a black man had real estate worth $300,000 and personal estate of $50,000.

39. Mary Virginia Montgomery's diary, Montgomery Papers, LC. There are dozens of references to her flower gardening throughout the first six months of the year.

40. Frank Luther Mott, *A History of American Magazines* (Cambridge, Mass.,

1938), 3:325–327, 388–389; Jane Trahey, ed., *Harper's Bazaar, 100 Years of the American Female* (New York, 1967), p. xii; Mary Virginia Montgomery's diary, Montgomery Papers, LC.

41. Mary Virginia Montgomery's diary, Aug. 19, Sept. 7, and passim, Montgomery Papers, LC.

42. Ibid., Montgomery Papers, LC; Mott, *American Magazines,* 3:41–42, 92, 281–286.

43. Merle Curti, *The Growth of American Thought,* 3rd ed. (New York, 1964), pp. 332–334; Harvey Wish, *Society and Thought in Early America* (New York, 1950), pp. 468–469; Mott, *American Magazines,* 1:447–448; 2:42, 87.

44. Mary Virginia Montgomery's Diary, Feb. 26, April 2, 3, and passim, 1872, Montgomery Papers, LC; Curti, *American Thought,* pp. 346–350, 578, 626–627.

45. Mary Virginia Montgomery's diary, Montgomery Papers, LC; Isaiah T. Montgomery and Martha Robb Montgomery, marriage license, May 4, 1871, certificate of marriage, May 11, 1871, Warren County, Miss., Marriage License Book 2, p. 189; *Weekly Clarion,* June 15, 1871.

46. Mary Virginia Montgomery's diary, June 19, 20, 22, 29, 30, Oct. 19, 20, 1872, Montgomery Papers, LC; William Still, *The Underground Railroad* (Philadelphia, 1872), p. 806.

47. *New Orleans Semi-Weekly Louisianian,* May 14, 1871; *Weekly Clarion,* May 11, 1871; Mary Virginia Montgomery's diary, May 1, 1872, Montgomery Papers, LC; Dun Credit Ledgers, Baker Library, Harvard University, vol. 2, p. 82.

48. C. Vann Woodward, *Origins of the New South, 1877–1913* (Baton Rouge, 1951), pp. 153–154; Mary Virginia Montgomery's diary, Jan. 29, April 7, 27, June 2, July 22, 28, Aug. 15, 25, Sept. 6, Oct. 13, Nov. 5, 1872, Montgomery Papers, LC.

49. Mary Virginia Montgomery's diary, Jan. 20, March 5, 8, 10, 11, 26, April 2, 10, June 2, 5, 19, July 2, Sept. 19, Nov. 11, 1872, Montgomery Papers, LC: Still, *Railroad,* p. 806.

50. U.S. Census, 1870, Population Schedule, Warren County, Miss., MDAH.

51. Mary Virginia Montgomery's diary, Feb. 2, 8, 21, March 4, 5, 7, 12, 20, April 10, 29, May 6, 8, June 27, 30, Sept. 27, Oct. 3, Nov. 1, 1872, Montgomery Papers, LC.

52. Ibid., Jan. 25, Feb. 2, March 10, 17, 22, April 21, May 28, 29, 31, June 3, July 8, 9, 10, 12, 16, Aug. 12, Sept. 4, 17, Oct. 2, 4, 20, 22, 23, Nov. 4, 1872, Montgomery Papers, LC.

53. Ibid., Jan. 23, 24, Feb. 6, 18, 20, March 5, 27, 31, April 17, May 25, June 12, 16, 19, 26, 30, July 14, 23, Aug. 4, 7, Sept. 2, 22, Oct. 3, 5, 13, 28, Nov. 10, 1872, Montgomery Papers, LC; Press to Hermann, May 18, 1978, in the author's possession.

54. Mary Virginia Montgomery's diary, Feb. 12, 14, 21, 29, March 6, 14, 15, 16, 21, May 14, 28, July 6, 12, 13, 29, Aug. 7, Sept. 16, 21, 26, 27, Oct. 11, 12, 27, Nov. 5, 7, 1872, Montgomery Papers, LC.

55. Ibid., Aug. 12, 13, 20, 28, 30, Sept. 9, 10, 12, 16, 19, 24, 25, Oct. 7, 8, 24, Montgomery Papers, LC.

56. *New National Era,* November 23, 30, December 14, 1871.
57. Mary Virginia Montgomery's diary, Sept. 5, Oct. 18, 19, 21, Nov. 1, 16, Dec. 29, 1872, Montgomery Papers, LC; *Catalogue of the Officers and Students of Oberlin College Year, 1873–1874; General Catalogue of Oberlin College, 1833–1908* (Oberlin, Ohio, 1909), p. 681; W. E. Bigglestone, archivist, Oberlin College, to Janet Hermann, October 26 and November 9, 1977. For the postwar role of freedwomen, *see* Leon F. Litwack, *Been in the Storm So Long* (New York, 1979), p. 246.
58. Mary Virginia Montgomery's diary, Jan. 17, 21, 31, Feb. 2, 5, 8, April 10, 11, 28, May 1, 5, 25, June 19, Sept. 22, 26, Montgomery Papers, LC; Loring and Atkinson, *Cotton Culture,* p. 131; bill of sale, John McMurray to J. E. Davis, for a $160 carriage, Jos. Davis Papers; Warren County Tax Rolls, 1871; U.S. Census, 1870, Agricultural Schedule, MDAH.
59. U.S. Census, 1870, Warren County, Miss., Population Schedule; Agricultural Schedule, MDAH.
60. Moore, "Mississippi During Reconstruction," p. 66; Loring and Atkinson, *Cotton Culture,* pp. 75, 106, 115, 137; U.S. Census, 1870, Population Schedule, Warren County, Miss., MDAH; Litwack, *Been in the Storm So Long,* pp. 244–245.
61. *New National Era,* April 20, 1871; Mary Virginia Montgomery's diary, March 29, May 20, Aug. 14, Sept. 30, 1872, Montgomery Papers, LC; Huntington and Pitkin to BRFAL, April 11, 1867, M826-6; Montgomery & Sons, per B. T. Montgomery to BRFAL, March 16, 1868, M826-7; rent vouchers for Freedmen's School, Davis Bend, Aug. 5, Sept. 3, 1867, Mississippi Superintendent of Education, Vouchers Approved, vol. 53; Capt. E. C. Platt to Joseph N. Bishop, Sept. 7, Oct. 14, 1867, Sub-Commissioner, Press Copies Letters Sent, vol. 273, BRFAL (Miss.), RG 105, NA.
62. *Vicksburg Daily Times,* November 21, 1866; Ben Montgomery to Davis, Sept. 9, 1869, Jos. Davis Papers, MDAH; Isaiah Montgomery to Booker T. Washington, Nov. 9, 1905, B. T. Washington Papers, LC, Box 847; U.S. Census, 1870, Population Schedule, Warren County, Miss., MDAH.
63. Oaths of Office of Registrars, 4th Military District, Office of Civil Affairs, LR, December 16, 1869, RG 393, NA, vol. 33, part I, p. 536; *Weekly Clarion,* December 18, July 28, 1870; Secretary of State (Miss.), Register of Commissions, 1871–1874, November 7, 1871, MDAH, p. 559.
64. *Weekly Clarion,* April 6, August 3, 1871.
65. Mary Virginia Montgomery's diary, June 25, July 18, 19, 20, 23, 24, 27, 31, Aug. 3, Montgomery Papers, LC; Wharton, *Negro in Mississippi,* p. 158; Garner, *Reconstruction in Mississippi,* p. 187.
66. Mary Virginia Montgomery's diary, Aug. 15, 16, 20, Sept. 18, 19, Oct. 16, Nov. 2, 5, 6, 7, Montgomery Papers, LC; Lynch, *Autobiography,* pp. 99–105. Grant's majority at Davis Bend was much greater than in the surrounding area, for he carried Warren County by only a two to one margin; McKee beat his Democratic opponent by a slightly greater majority, *Weekly Clarion,* November 15, 1872.
67. Quoted in Wharton, *Negro in Mississippi,* p. 264.
68. Mary Virginia Montgomery's diary, July 20, Aug. 4, Montgomery Papers, LC.

69. Ibid., March 27, April 30, May 1, July 3, 4, Montgomery Papers, LC.
70. Ibid., May 4, 20, 22, June 4, 18, July 13, Sept. 11, Montgomery Papers, LC.
71. Montgomery to Davis, April 26, 1869, Jos. Davis Papers, MDAH.
72. Mary Virginia Montgomery's diary, June 18, July 6, 9, Sept. 18, Nov. 3, 7, Montgomery Papers, LC.
73. Montgomery to Davis, Dec. 30, 1867, Jan. 27, Feb. 3, 1870, Jos. Davis Papers, MDAH.
74. Montgomery to Davis, July 29, 1867, March 4, April 5, Sept. 9, Nov. 4, 1869, Jos. Davis Papers, MDAH.
75. Mary Virginia Montgomery's diary, Feb. 4, May 4, Montgomery Papers, LC; Montgomery to Davis, Nov. 4, 1869, June 5, 1870, Jos. Davis Papers, MDAH.

Chapter 6

1. *Hinds County Gazette,* January 21, 1874.
2. Wharton, *Negro in Mississippi,* pp. 168, 171–172, 175–176; *Weekly Clarion,* December 17, 1874.
3. Bowmar to Davis, Aug. 13, 1873; Secretary of State, Register of Commissions, 1871–1874, Centennial Commission, June 20, 1874, MDAH, p. 45.
4. Register of Commissions, 1871–1874, Wharf & Harbor Master Commission, January 11, 1872, MDAH, p. 559; *Weekly Clarion,* May 11, 1871; Wharton, *Negro in Mississippi,* pp. 147, 173, 176.
5. Garner, *Reconstruction in Mississippi,* p. 333; *Daily Vicksburger,* July 21, 30, August 5, 8, 19, November 4, 28, 1874.
6. Garner, *Reconstruction in Mississippi,* pp. 332–337; Wharton, *Negro in Mississippi,* pp. 190, 221; *Daily Vicksburger,* December 4, 18, 20, 24, 30, 1874; *Weekly Clarion,* December 10, 17, 14, 1874; *Vicksburg Daily Times,* December 15, 1874; *Weekly Mississippi Pilot,* December 26, 1874; *Vicksburg Daily Herald,* January 20, 27, 1875.
7. Quotations from unnamed Jackson newspaper, 1874, in Loewen and Sallis, *Mississippi: Conflict and Change* p. 187; *Weekly Clarion,* December 17, 1874; Wharton, *Negro in Mississippi,* pp. 202–204; *Chicago Tribune,* May 7, 1879.
8. R. G. Dun Credit Ledgers, Baker Library, Harvard, vol. 21, pp. 81E., 170; John Hope Franklin, *From Slavery to Freedom* (New York, 1947), pp. 314–315; *Daily Mississippi Pilot,* August 1, 1875. The advertisement also appeared in issues of September 24, 25, 26, 30, and October 1, 2. It was carried by the *Weekly Mississippi Pilot* from January 16 through September 4, 1875.
9. Dun Credit Ledgers, Baker Library, Harvard, vol. 21, pp. 170, 198, 81E; Wharton, *Negro in Mississippi,* pp. 106, 127–128.
10. Elliott, *Flood Control,* p. 111; *Weekly Clarion,* August 20, 1874; Montgomery to Mrs. Lize M. Hamer, July 12, 1874, Lise Mitchell Papers, Tulane University; Hammond, *Cotton Industry,* vol. 1, appendix 1; *Chicago Tribune,* May 7, 1879.
11. *Laws of Mississippi* (Jackson, 1872), pp. 422–423; Davis v. Bowmar, MDAH, pp. 94–107.

12. Jefferson Davis to Varina Davis, Nov. 10, 1873, Jan. 21, 1874, Strode, *Private Letters,* pp. 371, 383; Davis v. Bowmar, MDAH, pp. 18–20, 170–172.

13. Davis v. Bowmar, MDAH, pp. 71–72, 438.

14. Ibid., pp. 113–114.

15. Ibid., pp. 110–114, 116–124, 176; Montgomery to Hamer, July 12, 1874, Lise Mitchell Papers, Tulane University.

16. Bowmar to Davis, Jan. 2, Feb. 20, 1875, May 14, 1877; Thornton Montgomery to Jeff. Davis, May 13, 1877, Confederate Museum, Richmond, Virginia; Virginia Montgomery to Jeff. Davis, March 11, 1875, Dunbar Rowland, ed., *Jefferson Davis, Constitutionalist* 7: 416.

17. Davis v. Bowmar, MDAH, pp. 405–430; Jefferson to Varina Davis, Oct. 23, 1874, May 6, June 5, 9, 14, Oct. 22, 1875, Strode, *Private Letters,* pp. 401–402, 408–409.

18. Warren County Chancery Court, Minute Book 3, p. 117; Jefferson to Varina Davis, Jan. 11, April 22, 1876, Strode, *Private Letters,* pp. 422–423, 428.

19. Lise Hamer to Walter Fleming, n.d., Fleming Papers, NYPL; Jefferson to Varina Davis, March 22, 1876, Strode, *Private Letters,* p. 426.

20. Dun Credit Ledgers, vol. 21, pp. 198, 81E, Baker Library, Harvard; Isaiah T. Montgomery Pension Record, Civil War, XC2997096, WNRC; Jefferson to Varina Davis, Dec. 9, 1876, Strode, *Private Letters,* p. 439.

21. Thornton Montgomery to Jeff. Davis, May 13, 1877, Bowmar to Davis, May 14, 1877, Confederate Museum, Richmond, Virginia; Loewen and Sallis, *Mississippi: Conflict and Change,* p. 187; Virginia Montgomery to Jefferson Davis, March 11, 1875, Dunbar Rowland, ed., *Jefferson Davis, Constitutionalist* 7:416; Estate of Benjamin T. Montgomery, Deceased, File No. 3029, Probate Docket, Chancery Court, Warren County, Miss.; U.S. Census, 1870, Population Schedule, Warren County, Miss. A letter from Jefferson Davis to his wife dated May 1, 1877 (Strode, *Private Letters,* p. 427), tells of the sudden death of Ben Montgomery, but it must be misdated since he did not die until May 12, 1877.

22. Estate of Benjamin T. Montgomery, Probate No. 3029, Warren Co.; Interview with Frank E. Everett, February 28, 1977, Vicksburg, Miss.

23. Jefferson to Varina Davis, May 1, 1877, Strode, *Private Letters,* p. 427; Dun Credit Ledgers, vol. 21, p. 170.

24. Jefferson Davis v. J. H. D. Bowmar, et al., *Reports of Cases in the Supreme Court for the State of Mississippi,* LV (St. Louis, 1879), 773–813; Warren County Chancery Court, Minute Book 3, June 1, 1878, March 29, 1879, April 13, 1880, pp. 411, 477, and 584, respectively.

25. Dun Credit Ledgers, vol. 21, pp. 81J, 198, Baker Library, Harvard; *1879 Directories of Vicksburg, &c.* (Vicksburg, 1879), p. 98; Press to Hermann, May 18, 1978.

26. *Chicago Tribune,* May 7, 1879; Secretary of State, Register of Commissions, 1878–1881, MDAH, p. 24; Isaiah Montgomery to Booker T. Washington, Nov. 9, 1905, B. T. Washington Papers, LC, Box 847; J. M. Gibson, *Memoirs* (Houston, 1929), pp. 9–10. Some years later, one of the politicians who had visited at Brierfield observed that he was amused when some of these white guests of the Montgomerys loudly criticized President Theodore Roosevelt for entertaining Booker T. Washington at a White House dinner.

27. U.S. Census, 1870, 1880, Agricultural Schedule, Warren County, Miss., MDAH; *Chicago Tribune*, May 7, 1879.
28. U.S. Census, 1880, Agricultural Schedule, Warren County, Miss., MDAH; *Chicago Tribune*, May 7, 1879.
29. Henry King, "A Year of Exodus in Kansas," *Scribner's Monthly*, XX, 2 (June 1880), 216; *Chicago Tribune*, May 7, 1879; Jefferson to Varina Davis, Oct. 22, 1875, Strode, *Private Letters*, p. 419.
30. Isaiah T. Montgomery to Gov. John P. St. John, May 28, 1879, Dept. of Archives, Kansas State Historical Society, Topeka, Kansas; Norman L. Crockett, *The Black Towns* (Lawrence, Kansas, 1979), pp. 10–12.
31. *Times-Democrat* (New Orleans), February 18, 1902; *Chicago Tribune*, May 7, 1879; Isaiah Montgomery obituary, unidentified newspaper clipping, n.d. (1924), Isaiah Montgomery Subject File, MDAH.
32. *Weekly Clarion*, June 25, 1879, reprinted from *Boston Herald*, n.d.; Nell Irvin Painter, *Exodusters* (New York, 1977), pp. 231–232; King, "A Year of Exodus," pp. 212, 215; Roy Garvin, "Benjamin or 'Pap' Singleton and His Followers," *Journal of Negro History*, vol. 33, no. 1 (January 1948), p. 13.
33. Warren County, Miss., Chancery Court Minute Book 4, pp. 75, 85, 145; Deed Book ZZ, pp. 529–532; Hamer to Fleming, n.d., Fleming Papers, NYPL; *St. Louis Globe Democrat*, October 24, 1886; Benjamin Montgomery to Joseph Davis, Dec. 30, 1867, Jos. Davis Papers, MDAH; Elliott, *Flood Control*, pp. 111 and passim.
34. *New York World*, September 28, 1890; Press to Hermann, May 18, 1978; Isaiah Montgomery Pension Record, XC2997096, WNRC; Wm. T. Montgomery Pension Record, Application No. 47101, Certificate No. 33531, NA. Record, Application No. 47101, Certificate No. 33531, NA.
35. U.S. Census, Population Schedule, 1870, 1880, Warren County, Miss., MDAH.
36. Joseph to Jefferson Davis, Jan. 2, 1861, Aug. 15, Sept. 16, Nov. 11, 1863, Jefferson Davis Papers, Transylvania University; Frank McKinney Deposition, Davis v. Bowmar, MDAH, pp. 405–414; U.S. Census, Population Schedule, 1870, 1880, Warren County, Miss., MDAH.
37. Burgess T. Montgomery to Varina Davis, Jan. 7, 1895, Strode, *Private Letters*, p. 510.
38. For evidence of the universal desire for landownership among freedmen, *see* Wharton, *Negro in Mississippi*, pp. 59–61; August Meier, *Negro Thought in America 1880–1915* (Ann Arbor, 1963), pp. 11–12.

Chapter 7

1. Booker T. Washington, "A Town Owned by Negroes," *World's Work*, vol. 14, no. 3 (July 1907), p. 9131.
2. Aurelius P. Hood, *The Negro at Mound Bayou* (Nashville, 1910), p. 58; Isaiah Montgomery to Jefferson Davis, Sept. 27, 1886, in Rowland, ed., *Jefferson Davis, Constitutionalist*, 9:490; Wharton, *Negro in Mississippi*, p. 270.

3. *The Appeal*, March 2, 1889; *Fargo Daily Argus*, September 23, 1884; W. M. House, *The North Dakota and Richland County Chart, 1897*, p. 49; *The Directory of Richland County, North Dakota, 1891*, Eagle Township, p. 83; Hiram M. Drache, *The Challenge of the Prairie* (Fargo, North Dakota, 1970), pp. 13, 200–201.

4. *Fargo Daily Argus*, May 19, October 27, 1884, June 24, 1885; *The Appeal*, March 2, 1889, October 17, 1891; Wm. T. Montgomery to Frederick Douglass, Oct. 27, 1888, Frederick Douglass Papers, LC, Reel no. 5.

5. Hood, *Negro at Mound Bayou*, p. 58; Washington, "A Town," pp. 9125–26; *New Orleans Times-Democrat*, February 16, 1902; A. R. Taylor, "A Brief History of the Town and Colony of Mound Bayou," Semi-Centennial Program, Mound Bayou, Miss., July 1937, p. 5; Geographical Site Location Report, Mound Bayou, Miss., May 7, 1888, Records of the Post Office Dept., Ser. 187, RG 28, NA; Press to Hermann, May 18, 1978. For a detailed description of the origin and expansion of the Louisville, New Orleans, and Texas Railroad, *see* Robert L. Brandfon, *Cotton Kingdom of the New South* (Cambridge, Mass., 1967), pp. 71–73.

6. Maurice Elizabeth Jackson, "Mound Bayou—A Study in Social Development" (M.A. thesis, University of Albama, 1937), pp. 29–30; *New Orleans Times-Democrat*, February 16, 1902; Washington, "A Town," p. 9126.

7. Jackson, "Mound Bayou," pp. 31–34; Washington, "A Town," p. 9126; Hiram Tong, "The Pioneers of Mound Bayou," *Century Magazine*, vol. 79, no. 3 (January 1910), pp. 393–394.

8. Washington, "A Town," pp. 9125–9127; Tong, "Pioneers," p. 394; Shepperd, "From Slavery," p. 186; Semi-Centennial Program, p. 6.

9. Washington, "A Town," pp. 9125–9127; Tong, "Pioneers," pp. 391–393; Rev. B. F. Ousley, "A Town of Colored People in Mississippi," c. 1904, Con. 376, B. T. Washington Papers, LC.

10. Washington, "A Town," pp. 9127–9128; Ousley, "A Town of Colored People," Con. 376, B. T. Washington Papers, LC; Semi-Centennial Program, p. 6.

11. Washington, "A Town," p. 9128; Brandfon, *Cotton Kingdom*, pp. 80, 88–89.

12. "Farmers Meeting," leaflet, Mound Bayou, Miss., January 22, 1906, B. T. Washington Papers, LC, Con. 328.

13. Washington, "A Town, pp. 9129–30; Tong, "The Pioneers," pp. 397–398.

14. Washington, "A Town," p. 9129; Tong, "The Pioneers," p. 398.

15. Washington, "A Town," pp. 9128–29.

16. Tong, "The Pioneers," pp. 398–399; Washington, "A Town," pp. 9132–34; Isaiah Montgomery to Varina Davis, April 25, 1902, Jefferson Davis Papers, University of Alabama; Ousley, "A Town of Colored People," Con. 376, B. T. Washington Papers, LC; *New Orleans Times-Democrat*, February 16, 1902.

17. Montgomery to Washington, Sept. 6, 1904, C. A. Buchanan to I. T. Montgomery, Sept. 10, 1904, Con. 292, B. T. Washington Papers, LC; Isaiah T. Montgomery "The Negro in Business," *Outlook*, Nov. 16, 1901, p. 733.

18. Isaiah Montgomery to Booker T. Washington, Nov. 9, 1905, Con. 847, B. T. Washington Papers, LC; Shepperd, "From Slavery," p. 188.

19. Typescript of I. T. Montgomery speech, Benjamin Montgomery Papers, LC; Wharton, *Negro in Mississippi*, pp. 211–212. The speech is also reprinted in the Semi-Centennial Program.

20. Semi-Centennial Program, p. 26; *New York World,* September 17, 27, 1890; Wharton, *Negro in Mississippi,* p. 212.

21. *New York Age,* October 11, 18, 1890; Henry F. Downing, circular letter, Sept. 27, 1890, in Louis R. Harlan, ed., *The Papers of Booker T. Washington,* (Urbana, Ill., 1974), 3:84.

22. Lynch, *Autobiography,* p. 342; Wharton, *Negro in Mississippi,* p. 212; Harlan, *Papers of Washington,* 3:85; J. Saunders Redding, *The Lonesome Road,* (Garden City, N.J., 1958), pp. 118–119.

23. Booker T. Washington, *My Larger Education* (Garden City, N.Y., 1911), p. 209, quoted in August Meier, "Booker T. Washington and the Town of Mound Bayou," *Phylon,* 15 (Winter 1954): 397; Isaiah T. Montgomery and James Hill to Frederick Douglass, March 16, 1894, Douglass Papers, LC, Reel no. 7; Montgomery to Washington, Oct. 14, 1895; Con. 113; Nov. 9, 1905, Con. 847, B. T. Washington Papers, LC.

24. Washington, *My Larger Education,* pp. 207–208; Harlan, *Washington Papers,* 1:182–183, 193; Shepperd, "From Slavery," pp. 231–234.

25. Report of Special Agent to the Commissioner, General Land Office, Washington, D.C., May 26, 1903, Con. 267; I. T. Montgomery to B. T. Washington, Jan. 5, 20, Con. 236; April 20, Dec. 17, 1902, Con. 234; W. T. Montgomery to Washington, July 14, 1903, Con. 267; I. T. Montgomery to Edgar S. Wilson, Jan. 1, 1902, B. T. Washington Papers, LC.

26. Emmett Jay Scott to B. T. Washington, June 21, 22, 1903, Con. 274; Theodore Roosevelt to Edgar S. Wilson, June 24, 1903, Con. 282; A. A. Sharp to Stuyvesant Fish, Aug. 7, 1903; Sharp to I. T. Montgomery, Aug. 31, 1903; Montgomery to Washington, Sept. 21, 1903, Con. 267, B. T. Washington Papers, LC; Brandfon, *Cotton Kingdom,* p. 93.

27. B. T. Washington to E. J. Scott, July 21, 1903, Con. 249; to Montgomery, Oct. 17, 1903, Con. 267, B. T. Washington Papers, LC.

28. I. T. Montgomery to Hon. Mr. Latta, Oct. 23, 1907; Wm. T. Montgomery to B. T. Washington, Oct. 23, 1907; Washington to Wm. T. Montgomery, Oct. 28, 1907, Con. 354; Richard L. Jones to I. T. Montgomery, Jan. 8, 1909; I. T. Montgomery to Washington, Jan. 13, 19, 20, 1909; Washington to Montgomery, Jan. 19, 25, telegram, Jan. 23, 1909; Remarks of Isaiah T. Montgomery at Lincoln's Birthplace, February 12, 1909, Con. 896, B. T. Washington Papers, LC.

29. William Collins to Montgomery, Aug. 31, 1904; Montgomery to Collins, Sept. 6, 1904; Montgomery to Sharp, Sept. 6, 1904; Montgomery to Washington, Sept. 6, 20, 1904; C. A. Buchanan to Montgomery, Sept. 10, 1904, Con. 292; Montgomery to Washington, Aug. 27, 1907, Con. 354, B. T. Washington Papers, LC.

30. I. T. Montgomery to F. B. Brown, Sept. 10, 1903, published in *Commercial Appeal,* September 13, 1903; W. T. Montgomery to Washington, Feb. 7, 1905, Con. 304, B. T. Washington Papers, LC.

31. Wm. T. Montgomery to Washington, July 6, 1904, containing clippings from *St. Louis Globe Democrat,* n.d., *Vicksburg Herald,* n.d., Con. 292; I. T. Montgomery to Washington, April 3, 1905, Con. 878, B. T. Washington Papers, LC.

32. I. T. Montgomery to Dr. A. F. Beard, Sec., American Missionary Society, June 8, 1900, Con. 179; Montgomery to Washington, Aug. 22, 1903, Con. 268; Jan. 29, 1909, Con. 896; March 24, 1909, Con. 395; Montgomery to E. J. Scott, Aug. 7, 1909, Con. 395, B. T. Washington Papers, LC; Semi-Centennial Program, p. 6; Meier, "Washington and Mound Bayou," pp. 397–398.

33. I. T. Montgomery to E. J. Scott, Sept. 3, 1908; Scott to Montgomery, Sept. 5, 1908, Con. 377, B. T. Washington Papers, LC; Tong, "Pioneers," pp. 396–397.

34. Tong, "Pioneers," pp. 396–397.

35. Washington to Banks, April 23, 1912; Washington to I. T. Montgomery, April 29, 1912; "Introduction to Mound Bayou," n.d.; Memo in re: Mound Bayou Community & Mr. Rosenwald, n.d.; Julius Rosenwald to Montgomery, June 3, 1912; Montgomery to Washington, June 7, July 3, 1912, Con. 459; Illinois Central Railroad, Report on Mound Bayou by J. C. Clair, n.d., with explanation, I. T. Montgomery, July 10, 1912, Con. 64; Montgomery to Rosenwald, Aug. 15, 1912; Montgomery to Washington, Aug. 29, 1912, Con. 460, B. T. Washington Papers, LC; Meier, "Washington and Mound Bayou," p. 398.

36. Dedication of Mound Bayou Oil Mill & Manufacturing Co., November 12, 1912, Con. 64, B. T. Washington Papers, LC.

37. Rosenwald to Banks, Feb. 25, 1913; Banks to Rosenwald, March 1, 1913, Con. 64, B. T. Washington Papers, LC; Meier, "Washington and Mound Bayou," pp. 398–399; Semi-Centennial Program, p. 6.

38. Washington to Banks, Sept. 5, 1913, Con. 64, B. T. Washington Papers, LC; Meier, "Washington and Mound Bayou," pp. 399–400; Jackson, "Mound Bayou," p. 47; J. Saunders Redding, No Day of Triumph (New York, 1942) p. 303.

39. Isaiah T. Montgomery Pension Record, Civil War, XC2997096, WNRC; Semi-Centennial Program, pp. 1, 6; Redding, No Day of Triumph, p. 304; Shepperd, "From Slavery," p. 218; I. T. Montgomery to Hon. Andrew Carnegie, April 18, 1912, Con. 64, B. T. Washington Papers, LC; Drache, The Challenge, p. 201; W. T. Montgomery Pension Record, Application No. 47101, Certificate No. 33531, NA.

40. Redding, No Day of Triumph, pp. 300–301.

41. Ibid., pp. 301–307; Crockett, Black Towns, pp. 72, 84, 142–143.

42. Redding, No Day of Triumph, pp. 289–293; Shepperd, "From Slavery," pp. 238–239.

Selected Bibliography

Manuscript Sources

Baker Library, Harvard University, Cambridge, Mass.
  R. G. Dun and Company. Mercantile Ledgers. Dun and Bradstreet Archives
Duke University, Durham, N.C.
  Jefferson Davis Papers
Library of Congress, Washington, D.C.
  Samuel D. Barnes Papers
  Benjamin Montgomery Family Papers
  Zachary Taylor Papers
  Booker T. Washington Papers
Mississippi Department of Archives and History, Jackson, Miss.
  Joseph E. Davis and Family Papers
  Jefferson Davis v. J.H.D. Bowmar et al., Warren County Chancery Court, July
    3, 1874–January 8, 1876, unreported
  William Burr Howell Collection
  John A. Quitman Papers
  Records of the Secretary of State, Record Group 28
  Mahala P. H. Roach letter, Miscellaneous Manuscripts
Museum of the Confederacy, Richmond, Va.
  Jefferson Davis Papers
National Archives, Washington, D.C.
  Military Records, 4th Military District, Record Group 393
  Office of the Adjutant General, Record Group 94
  Pension Records, Civil War
  Records of the Bureau of Refugees, Freedmen and Abandoned Lands, Record
    Group 105
  Records of the Post Office Department, Record Group 28

New York Public Library
  Walter Lynwood Fleming Collection
Old Court House Museum, Vicksburg, Miss.
  WPA Slave Narratives, Warren County, Miss., Record Group 60
Transylvania University, Lexington, Ky.
  Jefferson Davis Papers
Tulane University, New Orleans, La.
  Lise Mitchell Papers
University of Alabama, Tuscaloosa, Ala.
  Jefferson Davis Papers
University of Tennessee, Knoxville, Tenn.
  John Eaton, Jr. Papers

Books and Articles

Ames, Blanche Butler, comp. *Chronicles from the Nineteenth Century: Family Letters of Blanche Butler and Adelbert Ames.* 2 vols. Clinton, Mass.: privately issued, 1957.

Anderson, John Q., ed. *Brokenburn: The Journal of Kate Stone, 1861–1868.* Baton Rouge: Louisiana State University Press, 1955.

Baker, Henry E. "The Negro in the Field of Invention." *Journal of Negro History,* 2 (January 1917): 21–36.

Baldwin, Joseph G. *The Flush Times of Alabama and Mississippi: A Series of Sketches.* New York: D. Appleton, 1854.

Beaumont, Mrs. Betty (Bentley). *A Business Woman's Journal.* Philadelphia: T. B. Peterson & Bros., 1888.

———. *Twelve Years of My Life.* Philadelphia: T. B. Peterson & Bros., 1887.

[Benham, George C.] *A Year of Wreck: A True Story by a Victim.* New York: Harper & Bros., 1880.

Bentley, George R. *A History of the Freedmen's Bureau.* New York: Octagon Books, 1974.

Berlin, Ira. *Slaves Without Masters.* New York: Pantheon Books, 1974.

Bestor, A. E. *Backwoods Utopias.* Philadelphia: University of Pennsylvania Press, 1950.

Bettersworth, John K. *Confederate Mississippi: The People and Politics of a Cotton State in Wartime.* Baton Rouge: Louisiana State University Press, 1943.

Boynton, Charles B., comp. *History of the Great Western Sanitary Fair.* Cincinnati: C. F. Vent & Co., 1864.

Brandfon, Robert L. *Cotton Kingdom of the New South.* Cambridge: Harvard University Press, 1964.

Catalogue of the Officers and Students of Oberlin College for the College Year 1873–1874. Oberlin, Ohio: Oberlin College, 1873.

Clark, Thomas D. *Pills, Petticoats and Plows: The Southern Country Store*. Indianapolis: Bobbs-Merrill, 1944.

Cole, Margaret. *Robert Owen of New Lanark*. London and New York: Batchworth Press, 1953.

Curti, Merle. *The Growth of American Thought*. 3rd ed. New York: Harper & Row, 1964.

Davis, Reuben. *Recollections of Mississippi and Mississippians*. Boston: Houghton Mifflin, 1891.

Davis, Varina Howell. *Jefferson Davis, Ex-President of the Confederate States of America: a Memoir*. 2 vols. New York: Belford, 1890.

DeLeon, T. C. *Belles, Beaux and Brains of the '60's*. New York: G. W. Dillingham, 1909.

1879 Directories of Vicksburg &c. Vicksburg: Abel C. Tuttle, 1879.

The Directory of Richland County, North Dakota. N.p., 1891.

[Douglass, Frederick]. *Life and Times of Frederick Douglass*. New York: Collier Books, 1962. Reprinted from 1892 edition.

Drache, Hiram M. *The Challenge of the Prairie*. Fargo: North Dakota Institute for Regional Studies, 1970.

Eaton, John, Jr. *Grant, Lincoln, and the Freedmen*. New York: Longmans, Green & Co., 1907.

———. *Report of the General Superintendent of Freedmen, Department of the Tennessee and the State of Arkansas for 1864*. Memphis: published by permission, 1865.

Elliott, Dabney O. *The Improvement of the Lower Mississippi for Flood Control and Navigation*. St. Louis: Mississippi River Commission, 1932.

Everett, Frank E., Jr. *Brierfield: Plantation Home of Jefferson Davis*. Hattiesburg, Miss.: University & College Press of Mississippi, 1971.

Fogel, Robert William, and Engerman, Stanley L. *Time on the Cross: The Economics of American Slavery*. Boston: Little, Brown & Co., 1974.

Foote, Henry Stuart. *The Bench and Bar of the South and Southwest*. St. Louis: Thomas & Wentworth, 1876.

———. *Casket of Reminiscences*. Washington: Chronicle, 1874.

Franklin, John Hope, ed. *The Autobiography of John Roy Lynch*. Chicago and London: University of Chicago Press, 1970.

———. *From Slavery to Freedom*. New York: A. Knopf, 1947. 3rd ed. New York: Vintage Books, 1969.

Garner, James W. *Reconstruction in Mississippi*. New York: Macmillan, 1901. Reprinted by Louisiana State University Press. Baton Rouge, 1968.

General Catalogue of Oberlin College, 1833–1908. Oberlin, Ohio: Oberlin College, 1909.

Genovese, Eugene D. *Roll, Jordan, Roll*. New York: Pantheon Books, 1972.

Gibson, James M. *Memoirs of J. M. Gibson: Terrors of the Civil War and Reconstruction*. N.p.: J. G. Alverson, 1966.

Grant, Ulysses S. *Personal Memoirs.* New York: C. L. Webster & Co., 1885.

Hammond, Mathew B. *The Cotton Industry: An Essay in American Economic History.* Part I, *The Cotton Culture and the Cotton Trade.* New York: American Economic Association and Macmillan, 1897.

Harlan, Louis R., ed. *The Papers of Booker T. Washington.* 8 vols. Urbana: University of Illinois Press, 1972–1979.

Hood, Aurelius P. *The Negro at Mound Bayou.* Nashville, Tenn.: AME Sunday School Union, 1910.

House, W. M. *The North Dakota and Richland County Chart.* N.p., 1897.

Howard, O. O. *Autobiography of Oliver Otis Howard, Major General, United States Army.* 2 vols. New York: Baker & Taylor Co., 1907.

[Ingraham, Joseph Holt]. *The South West. By a Yankee.* New York: Harper & Bros., 1835.

King, Henry. "A Year of Exodus in Kansas." *Scribner's Monthly,* 20 (1880): 211–218.

Knox, Thomas W. *Camp-Fire and Cotton-Field.* New York: Blelock & Co., 1865.

Litwack, Leon F. *Been in the Storm So Long.* New York: Alfred A. Knopf, 1979.

———. *North of Slavery.* Chicago: University of Chicago Press, 1961.

Loewen, James W., and Sallis, Charles, eds. *Mississippi: Conflict and Change.* New York: Pantheon, 1974.

Loring, F. W., and Atkinson, C. F. *Cotton Culture and the South Considered with Reference to Emigration.* Boston: A. Williams & Co., 1869.

Lynch, James Daniel. *The Bench and Bar of Mississippi.* New York: E. J. Hale, 1881.

Lynch, John R. *The Facts of Reconstruction.* New York: Neale, 1913.

Macdonald, Donald. *Diaries, 1824–1826.* Indianapolis: Indiana Historical Society Publications, vol. 14, no. 2, 1942.

McFeely, William S. *Yankee Stepfather: General O. O. Howard and the Freedmen.* New Haven: Yale University Press, 1968.

McIntosh, James T., ed. *The Papers of Jefferson Davis.* Vol. 2. Baton Rouge: Louisiana University Press, 1974.

Meier, August. "Booker T. Washington and the Town of Mound Bayou." *Phylon,* 15 (1954): 396–401.

———. *Negro Thought in America 1880–1915.* Ann Arbor: University of Michigan Press, 1963.

Monroe, Haskell M., Jr., and McIntosh, James T., eds. *The Papers of Jefferson Davis.* Vol. 1. Baton Rouge: Louisiana State University Press, 1971.

Montgomery, Franklin A. *Reminiscences of a Mississippian in Peace and War.* Cincinnati: Robert Clark Co., 1901.

Mott, Frank Luther. *A History of American Magazines.* 5 vols. Cambridge: Harvard University Press, 1938–1968.

The National Cyclopaedia of American Biography. 50 vols. and index. New York: James T. White, 1898–1968.

Official Records of the Union and Confederate Armies in the War of the Rebellion. 73 vols. Washington: U.S. Government Printing Office, 1880–1901.

Olmstead, Frederick Law. *A Journey in the Back Country.* New York: Mason Bros., 1860. Reprinted by Schocken Books. New York, 1970.

Osthaus, Carl R. *Freedmen, Philanthropy, and Fraud: A History of the Freedmen's Savings Bank.* Urbana: University of Illinois Press, 1976.

Ousley, B. F. "A Town of Colored People in Mississippi," *American Missionary Association Bulletin, 1904.*

Owen, Robert. *A New View of Society.* London: 1813. Reprinted in *The Life of Robert Owen Written by Himself.* Vol. 1. 1857. Reprint. New York: Reprints of Economic Classics, 1967.

Painter, Nell Irwin. *Exodusters.* New York: Alfred A. Knopf, 1977.

Pease, William H., and Pease, Jane H. *Black Utopia.* Madison: The State Historical Society of Wisconsin, 1963.

Porter, Admiral David D. *Incidents and Anecdotes of the Civil War.* New York: D. Appleton & Co., 1885.

———. *The Naval History of the Civil War.* New York: Sherman Publishing Co., 1886.

Powdermaker, Hortense. *After Freedom: A Cultural Study in the Deep South.* New York: Viking, 1939.

Ransom, Roger L., and Sutch, Richard. *One Kind of Freedom.* Cambridge: Cambridge University Press, 1977.

Rawick, George P., ed. *The American Slave: A Composite Autobiography.* 19 vols. Westport, Conn.: Greenwood Press, 1972.

———. *The American Slave: A Composite Autobiography,* Supplement, Series I. Vols. 6–10, *Mississippi Narratives,* parts 1–5. Westport, Conn.: Greenwood Press, 1977.

Redding, J. Saunders. *The Lonesome Road.* Garden City: Doubleday, 1958.

———. *No Day of Triumph.* New York: Harper, 1942.

Reid, Whitelaw. *After the War.* Cincinnati and New York: Moore, Wilstach & Baldwin, 1866; Harper Torchbooks edition, 1965.

Riley, Franklin L., ed. *Diary of Martin W. Philips.* Jackson, Miss.: Publications of the Mississippi Historical Society, X, 1909.

Rose, Willie Lee. *Rehearsal for Reconstruction.* New York: Bobbs-Merrill Co., Inc., 1964.

Ross, Ishbel. *First Lady of the South: The Life of Mrs. Jefferson Davis.* New York: Harper, 1958.

Rowland, Dunbar, ed. *Jefferson Davis, Constitutionalist: His Letters, Papers, and Speeches.* 10 vols. Jackson, Miss.: State Department of Archives and History, 1923.

———. *Mississippi.* 3 vols. Atlanta: Southern Historical Publishing Association, 1907.

Rowland, Eron (Mrs. Dunbar). *Varina Howell: Wife of Jefferson Davis.* 2 vols. New York: Macmillan, 1927–1931.

Smedes, Susan D. *Memorials of a Southern Planter*. Baltimore: Cushings & Bailey, 1888.

Somers, Robert. *The Southern States Since the War, 1870–1871*. London and New York: Macmillan, 1871.

Still, William. *The Underground Railroad*. Philadelphia: n.p., 1872; reprinted Chicago: Johnson Publishing Co., 1970.

Stampp, Kenneth M. *The Peculiar Institution*. New York: Alfred A. Knopf, 1956.

Statistics of the Operations of the Executive Board of Friends' Association of Philadelphia for the Relief of Colored Freedmen. Philadelphia: Inquirer Printing Office, 1864.

Strode, Hudson. *Jefferson Davis, American Patriot, 1808–1861*. New York: Harcourt, Brace, 1955.

———. *Jefferson Davis, Confederate President*. New York: Harcourt, Brace & World, 1959.

———. *Jefferson Davis, Tragic Hero: The Last Twenty-five Years, 1864–1889*. New York: Harcourt, Brace & World, 1964.

———. *Jefferson Davis: Private Letters, 1823–1889*. New York: Harcourt, Brace & World, 1966.

Sydnor, Charles. "The Free Negro in Mississippi." *American Historical Review*, 32 (1927): 769–788.

———. *Slavery in Mississippi*. Baton Rouge: Louisiana State University Press, 1966.

Tong, Hiram. "The Pioneers of Mound Bayou." *Century Magazine*, vol. 79, no. 3 (1910): 390–400.

Trahey, Jane, ed. *Harper's Bazaar, 100 Years of the American Female*. New York: Random House, 1967.

Trowbridge, John T. *The South: A Tour of Its Battlefields and Ruined Cities; A Journey Through the Desolated States, and Talks with the People, etc.* Hartford: L. Stebbins, 1866.

U.S. Census Office. Sixth, Seventh, Eighth, Ninth, and Tenth Census (1840–1880). Mississippi Department of Archives and History.

———. Tenth Census (1880). Eugene W. Hilgard, Special Agent, *Report on Cotton Production of the State of Mississippi*. Washington: U.S. Government Printing Office, 1884.

U.S. Congress. *Senate Executive Document 53*. 38th Cong., 1st Sess. Washington: U.S. Government Printing Office, 1864.

———. *Senate Executive Document 27*. 39th Cong., 1st Sess. Washington: U.S. Government Printing Office, 1866.

U.S. Congress. *House Executive Documents 11, 70, 120*. 39th Cong., 1st Sess. Washington: U.S. Government Printing Office, 1866.

———. *Senate Executive Document 6*. 39th Cong., 2nd Sess. Washington: U.S. Government Printing Office, 1867.

———. *House Executive Document 1*. 39th Cong., 2nd Sess. Washington: U.S. Government Printing Office, 1867.

U.S. Department of Agriculture. *Report of the Commissioner of Agriculture for the Year 1867*. Washington: U.S. Government Printing Office, 1868.

Walker, Peter F. *Vicksburg: A People at War, 1860–1865*. Chapel Hill: University of North Carolina, 1960.

Wallace, Jesse Thomas. *A History of the Negroes of Mississippi from 1865 to 1890*. Clinton, Miss.: by the author, 1927.

Washington, Booker T. *My Larger Education*. Garden City: Doubleday, Page, 1911.

———. *The Story of the Negro*. 2 vols. New York: Doubleday, Page, 1909.

———. *The Story of Slavery*. Dansville, N.Y.: F. A. Owen, 1913.

———. "A Town Owned by Negroes." *The World's Work*, vol. 14, no. 3 (July 1907), 9125–34.

Wharton, Vernon Lane. *The Negro in Mississippi, 1865–1890*. Chapel Hill: University of North Carolina, 1947. Harper Torchbooks edition, New York: Harper and Row, 1965.

Wish, Harvey. *Society and Thought in Early America*. New York: David McKay Co., 1950.

Woodman, Harold D. *King Cotton and His Retainers*. Lexington: University of Kentucky Press, 1968.

Woodward, C. Vann. *Origins of the New South, 1877–1913*. Baton Rouge: Louisiana State University Press, 1951.

Work, Monroe N., ed. *Negro Year Book, 1921–22*. Tuskegee, Ala.: Tuskegee Institute, 1922.

Yeatman, James E. *A Report on the Condition of the Freedmen of the Mississippi Valley*. St. Louis: Western Sanitary Commission Rooms, 1864.

Newspapers

The Appeal (St. Paul, Minn.)

Cincinnati Commercial

Cincinnati Daily Gazette

Cincinnati Enquirer

Daily Clarion (Meridian, Miss.)

Daily Picayune (New Orleans)

Daily Vicksburger

Fargo Daily Argus

Hinds County Gazette (Raymond, Miss.)

Natchez Tri-Weekly Courier

New National Era

New Orleans Times-Democrat

New Orleans Tribune

New York Herald

New York Times
New York World
St. Louis Globe Democrat
Semi-Weekly Louisianian (New Orleans)
South-Western Farmer (Raymond, Miss.)
Vicksburg Daily Herald
Vicksburg Daily Times
Vicksburg Journal
Vicksburg Sentinel and Expositor
Vicksburg Times and Republican
Vicksburg Whig
Weekly Clarion (Jackson)
Weekly Mississippi Pilot
Woodville Republican
Yazoo Whig and Political Register

Unpublished Sources

Currie, James Tyson. "Vicksburg, 1863–1870: The Promise and the Reality of Reconstruction on the Mississippi." Ph.D. dissertation, University of Virginia, 1975.

Ganus, Clifton L., Jr., "The Freedmen's Bureau in Mississippi." Ph.D. dissertation, Tulane University, 1953.

Jackson, Maurice Elizabeth. "Mound Bayou—A Study in Social Development." Master's thesis, University of Alabama, 1937.

Moore, Ross H. "Social and Economic Conditions during Reconstruction." Ph.D. dissertation, Duke University, 1937.

Sanders, Phyllis, M. "Jefferson Davis: Reactionary Rebel." Ph.D. dissertation, University of California, Los Angeles, 1976.

Index

Agriculture at Davis Bend, 6, 22–26, 136; dictates rhythm of life, 150; diversification of, 153; in 1866, 102–103; in 1867, 133; in 1868, 138; in 1869, 152; in 1870, 152; in 1874, 201; in 1879, 208–209; and insect pests, 59–60, 131–133, 136, 185; and theft of crops, 191; in wartime, 41, 85. *See also* Cotton at Davis Bend

Agriculture at Mound Bayou, 223
Allen, Hagar, 204, 209, 214
American Freedmen's Inquiry Commission, 44–45
Ames, Adelbert, 130, 197
Army worm, 59–60, 131–133, 136, 185

Balmoral plantation, 137–138
Banks, Charles, 224–225, 233, 238–241
Barnes, Nicholas, 39–40
Barnes, Lt. Samuel D., 55, 56
Bedford, E. S., 67, 77, 86–87, 100; affidavit of, 97; as Freedmen's Bureau agent, 95; honesty of, 92; praise of, 96; takes Thornton Montgomery as partner, 99–100
Black Code in Mississippi, 87, 110
Blaine, James G., 228
Blake's plantation, 44
Bland, Thomas, 67, 69, 71, 83
Booze, Eugene P., 233, 241, 243
Booze, Mary Montgomery, 233, 242
Boston Herald, 210–211
Bowmar, J. H. D., 196, 197; as executor of Davis's estate, 147–150, 172–173; pleads Davis's case with President Johnson, 104, 110; postwar visits to Davis Bend of, 149, 172–173
Boyd, George W., 101
Bray, Granderson and Amanda, 214
Brierfield plantation, 13; antebellum crops on, 24–26; description of man-

sion at, 164; developed by Jefferson Davis, 13; 1867 crop on, 133; 1868 crop on, 138; 1879 crop on, 208–209; floods on, 116–120, 201; flower garden at, 165–166; Home Farm on, 53, 158; hospitality at, 170, 171–173; July 4, 1864 celebration at, 56–57; July 4, 1872 celebration at, 189; Montgomerys occupy mansion at, 157, 205; repair of buildings on, 115; slaves raid mansion at, 38–39; sold to Jefferson Davis, 211; sold to Montgomerys, 104, 109–110; unhealthy location of, 15, 55–56; value of, 109–110, 201, 208, 211–212; Yankees loot mansion at, 40
Broadwater, Thomas M., 67, 69, 71, 83, 196
Brooks, Martha, 164, 170
Bruce, Blanche K., 219
Burton, Enoch, 191
Burwell, Armistead, 78–79

Cardozo, T. W., 186
Carnegie, Andrew, 238, 241
Carter, J. H., 50, 58–59
Carter, P. G., 99
Charlton, Sam, 204, 209
Chicago Tribune, 167, 172–185, 209–210
Cincinnati Contraband Relief Commission, 51–52, 54, 57, 58
Clark, Sam, 191
Cleveland, Grover, 230
Constitutional convention in Mississippi: in 1817, 4; in 1890, 229–230
Cotton at Davis Bend, 136; antebellum crops, 22–26; cost of production, 152; 1865 crop, 85; 1866 crop, 102–103; 1867 crop, 133; 1868 crop, 138; 1869 crop, 152; 1870

283

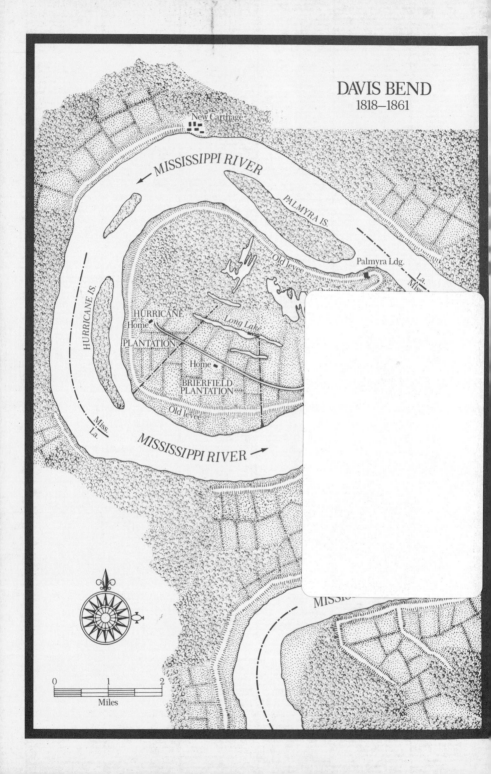

DAVIS BEND
1818–1861